THE ART OF BART

THE ART OF BART

Bilateral Affective Reprocessing of Thoughts as a Dynamic Model for Psychotherapy

Arthur G. O'Malley

KARNAC

First published in 2015 by
Karnac Books Ltd
118 Finchley Road, London NW3 5HT

British Library Cataloguing in Publication Data

A C.I.P. for this book is available from the British Library

ISBN 978 1 78220 135 9

Edited, designed and produced by The Studio Publishing Services Ltd
www.publishingservicesuk.co.uk
e-mail: studio@publishingservicesuk.co.uk

Printed in Great Britain

www.karnacbooks.com

CONTENTS

ACKNOWLEDGEMENTS ix

ABOUT THE AUTHOR xi

PREFACE xiii

INTRODUCTION: The art of bilateral affective reprocessing of thoughts (BART): a dynamic model for psychotherapy and peak performance xv

CHAPTER ONE
Concept of intuition and introduction to BART psychotherapy for both therapy and peak performance 1

CHAPTER TWO
Activation of the chakras using BART psychotherapy and peak performance 31

CHAPTER THREE
Neurodevelopment of the head-brain, heart-brain, and gut-brain 57

CHAPTER FOUR
Vibrational frequencies related to accelerated information processing in patients or clients 77

CHAPTER FIVE
Proposals for BART psychotherapy with special populations and effects of abuse and neglect on the developing brains of the patient or client 97

CHAPTER SIX
The mystery of consciousness 115

CHAPTER SEVEN
Development of thought and the role of BART psychotherapy and peak performance in reprocessing thoughts 133

CHAPTER EIGHT
Guidelines for practitioners on conducting a BART psychotherapy session 147

CHAPTER NINE
Taking a trauma and developmental history 161

CHAPTER TEN
Influence of some research in trauma therapy by neurobiologists and how this has affected my development of the integrative approach of BART psychotherapy and peak performance 175

CHAPTER ELEVEN
Living in a hypothetical world dominated by the left hemisphere's perspective, and summary of the five stages of BART psychotherapy 191

CHAPTER TWELVE
Using BART for peak performance in sport, business, academia, and any pursuit where anticipatory anxiety impairs results 211

CHAPTER THIRTEEN
Template for comprehensive assessment of the patient or client prior to BART psychotherapy or peak performance, and use of the Hermann brain dominance instrument 245

REFERENCES 269

INDEX 281

In memory of my father, Arthur, who died surrounded by family in 1993, aged eighty-two, and my sister, Grainne, who lost her battle with Crohn's disease in 1996 at the age of forty-two. May their guiding light continue to shine and may they rest in peace. To my mother, Joan, who, in her ninety-third year, continues to show resilience in the face of adversity. May she be bestowed with kindness by all who know her.

ACKNOWLEDGEMENTS

I would like to thank my wife, Maura, and our children, Sorcha, Oisin, and Cliodhna, for their support and encouragement during the arduous process of writing this book. I would also like to thank Sorcha O'Malley for her superb artwork in creating many of the illustrative drawings.

Steve Pratt, during one of our many supervision sessions, first encouraged me to write down my ideas. He and his wife, Carol, have been a constant source of support. It was from this seed that the idea for a book blossomed.

Jeff Hughes and Cathy Hamer gave me the opportunity in their St Helen's home to deliver my first presentation on the therapeutic ideas contained herein and they have continued to be a support throughout the process. I am grateful to all the friends who took the time to read early drafts, with a special thanks to Peter Eldridge, who provided meticulous notes to accompany his very helpful comments

My thanks to Nick Poole for looking after me when I lost consciousness and who, in many ways, has kept me on the path when it seemed easier to stray off it. To Andrea and Colin Willan for always being there when needed, thank you. Thanks also to Krys, Sandie, and Sarah, who have shown the enduring qualities of friendship. Fran S.

Waters from the USA encouraged me to submit an abstract on BART to the International Society for the study of Trauma and Dissociation (ISSTD). This allowed me to present at their annual conference in Montreal and galvanised my determination to see this work reach a wider audience.

My sisters, Maire McLoughlin and Una Wan, were always excited by the work and keen to hear of the latest instalments. When I presented my work to an audience in Sheffield, Sian Morgan from the Humanitarian Assistance Programme of the UK and Ireland EMDR association invited me to be the guest lecturer for a one-day workshop to raise funds for the HAP organisation. The day was facilitated by Mark Brayne and attended by seventy-five delegates. I received an overwhelmingly positive response. This was vindication for my ideas, as I was leaving myself open to criticism by promulgating a novel approach to therapy. I was reassured by speaking to David Grand, a psychologist based in New York. He trained, like me, in EMDR. He then went on to teach Natural Flow EMDR before stumbling on brainspotting, which he has been teaching around the world for ten years. My view is that new discoveries are emerging in relation to information processing in the human nervous system on a regular basis. It is up to each therapist to integrate this knowledge and apply it to the benefit of his or her clients and patients.

My family in Ireland remain a source of strength, none more so than my mother, Joan, whose wisdom stems in part from the upheavals in society experienced since her birth in 1921 at the time of the Irish Civil War.

I would like to thank Pat Scully from Rédacteurs Ltd for editorial assistance, and Denis, whose case history is part of the book. Ania Partakis helped prepare this transcript while Rod Tweedy and Constance Govindan of Karnac Books have held my hand along each step of the publication process. I am indebted to their professionalism.

Finally, I would like to thank my patients and supervisees, who always provide an opportunity for learning and growth.

ABOUT THE AUTHOR

Arthur G. O'Malley has worked as a consultant child and adolescent psychiatrist for the National Health Service (NHS) and in private practice since 2004 and became accredited as an EMDR consultant in 2008. He has been a member of the UK and Ireland EMDR Association since 2002 and was a member of the ninth European Annual EMDR Conference organising committee in 2008.

He was a speaker at the EMDR Annual Conferences of Glasgow, Manchester, and Dublin, and at the European Annual EMDR conferences of Paris and London. He has spoken widely on the subjects of trauma, neglect, and the developing brain, attachment and personality disorders, as well as emotional dysregulation in ADHD and ASD diagnosis and management.

Arthur O'Malley has developed Bilateral Affective Reprocessing of Thoughts (BART) for both psychotherapy and peak performance, which builds on his training in EMDR and psychotherapy.

In 2011, he was elected to the fellowship of the Royal College of Psychiatrists, and organised a conference on trauma-focused therapies, which was held at the Manchester Conference Centre and hosted by the Association for Child and Adolescent Mental Health (ACAMH). That same year, he presented his therapeutic approach at the twenty-eighth Annual Conference of the International Society for the Study of Trauma and Dissociation (ISSTD) in Montréal, Canada, and at the Bowlby Centre in London.

PREFACE

This innovative approach to therapy includes integration of third generation EMDR and sensorimotor psychotherapy. The dynamic new model is Bilateral Affective Reprocessing of Thoughts and is summarised in this book as the "Art of Bart".

The fundamental differences from both EMDR and sensorimotor psychotherapy are illustrated. The initiation of bilateral cerebellar stimulation is a key difference from the bilateral stimulation used in EMDR, and also, eye movements are not used in reprocessing.

Paying attention to the chakras' energy points is another key difference from these approaches. In addition; a protocol for peak performance is included which is absent from either traditional EMDR or sensorimotor psychotherapy.

Evidence for this approach is presented by references to recent research in neurobiology of trauma and dissociation and affective neuroscience.

In addition, I have recently developed a manual summarising the key aspects of the Art of Bart, and this will be made available to psychotherapists and business coaches who undertake training in the model.

Introduction: The art of bilateral affective reprocessing of thoughts (BART): a dynamic model for psychotherapy and peak performance

This book stems from my practice in child and adolescent psychiatry over the last fifteen years. More recently, I have become interested in ways of looking at our health from both an eastern and western perspective. My belief is that this whole approach to health benefits both ourselves and our patients and clients.

Chapter One provides the reader with an introduction to BART psychotherapy for both trauma focused therapy and peak performance. The concept of post traumatic growth is discussed. The links between the three brains of our central and peripheral nervous system are introduced.

Chapter Two illustrates the connections between the chakras and the body's endocrine system. These are discussed in relation to the body's window of tolerance and emotional regulation. This concept is alien to the majority of allopathic or conventional therapists. I aim to show the scientific basis behind these meridians and how accessing the chakra energies with BART psychotherapy can benefit patients.

Chapter Three outlines the stages of development of the embryo and clinical implications in terms of processing of the gut, heart, and head brains. The relationship to our core emotions is explained along with the implications for therapy. The peak performance approach of

Dr Peters is briefly outlined. Similarities to the top down and bottom up processing are found in the symbolism of *The Wizard of Oz* and the mythology of the ancient Egyptian Pharaohs.

In Chapter Four, the theory of vibratory intelligence is developed from the perspective of both the right and left cerebral hemispheres. The crucial role of the cerebellum has only recently been acknowledged within the affective neuroscience research community. My goal with this book is to harness the activation of each cerebellum using BART psychotherapy. The consequences of abuse and neglect in infancy have a profound deleterious effect on the infant brain which, if untreated, persists into adulthood. The different theories in relation to the vagal nerve and trauma are explained in detail. The relationship between the three parts of the cerebellum and its connections to the brainstem and frontal cortex are described and give rise to the unique technique of bilateral cerebellar stimulation, which is the foundation stone for BART psychotherapy. The historical descriptions of the autonomic nervous system have changed from those of John Langley to Walter Hess to Stephen Porges. The latter's polyvagal theory is discussed in relation to safe, unsafe, and life-threatening environments. There are links between our vagus nerve and that of our reptilian-brained ancestors. Understanding this connection helps to elucidate the body's reaction to stress and trauma.

Chapter Five explores the use of BART psychotherapy in two special client groups: autism spectrum and traumatic stress disorders. In the former, the goal is *B*ringing *A*ffective *R*egulation of *T*one. The implications for clinical practice are discussed. It is essential that practitioners understand the impact of abuse and neglect on the developing brain. This chapter covers the role of polyvagal theory in relation to infant development and the Jacksonian dissolution model of the autonomic nervous system. The term synaptic pruning is explained in detail, along with a discussion on why adolescents lack judgement and take risks. Finally, I explore briefly how to provide the ideal learning environment for children. This is based on Mercer and Littleton's work in schools (2007), and a learner profile for a child in secondary school is proposed.

Chapter Six explores the mechanisms for connecting the developing brain, the role of asymmetry and evolution in the function of our brains from our reptilian ancestors to the present day. A potential early common universal ancestor, the lystrosaurus, is proposed. The chapter provides a neurobiological explanation of why, when traumatised, our clients access instinctive brainstem responses and have the blood supply to their prefrontal cortex reduced. Hence, the patient can only respond rationally when they no longer feel trapped in an unsafe or life-threatening environment. This is very likely to be the case of in-patients, especially those admitted under sections of the Mental Health Act in the UK. Various locations for the neuroanatomical origin of consciousness are proposed, such as the periaqueductal grey matter in the midbrain. The philosophical origins are also mentioned. New insights, such as those once achieved by the Ancient Greeks at the Delphic oracle, are proposed. As we moved from the Age of Enlightenment to the age of reason in society, so did our world perspective shift from the right to the left hemisphere. This has had major implications in the field of psychiatry, with many more patients experiencing mental ill health by being cut off from their feelings. My book aims to redress this balance by guiding therapists to integrate their own thinking on western and eastern medicine before applying this to their patients or clients.

Chapter Seven examines a proposed evolution of human thoughts and how they can be reprocessed using BART psychotherapy. It is widely accepted that we use only five per cent of our brains capacity for conscious thought. The remaining ninety-five per cent is below the level of conscious control. Ways of exploring the potential of this part of brain processing are discussed. The concept of the connectome is introduced, along with its proposed role in the nature of memory. This work, described by Dr Sebastian Seung (2012), is at the cutting edge of scientific research into neural structure and function. The concept of the philosophy of Bertrand Russell (1946) is mentioned to explore avenues about how we might develop therapeutic conversations with our patients or clients. BART psychotherapy can benefit patients with a range of disorders, from anorexia nervosa, dissociative identity disorder, complex and developmental trauma, to patients with a history of both suicidal and non-suicidal self-injury.

Chapter Eight provides a detailed background to the techniques behind BART psychotherapy. If the reader starts here, they will miss the key developmental steps in earlier chapters. However, it is also reasonable to start with the techniques necessary for BART psychotherapy and then work backwards to the theory. The machine I commissioned provides the opportunity to apply a range of frequencies to the brain during reprocessing. My feedback from patients is that it is like having their brain suddenly switched on as they reach the brain frequency of forty–sixty Hertz, which may be necessary for thalamo-cortical information transfer. This makes BART psychotherapy different to all other psychotherapeutic approaches I am currently aware of. Matrix energetics, somatic experiencing, and brainspotting have some similarities, but do not use either the body of knowledge activator or the BART machine illustrated in this chapter, or apply a range of different frequencies of bilateral stimulation during reprocessing.

Chapter Nine introduces the assessment template for BART psychotherapy. This explains to therapists how to weigh up to what extent their patient has been overwhelmed by traumatic stress so that crucial sensory information was not integrated from initial episodic to later semantic memory during the traumatic episode. Of special relevance is any traumatic sensation perceived by the first cranial, or olfactory, nerve. The sense of smell is heightened during trauma and is directly transmitted to the amygdala, where it becomes associated to the fear response. Ways to assess involvement of the other cranial nerves are suggested. I suggest that any pathology could be based on aberrant functioning of the twelve cranial nerves and how this subsequently influences the patients' behaviour in either a safe, unsafe, or a life-threatening environment. Ways to overcome this pathology are suggested. A narrative seven-element relaxation exercise can be read to, or recorded for, the patient. The links of our eye movements to our thinking and feeling are proposed. This idea stems from neurolinguistic programming (NLP). Indeed, Francine Shapiro trained in NLP before going on to develop EMDR in 1989 (Shapiro, 2001). The main cranial nerve origin for eye movements at the superior colliculus in the brainstem is explained. This, I believe, has fundamental implications for the physiology of saccadic eye movements during the reprocessing of traumatic memories.

Chapter Ten discusses the contributions of Dr Bruce Lipton (2011), Dr Marcus Raichle (2007), and Professor James Austin (1999) in the field of psychotherapy for trauma. Dr Lipton, (2013), in his book, *Biology of Belief*, discusses how the environmental stimulus to the growth of a cell can be narrowed down to the frequency of either love or fear. Love has a higher vibration than fear and may interact positively with our deoxyribonucleic acid (DNA), to provide an opportunity for maturity and growth. Fear, on the other hand, sends a lower frequency signal to the cell to freeze at the level of the nucleus, so no cell growth occurs. Dr Ruth Lanius has done many MRI studies of patients who have experienced trauma and compared them to controls (Buczynski & Lanius, 2012). The affective neuroscience is pointing to the default mode network (DMN) as a key stage of development. Dr Marcus Raichle (2007) originally postulated this neural network, which comes into being at age eight or ten. If a child was abused or traumatised before then, their brain maintains that level of reprocessing ability until they receive effective trauma-focused therapy. It is vital for therapists to understand this and that their management and treatment strategies are fully informed by these governing principles of the cell and brain. Possible reasons for the fact that ninety per cent of DNA is categorised as "junk" and does not appear to be necessary for DNA replication are explored. It is, perhaps, by raising our resonant vibrational frequency that our cells will access this junk, or non-coding, DNA. The double and triple spiral symbols have been found all over the world. That in Newgrange is around 8,000 old, while at Gobekli Tepe in Turkey, the site might be 11,000 years old. It has been proposed that Stone Age man was communicating via these passage tombs. What was more important to communicate than the cellular structure of DNA? As yet, science has not yet been able to fully explain the mechanisms of alignment with the winter and summer solstice of Newgrange and Stonehenge monuments. These significant achievements of Stone Age man remain unexplained.

Chapter Eleven outlines the five stages of bilateral affective reprocessing of thoughts (BART). Each stage is explained in both images and words. This appeals to the strengths of the right and left hemispheres, respectively. The right hemisphere sees the whole image, whereas the left is more analytical in relation to receptive and expressive language. The aim is for therapist, patient, or client to have a coherent overall view of the process, which will enhance their therapeutic rapport. A key reason for the success of BART psychotherapy is that it is informed by affective neuroscience and neuroanatomical development. In the first six months of life, ninety per cent of neural information is transmitted to the same side of the body, that is, homolateral up to the level of the brainstem. After six months, it becomes ipsilateral and crosses to the opposite cortical hemisphere. When the baby starts to crawl, this cross lateralisation of the neural tracts starts to develop. This might explain why children who fail to crawl often develop dyslexia. This flow of information is enhanced using both figure of eight and ouroboros symbols, which enhance the visualisation of top down and bottom up reprocessing by the patient or client.

Chapter Twelve is devoted to achieving peak performance, either in a programme of its own right or following on from the fifth stage of BART psychotherapy. People whose target is peak performance are sportsmen and women, those seeking to achieve goals and objectives in business, actors with stage fright, and artists in any discipline, from music to dancing to painting. The maxim, "It takes ten thousand hours of practice to become a world champion" in any chosen discipline is explored. The optimum time to learn new skills is during the skill-hungry years from eight to twelve. The brains of these children are growing rapidly before pruning and strengthening of the most used reflexes occurs in adolescence. The achievers of peak performance are able to lose awareness of time, to be self-motivated for their chosen pursuit, to be able to hit the "sweet spot", metaphorically, and to be constantly improving as if on "automatic". The need for accurate feedback in relation to performance is discussed. The rest of this chapter is devoted to articulating the five steps towards achieving optimal or peak performance. The initial results using this technique are promising, but further study and research into PARTS one through to five is warranted.

Chapter Thirteen is the final chapter and provides an assessment, or health, questionnaire, which takes approximately two hours to complete. It is preferable if first-hand information in relation to the early childhood of the patient or client can be documented in relation to both adverse and other significant life events. Fundamental experiences from zero to five years could shape the rest of the person's life. The family history component comes from Barry Litt. He is currently offering an excellent seminar on the marriage of ego state therapy and EMDR with couple therapy in the USA. Two further assessment tools are included: the Herrmann Brain Dominance Inventory (1991), and a table of Brodmann brain areas (1909). These will help the therapist understand which parts of the head brain are most vulnerable in their patients or clients and perhaps enable them to target areas of brain function for development, growth, and, ultimately, peak performance.

CHAPTER ONE

Concept of intuition and introduction to BART psychotherapy for both therapy and peak performance

Introduction

During my childhood growing up in the area of Northern Ireland called South Armagh, I was only six when the "Troubles" started. We lived over a drapery shop on the main street in a rural village called Newtownhamilton. Soon, the region became known as bandit country and a large joint RUC–British Army base was established in the heart of the town less than one hundred metres from our house. In 1970, while leaving the kitchen, I was suddenly blown on to the floor by the force of an explosion, which had gone off without warning. What amazed me was the fact that I had no conscious awareness of what had happened. As I gingerly got up and realised the walls were still standing, I gradually came to comprehend what had happened. This was the first of over forty explosions, rocket attacks, shootings, and incendiary devices that the town's residents experienced over the years. The personal nadir for our family was when my parents and some workmen were held hostage while the IRA planted booby-trap explosive devices in our house and hardware shop. The British Army, in a controlled explosion, later razed this to the ground while our whole family were evacuated. One week later, my older brother was over from England on holiday. While walking over the rubble, he spotted a wire. The alarm was raised, as he had just stumbled over an unexploded bomb. We were again evacuated while the army bomb disposal squad made the device safe.

I relate this to explain where my interest in trauma resolution came from. When I specialised as a child psychiatrist, I started to investigate and train in trauma-focused therapies. These included:

1. Trauma-focused cognitive behaviour therapy. However, many of my patients were "unable to think" and in a state of speechless terror. They needed a different approach.
2. Eye movement desensitisation and reprocessing therapy (EMDR). I became an EMDR Europe accredited consultant in 2008 when very few child and adolescent psychiatrists had trained in this approach. In 2013, I renewed my accreditation as a consultant in EMDR for a further five years. I found this technique very useful with my patients. However, children's eye movements are immature and they are often unable to track across the midline. Therefore, I used tactile and auditory bilateral stimulation to good effect. However, part of the jigsaw was missing in relation to preverbal traumatic memories. This was partially addressed by attending training delivered by the wonderful paediatrician from California, Dr Joan Lovett, and summarised in her book, *Small Wonders* (1999). She recounts how she was several years recovering from a road traffic accident. This caused her to re-evaluate her life and dedicate her career to helping families with babies born prematurely and in incubators in neonatal intensive care, as well as other traumatised infants. I used this training, along with colleagues, to deliver a parental and infant mental health service in the National Health Service (NHS). However, it was clear to me that the instinctive responses of the body were not addressed by these techniques.
3. I spent one year training in sensorimotor psychotherapy at the training institute based in Lincoln. This approach was developed by Ogden, Pain, and Minton, who authored the book *Trauma and the Body: A Sensorimotor Approach to Psychotherapy* (2006). During the practical sessions of the training, I realised that my sensorimotor trauma memory could be accessed as easily as my episodic and semantic memories and would lead to more effective psychotherapy when combined with the other techniques.

4. This led to the dynamic model for psychotherapy and peak performance called "bilateral affective reprocessing of thoughts" (BART). It is a form of psychotherapy with universal application.

In this book, I will outline the art and science behind the technique. I started my life's journey in 1962 and now, fifty years later, in the words of Victor Hugo, "There is nothing more powerful than an idea whose time has come".

Background to BART for psychotherapy and peak performance

BART stands for bilateral affective reprocessing of thoughts. The first component represents various forms of bilateral stimulation from continuous auditory stimulation at the level of the mastoid processes, just behind each ear, to peripheral tactile stimulation using zappers applied at various frequencies. The second component represents access to the person's affective experience. Third, in ways that will be explained, repeated iteration of emotions, sensations, and feelings are reprocessed so that, finally, new thoughts emerge (recognition). This allows the patient or client to strive psychotherapeutically towards peak performance, which is the ultimate goal or target of therapy.

The relationship between the patient or client and therapist depends a lot on intuition for its effectiveness in helping to establish a therapeutic alliance. Intuition derives from the Latin term *intueor*, which itself comes from *intuitus*, meaning to look upon, to contemplate, and *tueor*, I look (whence, tutor and tuition). This is a key goal of BART psychotherapy and its activation via bilateral cerebellar stimulation. It is also the mechanism whereby the mind perceives either the agreement or disagreement of several ideas. It is how we become aware of the truth of things immediately, without reasoning and deduction. In a "sense", it is assumed in the body's experience (the technique of BART psychotherapy is grounded in acknowledging this experience).

There is an increasing awareness of the need to move from chaos towards coherence in the lives of our patients and clients and this can be represented by an integration of gut, heart, and head-brains. Cohere comes from the Latin words *co*, "for" and *hoero*, "I stick together". The organs of the body must stick together, that is, be in close contact, for information to flow freely and to form a connection or cohesive mass. In a coherent state, we optimise energetically, that is, emotionally, mentally, and physically. The heart, head, and gut-brains synchronise and operate efficiently when they are internally coherent. This is accelerated by BART psychotherapy when used both as a trauma therapy and for peak performance. In the body's neural networks, about eighty-five to ninety per cent of neural fibres travel from the body to the brain, especially via the different components of the vagus nerve. These dominate our decision making, creativity, and emotional state. During traumatic stress, this information can be blocked anywhere along the affected neural pathway.

The basic premise underpinning the mechanism of action of BART psychotherapy is that information is processed in three ways:

1. Reactively by the gut-brain.
2. Emotionally by the heart-brain.
3. Analytically by the head-brain (Figure 1).

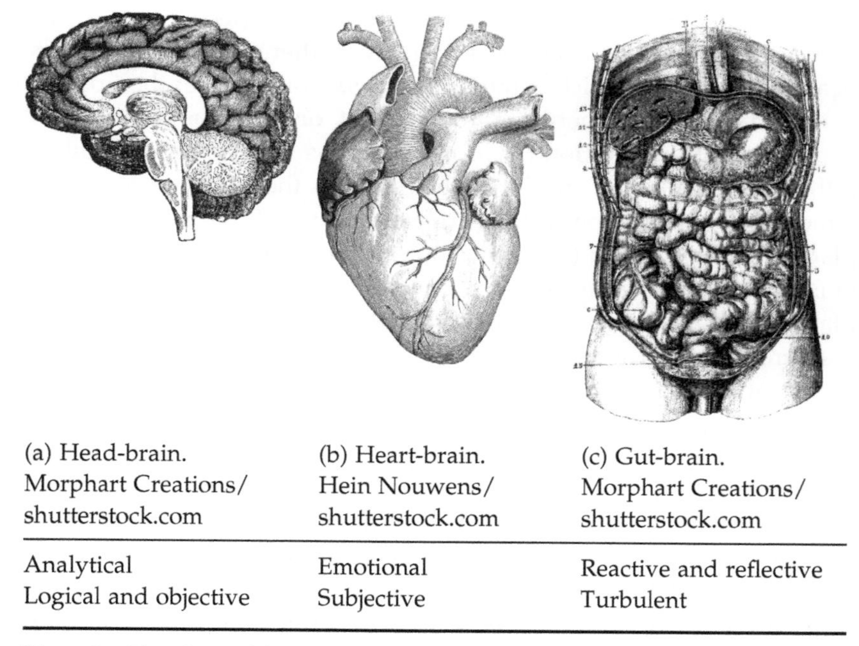

(a) Head-brain. Morphart Creations/ shutterstock.com	(b) Heart-brain. Hein Nouwens/ shutterstock.com	(c) Gut-brain. Morphart Creations/ shutterstock.com
Analytical Logical and objective	Emotional Subjective	Reactive and reflective Turbulent

Figure 1. The physical brain, heart-brain, and gut-brain.

The human nervous systems can be conceptualised as the gut-brain, which first registers sensations and feelings as a "gut reaction or instinct". This is followed by the heart-brain, or sympathetic and parasympathetic nervous system. These sensations are felt in the chest, and often relate to emotions of loss and delayed grief. The central and peripheral nervous systems work together to analyse this information, which leads to the production of thought and speech in the head-brain. This is the final stage of logical and objective thought and rational analysis. It is the linking of these separate processes that is unique to BART psychotherapy. For example, it is by recognition and inhibition of the sensation of butterflies in our stomach during reprocessing that we can ultimately achieve our objectives by engaging heart-brain and head-brain reprocessing capabilities.

The bilateral activation at the level of the mastoid processes resonates at the level of both cerebellums. This information appears to further access processing in the temporal, occipital, and parietal lobes. Finally, patients often report a tingling sensation in their frontal lobes. This appears to coincide with a release of energy from both the third eye and forehead chakras, correlating anatomically with the pituitary and hypothalamic glands. The techniques underlying this process are explained further in Chapter Eight.

The anatomical connections in patients or clients can be illustrated as follows: connection between the cardiac nervous system (heart-brain) and the central nervous system (head-brain) (Figure 2). The

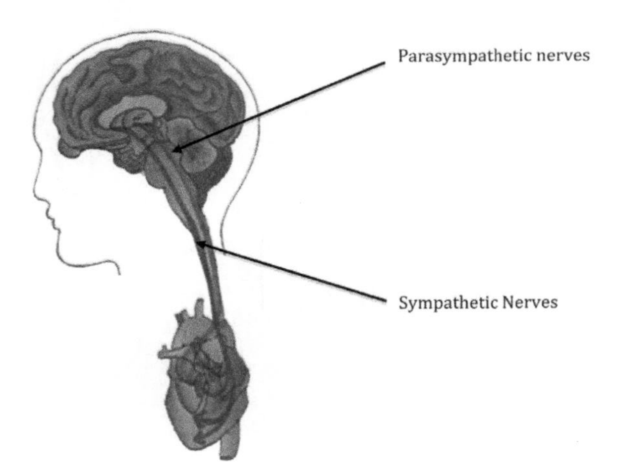

Figure 2. The heart–brain interaction and connections.

local circuit neurons in the heart are involved in coding of long-term memory in the hippocampus. The heart's functional memory via these heart neurons ensures that intuitive or heartfelt feelings are processed in the heart-brain. They also link directly with the gut-brain and head-brain networks. This builds on the widespread cultural belief that feelings registered at a heart level are as powerful if not more powerful than those of the gut-brain and head-brain.

Connections between the brain in the gastrointestinal tract (gut-brain) and the brainstem (head-brain) are illustrated (Figure 3). This is highly significant in anxiety resolution: there are layers of protection for the intrinsic neurones of gut plexuses from the contents of the gut mucosa. When the neural plexi afferents from and efferents to the head, gut, and heart are all connected, then maximal flow of information occurs. This appears to be possible using BART psychotherapy. The head-brain links up with the other systems via the sympathetic and parasympathetic nervous systems. The dorsal motor nucleus of the tenth cranial, or vagus, nerve has its origin in the brainstem and

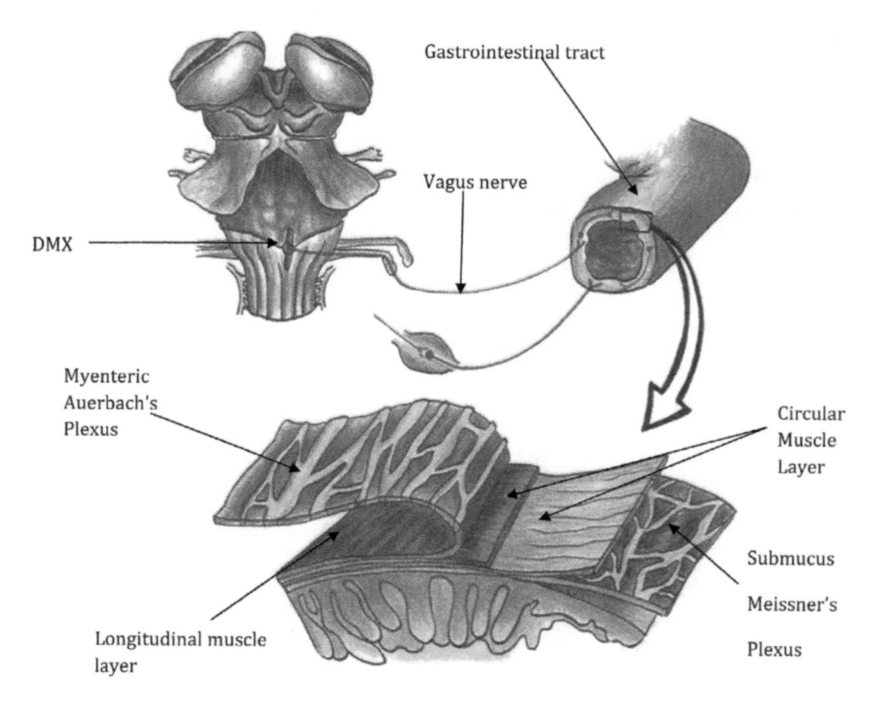

Figure 3. The gut connections with the brainstem.

synapses in the muscle wall of the gastrointestinal tract (GIT). In Figure 3, the black arrow shows a magnified section of the GIT containing the intrinsic neurones of the gut plexus. There are longitudinal and circular muscle layers containing Meissner's plexus in between them at the submucosa layer, which has only parasympathetic fibres. Auerbach's plexus also lies between the circular and longitudinal layers at the muscularis propria layer and has both sympathetic and parasympathetic input from the central nervous system.

The enteric nervous system (ENS), or gut-brain, has thirty different neurotransmitters and ninety per cent of the body's serotonin, as well as fifty per cent of its dopamine. It also has taste receptors which sense "sweetness" on the tongue and levels of glucose in the bloodstream. These taste receptors regulate insulin and are a good example of how the ENS really acts as our gut-brain and is capable of independent action. The processing of the gut instinct, or gut reaction, to incidents is a prerequisite for the BART therapeutic approach and is fully explained in Chapter Eight.

Research by Cryan and Dinan (2012a), reveals how the gut microbiota communicates with the CNS through neural, endocrine, and immune pathways. This provides scientific evidence for an influencing role in the regulation of anxiety, mood, cognition, and pain. The microbiota are integrated into the illustrated gut–brain axia and impact on the brain in states from satiety to stress.

A range of mechanisms have been proposed by which gut flora affect the CNS:

1. Altering composition of the gut flora. They can compete for dietary ingredients such as growth substrates, they can produce vitamins, reduce inflammation, and stimulate innate immune responses. All these can change gut–brain signalling.
2. Immune activation. The immune system interacts bidirectionally with the CNS. Also, indirectly, the gut flora affects the immune system, altering cytokine levels. These are both pro- and anti-inflammatory and directly impact brain function.
3. Vagus nerve. As illustrated below, this regulates bronchial constriction, heart rate, and gut motility. About eighty per cent of nerve fibres are sensory, conveying sensory information about the body organs to the CNS. Many of the effects of gut flora are

dependent on vagal activity. The mechanisms of vagal afferent activation by gut microbiotica have yet to be elucidated.

4. Metabolism of tryptophan. This essential amino acid is a precursor of serotonin. This metabolic pathway becomes dysregulated in many brain and gastrointestinal tract disorders. Two key enzymes involved in the metabolism are activated by inflammatory mediators and corticosteroids.
5. Microbial metabolites. Gut flora are essential in the production of bile acids, choline, and short chain fatty acids. Complex carbohydrates are digested and fermented in the colon by gut microorganisms into neuroactive short chain fatty acids.
6. Microbial neurometabolites. These neurotransmitters act on the enteric nervous system and may have anti-nociceptive properties.
7. Bacterial cell wall sugars. These may modulate neural signalling or act on afferent axons.

Knowledge of all these mechanisms of interaction of the gut enteric nervous system on the central nervous system lends credence to my hypothesis that reprocessing of the gut's emotional response can help to reduce a dysregulation of the gastrointestinal system. Also, continuing reprocessing of distressing sensations in relation to trauma at the level of the stomach can be signalled to the heart and brain via the vagus nerve. This will enable digestion and metabolism of these sensations at a cognitive level.

The vagus, or tenth, cranial nerve leaves the brainstem and tends to calm down all the organs of the body. The sympathetic nerves in red have the opposite effect and get the person ready to engage the "fight" response or mobilise the heart, lungs, and muscles for "flight" (Figure 4).

The five organs illustrated may represent the five stages of BART psychotherapy and peak performance. Thus:

1. Activation of the gut instinct or gut reaction at level of root and sacral chakras.
2. Stimulation of the pancreas with release of insulin and proposed direct link to anterior inferior and posterior inferior sections of insular cortex in cerebrum.
3. Energising of heart chakra and heart organ with reprocessing of loss and grief.

The vagus nerve "wanders" from the brainstem to the bodily organs to calm them down.

The sympathetic nerves travel to the bodily organs preparing them for a fight or flight reaction in times of stress

Stimulation of the vagus nerve shuts down inflammation at a cellular level. Immune system function is then enhanced throughout the body

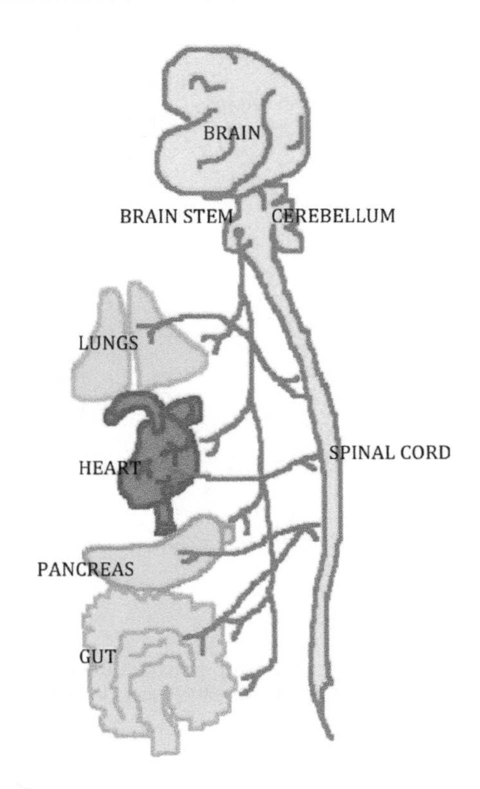

Figure 4. The path of the vagus nerve.

4. Inflation and deflation of lungs. This gives rise to the in and out breaths and helps stabilise any functional impairment due to anxiety and rapid breathing or panic attacks.
5. Continuous bilateral stimulation of head-brain so that the patient or client can take on board all of the information reprocessed at lower bodily energy levels.

The techniques of BART psychotheraapy are designed to boost the immune and endocrine systems and allow for neuronal rewiring (Figure 5).

Both cerebral hemispheres and the gastrointestinal tract develop from the neural crest at ten weeks gestation. Thus, they have the potential to communicate interneuronally. It takes both the gut mucosa and the brain four years to develop protective myelin sheaths.

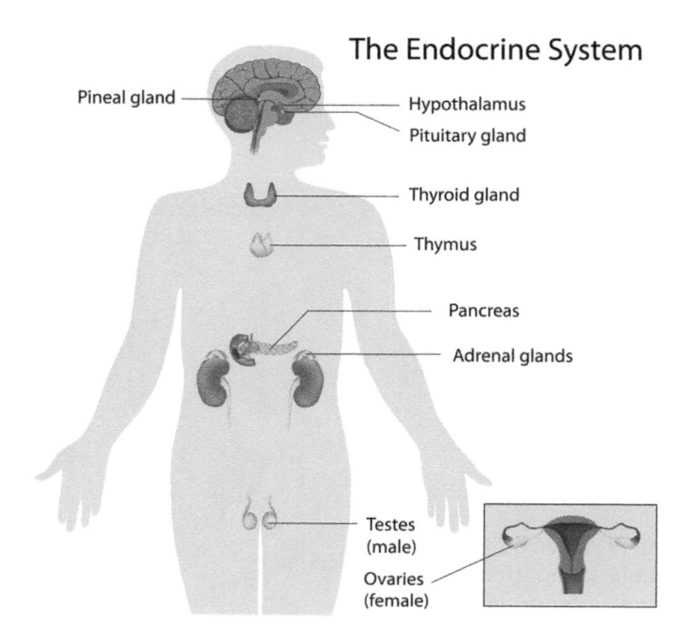

Figure 5. Relationship between the endocrine system and BART psychotherapy. Alilia Medical Media/shutterstock.com

Thus, children younger than four are especially prone to infections, food allergies and intolerance, and the developing brain is susceptible to abuse and neglect. This is further discussed in Chapter Six.

The heartbeat develops at eight weeks gestation and sets the basic rhythm experienced throughout life. The heart has its own independent neural network. BART psychotherapy enhances the gut, heart, and brain neuronal and energetic communication.

At the head-brain level, BART psychotherapy promotes inter-hemispheric integration. The patient or client is mindful of feelings and reprocessed thoughts.

The intrinsic nervous system of the heart triggers a heartbeat from the eighth week of gestation. The 40,000 functional group of autonomous nerve cells in the heart can register heartfelt emotions and sensations linked to loss and traumatic grief. The heart has evolved from a single tube in fish, two chambers in frogs, three chambers in reptiles, to the four-chamber human heart. With each evolutionary stage has come greater neuronal sophistication.

The pancreas and intestines are part of the gut-brain. They give rise to the patient or client's gut instinct or reaction. The pancreas produces insulin, which may be directly detected by the insular cortex of the head-brain. The gut's enteric plexus contains one hundred million nerve cells. These can function independently to the central and cardiac nervous systems. This is particularly true in children. Most parents will recognise the scenario: John or Mary does not want to go to school. It is Monday morning and they are complaining of a pain in their tummy. Concerned, you pay a visit to the doctor. The examination proves inconclusive and the diagnosis of acute non-specific abdominal pain, or ANSAP, is made. I would interpret the pain in emotional terms and, as a child has not yet fully developed the capacity for abstract thought, they are unable to put into words the reasons for their emotional distress. Using the techniques described later in the book, therapists will discover how to link the sensations of the gut-brain to the thought processes in the head-brain.

The adrenal glands and kidneys are positioned bilaterally and can give rise to a patient or client who says, "I feel it in my water". The circulating adrenaline transmits these feelings of fight, flight, fright, freeze, falling, and feigned death around the endocrine system. BART psychotherapy promotes the reprocessing and resolution of sensations, feelings, emotions, and thoughts at each brain level.

The activation of the root, or base, chakra energies will be related to processing of testosterone from the testes in the male and oestrogen from the ovaries in the female. This is especially relevant in patients who are victims of sexual abuse, which remains unresolved. (See Figure 5.)

Composition of neuroreceptors in the heart-brain, or cardiac neural plexus

Twenty per cent of heart neurons are receptive, that is, detect mechanical pressure in the heart. Chemoreceptor neurons account for the remaining eighty per cent. These are sensitive to hormones and neurotransmitters. This information accumulates in the heart-brain for decision making at a local level. It connects to brain, gut, skin, lungs, and other visceral organs, subsequently. The patient benefits by paying attention to this bodily information. The heart-brain synchronises with the patient's head-brain and thalamus. Fluent heart rate variability (HRV) results. Mindful breathing helps induce a harmonious mental state in the patient, and regulates HRV, helping to calm the patient or client's dysregulated, emotional state. Quantum coherence leads to the occurrence of synchronised electrical activity emanating from the heart to the thalamus to the frontal cortex. This allows for better focusing and reprocessing of patient or client reactions, which are appropriate to the situation and within their window of tolerance. (See Figure 9.)

Role of the gastrointestinal tract in processing food and emotional reactions and hypothetical link to insular cortex in cerebral hemispheres, or head-brain

The gut absorbs and processes food, which increases glucose concentrations in the bloodstream. The pancreas produces insulin (from the islets of Langerhans). The insular cortex in the brain may directly perceive this hormone. It is divided into the anterior insular cortex (AIC) and posterior insular cortex (PIC) and helps to give us insight into our basic gustatory feelings. Indeed, its phylogenetic origin is from the gustatory cortex, which, in mammals, enables the processing of taste and leads to the perception of disgust.

A recent review by Kennedy and colleagues (2012) examined the neural pathways connecting the brain to the gut and vice versa. Thus, the gut viscera influences brain functioning. Stress, mood, thoughts, and emotion affect gut function via the vagal pathways of the autonomic nervous system. The immune system affects functioning of the enteric nervous system, which then influences the central nervous system. Other mediators include neurotransmitters and neuropeptides such as serotonin, noradrenaline, and corticotropin-releasing factor. This led to the hypothesis of cognitive dysfunction and stress as important in the aetiology of gut disorders such as irritable bowel syndrome.

Both AIC and PIC components of the insular cortex (IC) have a role to play in the integration of social emotions, from empathy, disgust, and pain to experiences of joy, compassion, admiration, and fairness. The left and right AIC may code for positive and negative affect in the prefrontal cortex (PFC), as suggested by Davidson (2004). This provides further scientific evidence for the benefit of continuous bilateral cerebellar stimulation in the twin approaches of BART psychotherapy for resolving trauma and achieving peak performance.

The insular cortex has visceral and sensory neural connections. It encodes body temperature, sensations from the musculature, viscera, and levels of arousal. This leads to a gradual process of interoceptive awareness, which is consistent with the five stages of BART psychotherapy. Initial gut instinct such as visceral or somatic bodily feelings is at the genesis of human emotional experience (Kennedy, Clarke, O'Neill, et al., 1962). Integration and appraisal of this information allows the patient or client to progress to interpretation and action based on their instinctive or conscious experience. Thus, a sensation such as "stomach tension" could be associated with feelings of fear or pleasure. The individual patient or client is helped by the BART psychotherapist to correctly identify the emotional memory linked to the stomach sensation.

The insular cortex plays a critical role in mapping internal bodily somatic and feeling states. Once mapped, they can form the basis for predictions of further bodily reactions to emotional or sensory stimuli directly related to the self.

It appears that painful stimuli map on to the PIC while affective stimuli related to the self map on to the AIC. It is my hypothesis that this part of the cortex was named after the pancreas, which produces insulin. It is as if this hormone, which monitors glucose levels in the gut, has a direct neural link to the insular cortex to provide the same role for cortically expressed emotions. Thus, there is an integration of feeling, empathy, and uncertainty in the insular cortex. This is appraised by the cerebral hemispheres, as explained in Chapter Twelve.

The insular cortex has emerged as the key structure in the brain to be activated for trauma resolution, according to one of the world's foremost experts on emotion and behaviour, Professor Ray Dolan, of Queen's Square Hospital for Neurology and Neurosurgery in London. It is involved in processing internal bodily signals (interoception). In addition, it integrates the patient or client's mental map with incoming sensory information to create a definitive sense of self (Rusbridger, 2014).

This is the putative site for registration of gut feelings in the brain. Coherence allows information from the head-brain, heart-brain and gut-brain to be synchronised and balanced. The autonomic nervous system (ANS), endocrine and immune systems are similarly co-ordinated. Eventually, the aim is for them all to fire at the same rate. Those that fire together wire together (i.e., work well interactively). Synergistic adaptive growth ensures that, with healthy evolution, HRV varies when an emotional stimulus is about to be shown. Thus, four or five seconds before it is actually shown, the prefrontal cortex (PFC) registers this intuitively. The PFC then modulates heart rhythm 250 ms later. We become attuned (from sound or stretch) to the heart's rhythm.

Unconsciously stored information is intuitive until it is reprocessed from the body-mind into our consciousness. BART psychotherapy accelerates that process in the fourth stage of activating our brain's axons, which are rewired for transmission (cf. stage four of BART psychotherapy).

Figure 6 shows how the gut has sensory and motor control independent of the peripheral and central nervous systems. The intrinsic and extrinsic pathways are shown.

Doc Childre founded the Institute of Heartmath in 1991 and sought to explore the effect of stress on human body systems. The heart is the most powerful generator of electromagnetic energy in the human body. As such, it is uniquely positioned to connect the gut-brain, head-brain, emotions, feelings, sensations, and spiritual awareness. To quote Childre and Rozman (2002),

> Since emotional processes can work faster than the mind, it takes a power stronger than the mind to bend perception, override emotional circuitry and provide us with intuitive feeling instead. It takes the power of the heart. (p. 86)

The heart's magnetic field

The magnetic field emanating from the heart is 5,000 times larger than that from the brain and measurable up to several metres from the body (McCraty, Atkinson, & Tomasino, 2001). Augmentation of this magnetic field is a goal of future BART psychotherapy. The heart's electrical field is sixty times greater in amplitude than the electrical activity generated by the brain. The heart communicates with the brain and body in four ways via:

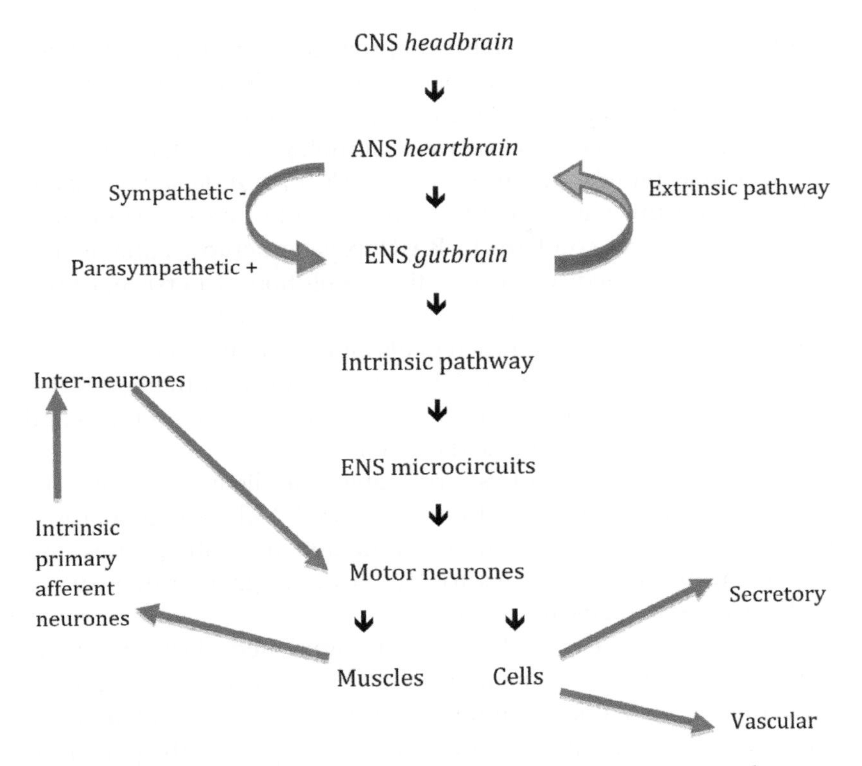

Figure 6. Diagram of the head, heart, and gut pathways. CNS = central nervous system, ANS = autonomic nervous system, ENS = enteric nervous system.

- nervous system or neurologically;
- pulse waves of blood pressure or biomechanically;
- hormones or biochemically;
- electromagnetic fields or energetically.

These different forms of heart–brain communication affect how we perceive and react to the world. The heart-brain talks to the head-brain and gut-brain. The gut-brain communicates to both heart-brain and head-brain. Finally, the head-brain digests and replies to the signals from both the heart's nervous system and the enteric nervous system. It is a highly integrated neural network right down to the cellular level. The initial gut reaction accessed during incident reprocessing in BART psychotherapy reaches the heart, which acts as a focal point for connection to relevant bodily sensations, feelings, emotions, cognitions, and spiritual insights. Reprocessing of negative feelings leads to generation of positive ones, for example, compassion. The brain's perception of these feelings is altered and we feel better. A key goal is the development of positive psychological change. This is a topic of David Blore's PhD thesis: *In Search of the Antonym to Trauma* (2012). It is for this reason that the achievement of peak performance is seen as a natural corollary to BART psychotherapy. Patients and clients are encouraged to imagine that resolution of persistent traumatic stress opens a window of opportunity to achieve optimal or peak performance in their chosen goals and future templates.

The heart's electromagnetic field extends out from the body. This can be conceived as part of Sheldrake's extended mind hypothesis and his theory of morphogenetic fields (1988).

When two people (therapist and patient or client) communicate, we get the following potential for interaction. BART psychotherapy is aimed at making this a positive interaction for both parties and maximising the opportunities for post-trauma growth or positive psychiatric/psychological change.

When humans interact, there is an augmented electromagnetic field in the gap between them. This might enhance the prospect of non-verbal or telepathic communication. This shows the potential for enhanced progress in the suitably attuned therapist for the patient or client. Part of the therapeutic alliance rests on finding a suitable distance between therapist and patient or client to optimise this resonance. This is taught in both somatic experiencing and somatomotor therapeutic approaches.

Schumann (earth) resonances

The Schumann resonances reported by Cherry (2002) occur between the earth and ionosphere and start at 7.83 Hertz (Figure 7). We may send intentions in the form of a radio wave. The particles may consist of neutrinos that can travel faster than the speed of light. It is now believed that they warp in a different quantum or dimension previously undetected by science. As we emit positive neutrino light energy there is greater resonance with the earth's geomagnetic energy field. The atmosphere becomes more coherent (from Latin: *cohere*, to stick together). The earth's magnetic field is changing and the Institute

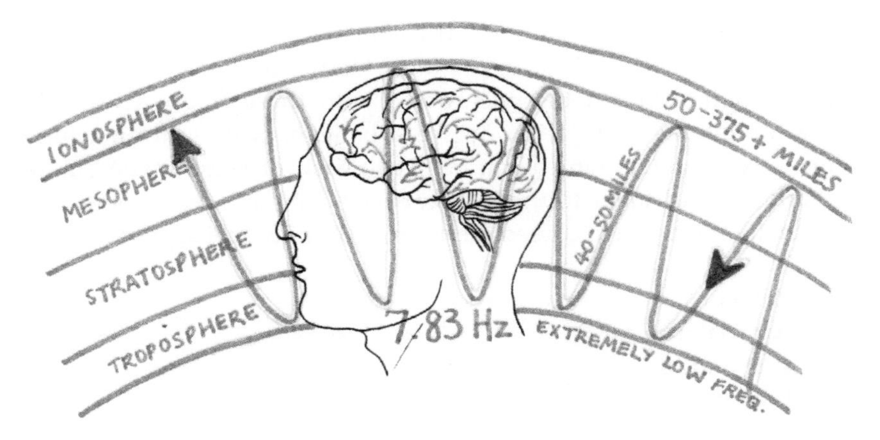

Figure 7. Schumann resonance and the planetary ionosphere.

of Heartmath are recording this through their Global Coherence initiative. By uniting people to speak and feel from the heart-brain, a shift in consciousness can occur. The human population can move from a state of instability and disharmony to one of balance, cooperation, and peaceful coexistence. By raising the vibration of one person, then one hundred quantum shifts in consciousness are possible. The hundredth monkey effect (Keyes, 1984) discusses this possibility. Human thought and aspiration can interact with the wider environment and effect changes at the planetary level of the earth's magnetic field.

The interaction between Schumann resonance vibrations in the human brain and geomagnetic atmospheric resonances in planet earth is shown in Figure 7. The hypothesis is that our biological systems have been exposed to these vibrations since the beginning of our evolution. Scientific measurements suggest that the average Schumann resonance in the ionosphere has increased from 7.83 Hz to approximately 11 Hz.

It is likely that our biological systems will also start to resonate at a higher frequency. The thrust of BART psychotherapy is to start at the lower vibratory energies at the levels of the root and sacral chakra. As reprocessing ascends, the higher chakras are activated and ultimately the brain experiences exposure to a vibratory resonance of 40–60 Hertz, triggering thalamocortical connections and coherence (see Figure 8).

The Schumann resonance of earth contains seven subtle vibrations. These are 7.83, 14, 21, 26, 33, 39 and 45 Hertz. Are our body's chakra energy points meant to synchronise with these frequencies? My BOKA bilateral stimulation device, I believe, is the only machine currently available which can be set to each of these seven subtle vibrations equivalent to those of earth's Schumann resonances. For psychotherapy, I have coined the term ZAPPERS, which stands for:

Zone of
Arousal of
Past and/or
Present
Emotions
Reprocessed
Successfully

These zappers can be set to coincide with the five stages of BART psychotherapy and peak performance:

1. Stage 1: 1–9 Hz average 7.8 Hz.
2. Stage 2: 10–19 Hz average 14 Hz.
3. Stage 3: 20–29 Hz includes Schumann resonances of 21 and 26 Hz.
4. Stage 4: 30–39 Hz includes Schumann resonances of 33 and 39 Hz.
5. Stage 5: 40–60 Hz includes gamma wave frequency of 45 Hz.

As the patient or client progresses through the stages of BART psychotherapy, they report feeling lighter, consistent with resonance at a higher, more intuitive frequency. They often leave the therapeutic session feeling as if a weight or burden has been lifted from their shoulders.

Benefits of a coherent atmosphere for trauma reprocessing and peak performance

Focused coherence in the patient or client is self-reinforcing and the beneficial effects of BART psychotherapy are amplified. The human brain operates best when the thalamus can resonate at a frequency of 40–60 Hertz. It is at this frequency that thalamocortical circuits are activated with increased capacity for reflective thought. Using the latest multi-user BOKA machine, I am able to apply an external frequency of 40–60 Hertz bilaterally at the level of the left and right mastoid process. Theoretically, this can increase the vibratory resonance within the body particles of each cerebellum. Thus, atoms and molecules of the gut-brain, heart-brain, and head-brain (or body-mind) can coalesce to enable the client or patient to reach a higher state of conscious awareness.

We now know from CERN research at the Large Hadron Collider (LHC) in Switzerland that the elusive Higgs–Boson particles have been discovered and give mass and impetus to this process. The mastoid process is chosen for the site of bilateral stimulation using specially adapted headphones. I have found that placing the bilateral auditory signal over the ears interfered with the patient or client's therapeutic alliance and inhibited their opportunities for direct feedback during BART psychotherapy. The mastoid process is derived from the Greek word for breast. It acts as a point of attachment for the muscles splenius capitus, longissimus capitus, posterior belly of digastric and sternocleidomastoid. It acts as a focal point of auditory resonance for the cerebellum, which helps to dampen instinctive brainstem responses and connect to the prefrontal cortex pathways modulating sensations, feelings, emotions, and cognitions. Stimulation of these muscles allows for:

- head extension, lateral flexion, and rotation of the cervical spine;
- flexion of the head and neck to the same side and bilateral extension of the vertebral column;
- allowing the jaw to open;
- lateral flexion and rotation of the head to the opposite side (unilateral contraction). Dorsal head extension (bilateral contraction) and support for inspiration when the head is still.

Role of the thalamus in the brain

Thalamus means "inner chamber" in Greek. It surrounds the third ventricle, which contains cerebrospinal fluid and is divided into two walnut-shaped halves with the nutshells positioned horizontally. It now appears to have seven discrete functions.

1. Relay station for somatic sensations apart from smell and cerebellar motor pathway.
2. Integrating centre for somatic sensory, visual, visceral, and motor in cerebellum, namely corpus striatum.
3. Regular maintenance of alertness, attention, and consciousness.
4. Emotional reprocessing, hence theory of bilateral affective reprocessing.
5. Pain now conceived as emotion.
6. Regulation of sleep-wake cycle.
7. Via connections to the mesio-temporal lobe, it is believed to be involved in memory recall and familiar memory.

Many of the functions of the thalamus remain poorly defined and understood. It is hoped that the human brain project will further our understanding of this inner chamber. In the great pyramid of Giza, the positioning of the King's chamber and Queen's chamber may represent the pineal gland and pituitary gland, respectively.

Schwaller de Lubicz (1949) wrote *Le Temple dans l'homme* (*The Temple in Man*). He theorised that the Triple Sanctuary in the Temple of Luxor (lux = light and/or gold) corresponded to the human skull and its three endocrine glands, or power centres. He claimed that the thalamus was associated with the experience of enlightenment. In BART psychotherapy, activation of the sensory thalamus leads to information transfer to the cortex. This, in itself, can be seen as a type of enlightenment.

In *God-man: The Word Made Flesh* (Carey & Perry, 2013), the King's Chamber was the Holy Grail.

> Their eyes will become opened. The Great Pyramid will reveal us the sacred claustrum and the Door of Brahm. Before entering the King's Chamber are the four grooves named the, 'granite leaf'. These may correspond to the four eminences or the colliculi of the corpora quadrigemina in the midbrain. (p. 66)

The superior colliculi act as the visual reflex centre and the inferior colliculi are the auditory reflex centre. They are directly activated by the peripheral bilateral stimulation process integral to BART psychotherapy.

In Figure 8, the arrows show where the sensory information from the thalamus is transferred when rapid eye movements REM occur during ninety-minute sleep cycles. It is my hypothesis that this state of thalamocortical transfer of information, as represented by the arrows emanating from the thalamus, can be achieved during a two-hour therapeutic BART psychotherapy session. Most patients report a profound state of calm at the end of a session and yawn as if they have just had a good night's sleep. The lines coming from the cerebellum illustrate the dampening effect on the brainstem that I hypothesise can happen during the therapeutic session as both cerebellums receive direct mechanical input via auditory bilateral stimulation.

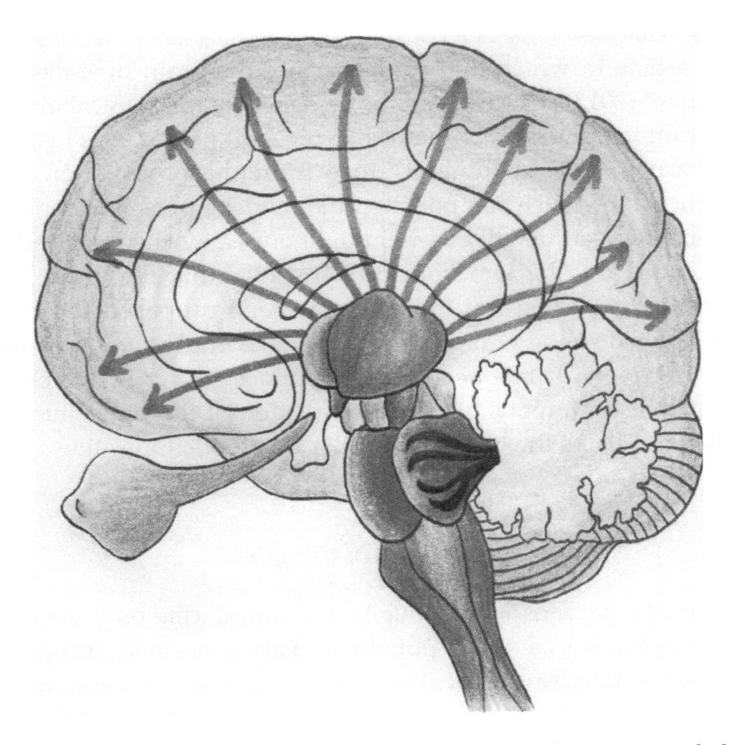

Figure 8. The cortex under the influence of an optimally resonant thalamus during sleep.

The role of the cerebellum in human evolution

Stringer (2012), in his book, *The Origin of Our Species*, has discussed how the cerebellum plays a role in higher brain functions such as information processing and learning. Initially, around two million years ago, the increased size of the brain was due to an increase in the size of the cerebral cortices. In recent human history, the reverse has occurred, with archaeologists reporting that the cerebellum has become larger, with the brain overall shrinking in size by ten per cent over the past twenty thousand years. It has been hypothesised that the larger cerebellum enables the brain to process information more efficiently. There might also be a connection to the gradual decrease in size of the connecting fibres between the hemispheres known as the corpus callosum.

This lends support for my direct stimulation of the cerebellum by auditory sound waves activated bilaterally at the level of the mastoid process. Anathaswamy is a consultant for *New Scientist* and has written an article in which he postulates that the brain operates, "like clockwork" (2013). This reviews the evidence for mechanical influence on the running of the brain that is like the springs and cogs in a finely tuned watch. The hypothesis arose from the observation that a mechanical blow, such as a punch, could render a person unconscious. The brain has traditionally been thought of as a biochemical and electrical organ. Yet, the knockout punch shows that the brain is also responsive to mechanical input. It has been proposed that sound waves applied to the brain can help to make our thoughts go round more effectively. It has been my experience, using BART psychotherapy, that continuous bilateral stimulation of the cerebellum does just that and helps the brain to run like a well-oiled machine.

The buzz of thought

Traditionally, neurons were thought to communicate only via electrical signals known as action potentials. This is normally propagated from axon to dendritic spine. However, on receiving a nerve impulse when a chemical neurotransmitter binds to its receptor, these spines bend and sway as if also affected by a mechanical sound wave. This movement also acts to progress the transfer of information, potentially making our thoughts go round more effectively. These changes have been hypothesised to help store information during learning about stored memories. Another mechanical influence on nerve transmission has been observed. Forces are transferred between dendritic spines as microtubules store energy like a spring. Mechanical stimulation of one dendritic spine causes a transfer of forces to adjacent ones via this bed of proteins. This has been proposed to help the individual adapt to the situation at hand and tune neural networks so that the brain could hum at a higher resonant frequency. The overall conclusion is that mechanical vibrations in brain tissue such as the cerebellum can cause beneficial changes in neural activity. This provides scientific evidence for the mechanism of action of BART psychotherapy, which has as a central component continuous bilateral auditory stimulation of the brain.

The brain thinking has been compared to a waterwheel going round and round. When the flow of water into the wheel increases, then more thoughts are secreted or produced. On the other hand, at times when the flow of water is reduced, for example, meditation or sleep, the output of neural activity or thoughts decreases. Depression has been likened to a state where the flow of water stops, the waterwheel grinds to a halt, and the patient is unable to think straight or, sometimes, even communicate. From my earlier discussion, there is every possibility that the BART psychotherapist will make a difference to the depressed patient's mental state. This can be the subject of future research.

The reprocessing of traumatic memories during BART psychotherapy can mimic thalamocortical projections. This is reflected in the verbal feedback from the patient in relation to cerebral sensation, which appears towards the end of a therapy session. As reprocessing ascends past the level of the throat chakra, or thyroid gland, patients often report sensations and feelings at the level of the right and left cerebral hemispheres. As reprocessing continues, they point to their forehead as if activating the brow or third eye chakra. They are then able to reflect on the learning and meaning from the experience by engaging with the functionality of their prefrontal cortex. This has relevance to the concept of the Mer-Ka-Ba discussed later. It has been proposed that to achieve the meditative state needed for the Mer-Ka-Ba experience the client or patient must relearn how to breathe through their third eye, which is located at the site of the sixth chakra, or pineal gland.

The most exciting research in neuroscience is pointing us towards the potential for coherent thought when thalamic neurons are exposed to a frequency of 40–60 Hertz or a range of gamma band activity. This is believed to facilitate thalamocortical binding.

Influence of the Dalai Lama on meditative practice and neuroscience

From presentations I attended given by the fourteenth Dalai Lama in Manchester in June 2012, there is a need for increased conscious awareness and compassion of all like-minded people on earth if we are to better live in harmony with both ourself and those around us. The Dalai Lama mentioned conversations he had with Professor Aaron Beck, the father of cognitive behaviour therapy (CBT). Professor Beck believed that ninety per cent of a person's negative emotions were due to mental projection. The Dalai Lama said this was similar to the Buddhist belief that reality is influenced by one's projections. He mentioned the benefits of taking a strong stand against those engaging in destructive behaviour by cultivating compassion towards them. This process contrasts with being self-centred, which leads to mental unhappiness. When people are selfish, they become oblivious to others and end up creating their own unhappiness, according to the Dalai Lama.

He went on to state that placing the welfare of others at the centre of your life means that your own self-interest is generated as a by-product. The Dalai Lama spoke about the nature of mind being equivalent to a clear light with space for love. The activation of the chakras discussed in this book is consistent with this eastern world philosophy. The Buddhist view of enlightenment is to quieten or neutralise the sensorial mind. The goal is to deliberately stop reminiscences on the past and projections about hopes for the future. By remaining in that empty space of present awareness, you will then get a picture of the true nature of consciousness, wisdom, or knowing. The clarity involved in cultivating this mental state means enlightenment will suddenly dawn on you, according to Buddhist tradition. The goal is to seek a deeper understanding of the emptiness of mind by meditating and reflecting on its nature.

The Dalai Lama also sought to explain the environmental conditions present before humanity was aware of consciousness. He stated that particle matter was already there before the Big Bang. Researchers such as Professor Turok (Leonard, 2010), at the Perimeter Institute in Toronto, Canada, also believe that and discuss a series of bouncing big bangs, with one coming to an end before the next one starts. In this theory on the origins of the universe, there is a pause between big bangs when only particle matter exists. This shows the compatibility of beliefs between traditional Buddhism and modern theoretical physics. In addition, quantum theory is delving into exploring the concepts of dark matter, empty space, and why gravitational forces are so weak. In my opinion, the philosophic and scientific standpoints of east and west are coming full circle and meeting once again in the middle.

This is reminiscent of the parable of the two eagles, one male and one female, who were released from heaven by Zeus. According to legend, both flew around the universe in opposite directions. When they met up, he allegedly pronounced, "The eagles have landed". A nest was formed and great wisdom emanated from this location. It became known as the Delphic Oracle and is now a highly revered site from ancient Greece or modern day Delphios.

A good word to summarise the philosophy of the Dalai Lama is mindfulness (Gilbert & Choden, 2013). This has now been adopted by mental health services in the west as a key component in the patients' journey towards wellness. The compassionate mind approach and practice of Professor Paul Gilbert are good examples of the infiltration of this approach into the NHS.

I believe the first step in achieving mindfulness is an increase in the individual's level of conscious awareness. This can be achieved using the staged process of BART psychotherapy both for trauma resolution and peak performance.

Further aspects of the concepts of consciousness in relation to the experiences of the patient or client

This also taps into the ideas of archetypes and personal and collective unconscious first discussed by Sigmund Freud and Carl Jung and illustrated in Figure 9 (Freud, 1900a).

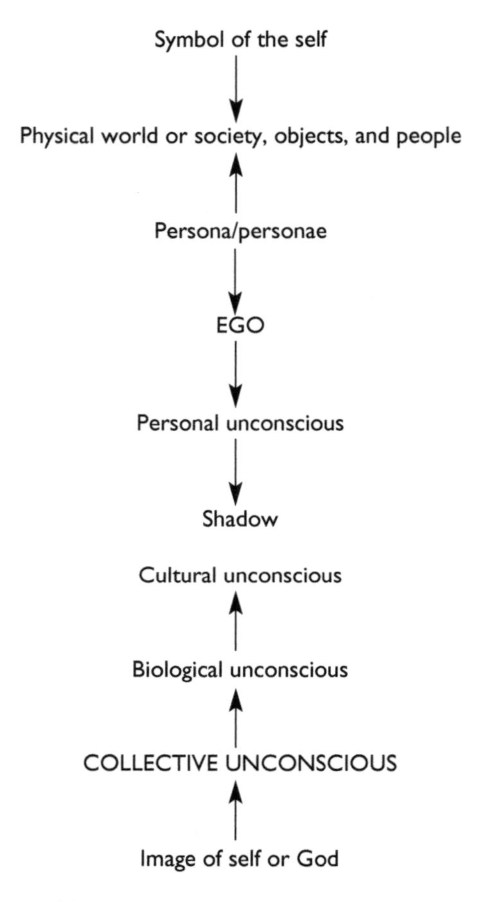

Figure 9. Psychic world comprising complexes and archetypes.

This is like a ripple spreading from the centre with the overarching influence of the ego. Jung proposed shadow and archetypal projections into the physical world. This was further expanded in Assagiolis's conception of the different strands of consciousness.

Assagiolis (1975) developed the concept of psychosynthesis. He saw similarities between this concept and Jung's ideas. The task of therapy is to transform the individual's personality and develop the higher psychic functions, such as the spiritual dimension. He said that Jung differentiates four functions: sensation, feeling, thought, and intuition. He believes imagination or fantasy is also a distinct function.

He also placed the will at the heart of self-consciousness or the ego. The debate on consciousness continues to this day and knowledge of past theories will inform future research. The five functions can be likened to the five stages of BART psychotherapy.

1. Sensation from the peripheral nervous system.
2. Feeling from the heart-brain and first three chakras.
3. Thought from the head-brain.
4. Intuition from the pituitary gland and higher chakras.
5. Imagination or fantasy from the pineal gland and the Mer-Ka-Ba.

Interhemispheric connectivity: use of a medical device, body of knowledge activator (BOKA), during BART psychotherapy and peak performance

Dr Gerard Karl from Karlware Gmbh in Germany built this machine according to my specifications over the period 2010–2012. The acronym BOKA stands for "body of knowledge activator". As levels of emotional turmoil subside, thought that is more rational allows information to flow more freely to become a source of knowledge. The advantage of this unique machine is that frequencies of bilateral stimulation can be set to reflect the alpha, beta, theta, delta, and gamma waves produced by the brain according to its level of awareness. The final prototype was delivered after several modifications. This is the first of his machines to calibrate the frequency of bilateral stimulation using multiple tactile and auditory socket outlets. It is electrically operated and can be switched off by remote control. The machine itself has a position switch with which the frequency in Hertz of bilateral activation is selected. The bilateral stimulation can be applied to the patient or client either separately or combined. The second position anticlockwise selects the click frequency for bilateral cerebellar resonance in the combined mode, that is, clicks delivered simultaneously. The third position anticlockwise selects the tactile frequency in Hertz.

The machine surface has five circular switches and three flick switches. The upper left switch controls the speed for the left channel. The upper right switch controls the click speed for both right and left channels. Flick switches set high and low speeds for either separate or combined channels. Speed settings can be set individually. Circular switches are used to adjust vibration intensity and frequency of vibration for tactile devices. A final switch for the volume of the headphones completes the controls. The digital display on the angled surface of the device gives read-out of the frequency in Hertz of the bilateral stimulation applied to the patient or client. (Range: 0.1 to 60 Hz.)

The auditory clicking of the BOKA machine is applied externally to the mastoid processes bilaterally. This can induce an internal state of entrainment, increasing resilience and flexibility when the patient is in a crisis. Entrainment means that by exposing one cerebellar hemisphere to a frequency of 30 Hertz and the other cerebellar hemisphere to a frequency of 10 Hertz, we entrain both hemispheres to resonate at a frequency equal to the difference, that is, 20 Hertz. This machine incorporates the apparatus for up to six individual medical devices. It is the only prototype in which the bilateral stimulation can be delivered to up to twelve patients or clients simultaneously. In addition, it is the only machine currently available in which the frequency can be set ranging from 1–60 Hertz and varied bilaterally. The main advantage of this machine is that groups of patients or clients can be seen simultaneously. This would benefit a family who had experienced the death of a loved one from an accident involving a motor vehicle or suicide. In terms of members of a sports team, they could be helped to prepare for competition by activating their imagination and promoting development of resilience.

This is the first prototype of a bilateral stimulation multi-user machine. It integrates bodily experience with cerebral knowledge and can help the patient or client process their traumatic experiences before going on to become activated towards optimal or peak performance.

I integrate foot-tapping by the patient or client into the process of BART psychotherapy. This way I am able to kick-start the integration of bottom-up neurological processing with top-down neurological processing of information from the cerebral hemispheres. As the left foot taps, the sensory and motor aspects of the right hemisphere are activated. This information is passed along the fibres of the corpus callosum and, as the right foot starts to tap in synchrony, the signal reaches the left hemisphere, increasing interhemisphere connectivity and, hence, coherence.

Further use of this machine can be to help people and their companies with increased levels of behavioural organisation. The main distinction between good and bad bosses within companies is the extent of their good or bad behaviour. Rarely does an employee complain that their boss was a bad accountant, engineer, or surveyor. Rather, they will complain of his being a bully, ignorant, and having a blame culture.

There is an altered frequency of waves produced by the brain with increasing states of wakefulness. Delta waves (0.5–3 Hz) are produced during deep sleep. Theta waves (4–7 Hz) are produced during deep meditation and dreaming. Alpha waves (8–13 Hz) occur during visualisation and meditation when the eyes are closed. Beta waves (14–40 Hz) are produced during wakefulness. Finally gamma waves (<40 Hz) are associated with heightened states of perception and awareness. Further research could identify to what extent externally applied frequencies compare with the brain waves recorded during a BART psychotherapy session. The ultimate goal is to stimulate gamma waves equivalent to a state of heightened perception. My hypothesis is that using the BOKA machine at a frequency of 40–60 Hertz will initiate this state of heightened awareness and improved reprocessing. This can benefit both clients in the business sector and patients in the health sector.

Summary

In this chapter, I have introduced the concept of BART psychotherapy. This is based on the processing of information from the enteric nervous system (gut-brain) cardiac nervous system (heart-brain) and central nervous system (head-brain). The interrelationship of the gut-brain and heart nerve pathways is explained along with the role of the heart's magnetic field. Schumann resonances are proposed to have an effect on the five stages of BART psychotherapy. The changing evolution of the brain is discussed as well as reduced size of the cerebral cortices and corresponding increase in size and functional importance of the cerebellum bilaterally. Recent research on the mechanical influence of sound waves on the brain propagating neural activity is mentioned. This is felt to help make our thoughts go round and I believe provides scientific evidence for the mechanism of action of BART psychotherapy. The benefits of coherence of thoughts via inter-hemispheric connectivity are explained. This is influenced by thalamic rhythms acting on the cortex during sleep. It is proposed that this state can be achieved during BART sessions of psychotherapy. The thoughts of the Dalai Lama on meditative practice and their links to neuroscience are discussed. The concepts of consciousness are discussed from the perspectives of Carl Gustav Jung and Roberto Assagiolis. My bilateral stimulation machine for administering BART psychotherapy is discussed. The different brainwave frequencies are shown with the proposal that the gamma wave frequency correlates to a state of heightened perception.

CHAPTER TWO

Activation of the chakras using BART psychotherapy and peak performance

Another aspect of this multi-user machine is achieving an ascending kaleidoscope of body chakra activation. The following description outlines the nature of the main chakras, both internal to the body itself and external. These are illustrated on the following colour plate: in ascending order, the most well known chakras are root chakra (Figure 10), sacral chakra (Figure 11), solar chakra (Figure 12), heart chakra (Figure 13), throat chakra (Figure 14), third eye chakra (Figure 15), crown chakra (Figure 16), earth star chakra (Figure 17), soul star chakra (Figure 18), stellar gateway chakra (Figure 19), and universal gateway chakra (Figure 20). In ascending order, the pattern starts with the earth star, or subpersonal chakra (Figure 17).

Earth star (or subpersonal chakra

Manifestation centre.
It connects us to earth's life force energy and electromagnetic fields.
This links to both the metatron cube's sacred geometry and the seven-element relaxation exercise for grounding patients or clients (discussed further on p. 154).

Figure 16. Crown chakra.

Figure 15. Third eye chakra.

Figure 14. Throat chakra.

Figure 13. Heart chakra.

Figure 12. Solar chakra.

Figure 11. Sacral chakra.

Figure 10. Root chakra.

Figure 20. Universal gateway chakra.

Figure 19. Stellar gateway chakra.

Figure 18. Soul star chakra.

Figure 17. Earth star chakra.

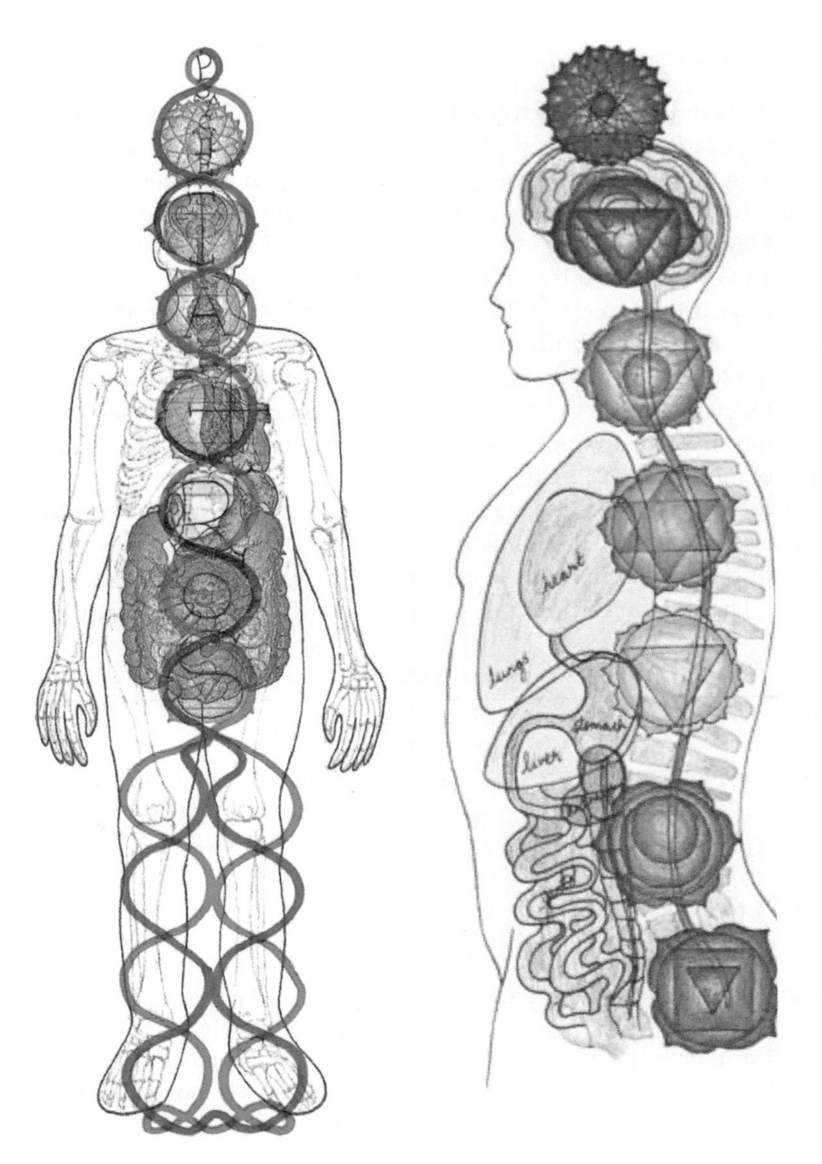

Figure 21. Chakras and organs. *Figure 22*. Chakras and organs, lateral.

First (spinal cord/root) chakra (Lotus Muladhara)

This is believed to be the grounding energy centre. It can be seen as anchoring spiritual reality in physical reality. The Tau symbol sits on the heart symbol and both are contained within the four-petal lotus.

The Muladhara chakra is shown as having four petals, bearing the Sanskrit letters *va*, *scha*, *sha*, and *sa*. The seed sound in the centre is *lam*. The earth is shown as a red triangle (see Figure 22).

There is little perception at this level and BART psychotherapy activates the patient's built-in survival instinct in a containing way. This helps to establish belief in a reality greater than the root chakra's sense of separateness. An imbalance here is experienced as insecurity. There may be a history of insecure attachments in early childhood (from six months to 3.5 years) (Table 1).

For diagnosis of these, see initial section of comprehensive mental health assessment in Chapter Thirteen.

Healing this chakra helps to restore security, well-being, and self-esteem. The physical body is mastered with increased stability,

Table 1. Spinal cord, or root chakra, functions.

Mantra	Lam.
No. of petals	Four.
Physical functions	Gives vitality to the physical body. Associated with being "grounded" and survival instincts.
Metaphysical functions	
Endocrine glands/organs	Adrenals, kidneys, spinal canal, colon (for digestive action), legs, feet, and bones.
Symptoms if chakra is "out of balance"	Violence, greed, anger, concern over physical survival.
Lessons learnt once chakra is activated using BART psychotherapy	Mastery of one's physical body, "grounding" one's individuality, stability, security, stillness, health, courage, and patience. Helps to develop emotional well-being and self-esteem.
Gemstones that crystallise this energy	Ruby, garnet, obsidian, red jasper, smoky quartz.
Element	Earth.

courage, and patience. The second (II) or sacral chakra can now be activated during continuation of BART psychotherapy.

Second (sacral) chakra (Lotus Svadhisthana).

This is believed to be the centre for both relationships and social interactions. It can be seen as the centre for dealing with issues related to the inner child aspects of our personality (Table 2).

Third (solar) chakra (Lotus Manipura)

This is believed to be the centre of personal power. It can also be seen as a centre of both chi energy and intuition. In addition, it is believed to give rise to functions of the auras, etheric and astral sensitivity. Here, ten petals, each with their own individual symbol, contain the yellow

Table 2. Second, or sacral, chakra functions.

Mantra	vam.
No. of petals	Six.
Physical functions	Oversees personal belongings, partnerships, and relations. Seat of creativity and procreation. Involves making money and achieving financial support or investment.
Metaphysical functions	Vitality, sexuality, procreation. Linked to conscious creativity and inner child.
Endocrine glands/organs	Genital, spleen, bladder, kidneys. and uterus.
Symptoms if chakra is "out of balance"	Insecurity, violence, greed, anger, sciatica, arthritis, anorexia nervosa.
Lessons learnt once chakra is activated using BART psychotherapy	Emotional balance, love, intake of new ideas, working harmoniously and creatively with others.
Gemstones that crystallise this energy	Amber and carnelian.
Element	Water.

sun, which, within its triangle, reveals the symbol of power in chi, aura, etheric, and astral realms. These are based on the gut instinct or reaction, which is the starting point for BART psychotherapy (Table 3).

As the feelings, sensations and emotions of the patient are vibrated at higher frequencies, the third chakra, or solar plexus (as outlined above), actively links to the gut feelings of the enteric plexus, or gut-brain. Its colour is yellow and it generates warmth, like the ambient radiation from the sun (*sorcha*, Irish word for sun).

Opportunities and willpower emerge from the location of the third chakra. Intellect from the head-brain registers through the reprocessing of the patient's gut feelings. Self-control and discerning behaviour are experienced. If this chakra is out of control the patient remains in an angry, aggressive state. The ability to appraise genuine threat occurs at the level of the solar plexus. With BART psychotherapy, the patient can choose the battles that are of importance to them, allowing them to refrain from being in a continual state of anger ("battle mind").

The key goal of aligning willpower with intellect starts to occur through activation of the appropriate neural networks. Breathing into

Table 3. Third, or solar, chakra functions.

Mantra	ram.
No. of petals	Ten.
Physical functions	Sympathetic nervous system, digestion, metabolism.
Metaphysical functions	Seat of emotions, clairsentience, and spirituality.
Endocrine glands/organs	Stomach, pancreas, gall bladder, liver and central nervous system.
Symptoms if chakra is "out of balance"	Abusive power, anger, ulcers, hypoglycaemia and diabetes mellitus
Lessons learnt once chakra is activated using BART psychotherapy	Authority, mastery of desire, awakening of consciousness, transformation of self, laughter, and morality.
Gemstones that crystallise this energy	Amber, yellow tourmaline, citrine, and topaz.
Element	Fire.

and holding the solar plexus pulls the heart-brain and head-brain into synchrony with the gut-brain, allowing focus and decision to emerge for the patient.

Blood flow changes in our patients and clients in the context of perceived threat. Blood is withdrawn from the prefrontal cortex at the moment of traumatic stress (thus, the patient or client cannot think) and the brainstem receives increased blood flow, orientating the person towards survival strategies. These are often still engaged once the threat has passed, and BART psychotherapy can reverse this blood flow, allowing more realistic appraisal of threat and the patient or client time to develop thinking space and a rational response.

At the moment of trauma or stress, blood is diverted to the amygdala, which perceives and reacts automatically to threat. Only information perceived as relevant to survival is processed, leaving the individual vulnerable to instinctive reactions.

BART psychotherapy encourages the patient to be fully conscious and mindful, with one foot in the present and the other in the memory of the past event being processed. Once the energetic levels of the first three chakras are balanced, the patient's senses awaken and they experience creativity with an appreciation of beauty. In my dissociation model (O'Malley, 2011), I encourage patients to imagine being soothed by the calm WATER level (Window of Affect Tolerance and Emotional Reprocessing, see Figure 23b). Together with the patient or client, we reprocess sensations or feelings associated with the hyperarousal state RAPIDS (see Figure 23a), or the hypoarousal state FROZEN (see Figure 23c) (see p. 42 for explanations of these acronyms). Often, I will explain these different states of arousal to the patient or client prior to therapy. Along with the seven element relaxation exercise, this helps to prepare them for any distressing emotions experienced as a necessary prerequisite to effectively reprocessing their trauma and stress and enabling them to move on in their lives.

Fourth (heart) chakra (Lotus Anahata)

This is believed to be the centre of emotional empowerment. It can be seen to deal with the expression of feelings through the heart such as grief, loss, and love. By resonating with this chakra through BART psychotherapy, our patients and clients can become more receptive to love and emotional healing. The green heart in the centre of this chakra has twelve petals surrounding a six-pointed star. The central symbol represents emotional healing. The symbol strikes me as resembling a person holding and soothing a baby (Table 4).

Further BART psychotherapy brings the patient towards the "path of the heart". They are able to let go of their psychological defences. As one patient explained to me, he felt that an arrow tipped with a

Table 4. Fourth, or heart, chakra functions.

Mantra	Yam.
No. of petals	Twelve.
Physical functions	Centre of personal self-esteem, power and ethics. How a person makes decisions, handles crises, and takes risks. Conquers fear and creates happiness and satisfaction. Responds to appreciation with empowerment.
Metaphysical functions	Anchors a higher self. Direct link to the intuitive, or sensing, right hemisphere. Opens awareness to universal energy (to love one's neighbour as oneself).
Endocrine glands/organs	Thymus, lungs, arms, hands, and circulation.
Symptoms if chakra is "out of balance"	Disturbed emotions, repression of love. Asthma, high blood pressure, lung and heart disease.
Lessons learnt once chakra is activated using BART psychotherapy	Oneness with life, forgiveness, compassion, understanding, balance, conscious awareness, acceptance, peace, openness, harmony, and contentment.
Gemstones that crystallise this energy	Emerald, tourmaline, jade, and rose quartz. Primary colour is green. Secondary colour is pink.
Element	Air.

rose was released from an angelic "Eros" before gently entering his heart, leaving him with a feeling of warmth and love. This is an example of how activating the fourth chakra, using BART psychotherapy, can connect the individual energy of the first three chakras with their universal life energy. The patient's personal and spiritual life energies become integrated, both bilaterally and vertically. This allows mindfulness to emanate from the heart centre towards higher chakra levels.

Fifth (throat) chakra (Lotus Vishuddha)

This is the centre for the encouragement of communication. It is also believed to be the centre of truth, personal expression, responsibility, faith, and creativity. The blue throat chakra contains sixteen petals and the symbol within the equilateral triangle represents truthful expression, responsibility, faith, and creativity (Table 5). During BART psychotherapy, the patient often experiences a lump in his or her throat. This must be cleared before reprocessing can be completed. It is often a reflection of aspects of the traumatic event that the patient or client has not been able to speak about because of the associated dysregulated affect. At the time of the traumatic event, the inflow of sensory information was so great that the neural fibres leading to the switching station of the thalamus became overwhelmed. This meant that the amygdala was only able to detect an unsafe or life-threatening situation. The key goal was survival and the fight, flight, or freeze neural pathways were activated. The speech pathways involve the left frontal cortex of Broca's area and the inferior frontal gyrus of Wernicke's area for expression and comprehension. As no information was being allowed through from the thalamus to these cerebral cortices, the patient or client did not have sufficient time to comprehend, evaluate, or talk about his experience. Indeed, being rendered speechless would have dramatically increased his chances of survival. However, many carry the speechlessness for months or years after the event. BART psychotherapists can reverse that process. Simon Weston was severely wounded following a bomb explosion on *HMS* Sir Galahad during the Falklands conflict in 1982 between the UK and Argentina. For six months he was not expected to live, and he has since been operated on eighty-seven times and received five hundred units of blood or blood products. He relived the explosion every night in nightmares

Table 5. Fifth, or throat, chakra functions.

Mantra	Ham.
No. of petals	Sixteen.
Physical functions	
Metaphysical functions	Seat of communication. Centre of speech, sound and clairaudience. To show increased abundance.
Endocrine glands/organs	Mouth, thyroid, parathyroid, and hypothalamus.
Symptoms if chakra is "out of balance"	Problems with speech, communication, and hearing. Ignorance, depression, lack of discernment. Unwise use of knowledge. Sore throat and thyroid dysfunction.
Lessons learnt once chakra is activated using BART psychotherapy	True communication of the spoken word. Creativity in speech, writing and the arts. Peace, truth, knowledge wisdom, honesty, reliability, gentleness, and kindness. Throat chakra mediates between the head thoughts and the heart feelings. It is the seat of willpower, courage, and guidance.
Gemstones that crystallise this energy	Lapis lazuli, azurite, turquoise, aquamarine, celestite, and blue topaz.
Element	Akasha (ether).

for twenty-four years after the explosion. He woke up in a sweat each night, unable to process the experience. He was still in survival mode and speechless. Then, one night, the metaphorical elastic band around his chest snapped. He was able to dream about the experience and talk to his dead colleagues in the trenches. I would hypothesise that the tightness around his chest was a constricted heart chakra. Once this was activated, the blockages at the level of the throat chakra could be addressed. This, in turn, allowed the thalamic circuits to switch off from survival mode. Nightmares or non-REM sleep phases were negotiated without waking up in a sweat. The REM dreaming circuits were switched on. This transferred healthy imagery and emotional experiences to the left cerebral hemisphere. This activated Simon's comprehension and expression. He has since been able to eloquently ascribe meaning to his ordeal. I would suggest that had Simon been able to avail himself of the staged approach of BART psychotherapy, he would not have had to wait twenty-four years for his own spontaneous healing reprocessing to occur.

In my experience, using BART psychotherapy, patients tend to "get stuck" at the level of the throat chakra. This is felt to be "like a lump in the throat" and represents an emotional or mental block in their traumatic memory. Their fifth chakra is their source of expression of emotions, feelings, and creativity. By direct bilateral stimulation of the throat, patients are able to shift this "blockage". They are then able to "find their voice" and speak truthfully and calmly in relation to the traumatic memory. The throat chakra has a sky-blue colour and resonates with clarity of speech and sound when activated.

During BART psychotherapy, it is essential to manage the patient's reprocessing within their Window of Affect Tolerance and Emotional Regulation (WATER), otherwise hyper- or hypo-arousal can occur. The resultant anxiety can trigger panic attacks and nervousness. Safely negotiating this stage allows the emergence of inspiration and intuition for the patient or client. By now, a quantum leap in consciousness has occurred and the patient is ready to ascend to the vibrational levels present in the quintessential mind. Individual and collective unconsciousness start to merge and innovative thinking merges with knowledge acquisition. The patient starts to view his life with a new perspective.

Explaining hyperarousal, hypoarousal, and dissociation to the patient or client

Figure 23(a,b,c) illustrates the model used to explain the interrelationship between levels of arousal, dissociation, and integration of emotional states of the patient or client (O'Malley, 2011).

The middle picture is of Narrow Water Castle in Warrenpoint, County Down, Northern Ireland. This was the location for the greatest loss of life in the security forces in the Troubles in Northern Ireland

RAPIDS

Racing thoughts

Affective dysregulation

Partitioned personality

Impulsivity

Distress

Suicidality

(a) Hyperarousal and dissociation.

WATERS

Window of

Affect Tolerance

Emotions

Regulated and

Stabilised

(b) Integration of emotional states.

FROZEN

Freeze Reaction

Oblivious to the outside world

Zonked out

Emotionally

Numb

(c) Hypoarousal and dissociation.

Figure 23. RAPIDS, WATERS, and FROZEN in BART psychotherapy.

and occurred in 1979. It is designed to illustrate how the state of calm represented by "WATERS" can change in seconds to the destructive states of chaotic "RAPIDS" and numbing "FROZEN". This can lead clinically to the dissociative states described above. The consensus view of trauma therapists is that the state of hyperarousal is also a form of dissociation. Patients in either the RAPIDS or FROZEN state require a different therapeutic approach to restore their state of equilibrium to calmer WATERS.

Plans were at an advanced stage to erect a bridge over this span of water near Warrenpoint, which, metaphorically, can be seen to represent new neural networks spanning the twin states of being either frozen or in the rapids. This could be symbolised by an arc or rainbow of light reaching over the murky depths of water below.

If we play with the initial letters of the name Narrow Water Castle, we can describe how, with experience, the nerves and synapses make new connections.

*N*erves
*A*ctually
*R*epeatedly
*R*ewire
*O*pening the
*W*idth of the
*W*indow of
*A*ffect
*T*olerance and
*E*motional
*R*egulation

*C*ontaining/*C*omputing/*C*onverting
*A*ny
*S*ignificant or
*T*raumatic
*L*ife
*E*xperiences

As the neural synapses fire, they rewire, and this allows the window of tolerance to widen as if the banks of the river in the photograph have been strengthened to protect against flooding and being frozen over. This allows the patient or client to tolerate greater degrees of affect and also to better regulate all their emotions. By strengthening this reservoir using the seven-element exercise described on p. 154, they can safely contain any dysfunctional emotional state. The information is then taken up to the sensory gateway known as the thalamus. Here, there is a low-grade level of analysis computing any signs of danger. This could be high winds and turbulent waters or the hidden danger of an iceberg. Once the danger has passed, the cortex is able to convert any significant or traumatic life experiences so that meaning can be made from the event. Unfortunately, the EU funding of £14.5 million for the bridge construction has been withdrawn as matching funding was not forthcoming from the Irish and Stormont governments (*BBC News*, 2013).

Case example 1

One patient described to me his vision of a fish with bulbous eyes, as if linked to the earliest reptilian evolution of visual perception. This became linked to the image of a dolphin riding the crest of a wave and diving into the deep ocean. Since their evolution, dolphins are believed to have retained the consciousness emerging from the planetary grid of earth. In Professor Brian Cox's documentary, *Wonders of Life* (2012), the evolution of human senses are discussed. When jawless fish existed, they breathed via sets of gills. As evolution proceeded, these gills formed arches and gave rise to fish with jaws. These bones then further receded to form the internal ear ossicles, the stapes, incus, and anvil. Similarly, our eyes have evolved from these primitive ancestors. The most primitive aspect to our visual pathway has been incorporated into the brainstem and is known as the superior and inferior colliculi, or corpora quadrigemina. Thus, peripheral bilateral stimulation during BART psychotherapy can trigger visual imagery for our patients and clients as in this example. Furthermore, many lizards have a third eye which reacts to light and dark. This is symbolic of the brow, or third eye, chakra, which is associated with inner sight or intuition. In many meditative practices, practitioners visualise breathing in through the pineal gland, or third eye. This is believed to have the effect of activating both the lower and higher chakras.

Figure 24 shows a schematic drawing of the dorsal view of the goldfish brain shows the main brain divisions: forebrain (the olfactory bulbs and telencephalon), midbrain (mesencephalon) with the optic lobes, cerebellum, and vagal lobes. The floor of the telencephalon is the evolutionary primitive structure for the basal ganglia in higher vertebrates. The roof of the telencephalon is the precursor to the hippocampus. The optic lobes and the cerebellum have their usual higher vertebrate equivalents. The vagal lobes are the locus of cell bodies for the glossopharyngeal nerve, which is important for taste. The mesencephalon is not visible from a dorsal view and is located at a rostral and caudal position, respectively, underneath the midbrain's optic lobes. The schematic drawing of the lateral view of goldfish brain shows the level of the sections in the lower part of the diagram. These can be compared with the embryological divisions of the human brain shown in Chapter Eight. It is interesting to observe how

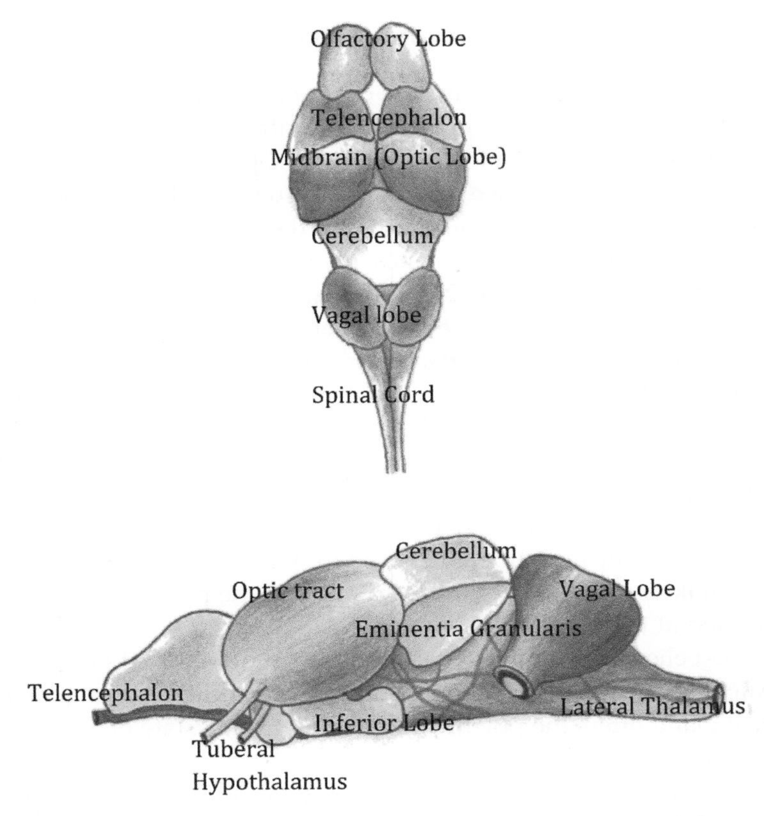

Figure 24. Dorsal view of the goldfish brain above and lateral view below.

the vagal lobe of the goldfish has evolved into the human brainstem. This provides further neuroanatomical support for the theoretical validity of BART psychotherapy, where a key consequence of bilateral cerebellar stimulation is activation of the brainstem of the patient or client. Further BART psychotherapy activates neural synapses and often a tingling sensation is experienced, as I believe new synaptic connections are made and axon rewiring occurs. An independent mind finds verbal expression easier as emotional blocks are overcome and creativity flows more freely. Broca's area (expressive language) and Wernicka's area (receptive language) become activated. Blood flow increases in the prefrontal cortex, thus better transmission of information is possible.

Sixth (brow) chakra

This is also known as the third eye chakra (Lotus Ajna). It is believed to be the centre of psychic energy. This centre is the origin of insight and a doorway into the unconscious mind. Opening the third eye can assist our patients and clients in their exploration of higher realms. Of note, there are only two petals in the third eye chakra (Table 6). Anatomically, this is the site of the pineal gland. There is a sculpture representative of the pineal gland in the Vatican attesting to the significance of this endocrine gland in Catholic belief. This is the largest sculpture representative of the pineal gland in the world (Figure 25).

Many patients experiencing BART psychotherapy end their journey of self-realisation here, as they find sufficient meaning from their experiences. Further insight is possible with activation of the seventh, or crown, chakra. This can provide a link for the patient or client with what Jung termed "collective unconsciousness".

The pine cone sculpture is believed to symbolise the opening of the brow chakra, equivalent to the third eye and the pineal gland, which is located at the centre of the brain.

It is believed to link us to the frequency of our soul energy and greater self-awareness and knowledge. Opening the brow chakra and pineal gland offers the potential of moving from a state of dualism to oneness.

This can be achieved by those who meditate for prolonged periods. They are said to become intuitive by opening up their third eye, sixth chakra, or pineal gland. Their pineal gland has enlarged to the size of a real pine cone. The average size in someone who does not meditate is the size of a pea, apparently.

This area in the forehead is marked by many eastern cultures with a *bindi*. This comes from the Sanskrit *bindu*, meaning 'a drop, small particle, or dot". It is believed to be the seat of concealed wisdom and the exit point for *kundalini* energy. The *bindi* is said to retain energy and strengthen concentration. *Bindis* come in different shapes and colours, according to their meaning. Red represents honour, love, and prosperity, whereas yellow symbolises the power to influence the intellect.

In many eastern traditions the energy, prana, or chi is inhaled through the third eye. Some animals, notably lizards, have a vestigial third eye which is sensitive to light and dark. The inhaled energy is

Table 6. Sixth, or brow, or third eye, chakra functions.

Mantra	om.
No. of petals	Two.
Physical functions	Visualisation of the brain stem, and cerebellum. Vision and balancing of the two cerebral hemispheres.
Metaphysical functions	Clairvoyance and insight.
Endocrine glands/organs	Pituitary, nose, left eye, and ears.
Symptoms if chakra is "out of balance"	Lack of concentration, cynicism, tension headaches, nightmares, and disturbed vision.
Lessons learnt once chakra is activated using BART psychotherapy	Realisation of the soul, insight, imagination, peace of mind, concentration, wisdom, and perception beyond duality.
Gemstones that crystallise this energy	Fluorite, tourmaline, azurite, quartz, and ophrys.
Element	Light.

Figure 25. Two views of the pine cone sculpture, or pigna, outside the Vatican.

directed upward to the crown chakra and then downward, infusing all the remaining chakras until it exits the earth star chakra.

As we ascend further to the level of the sixth (brow) chakra, we link to Maslow's (1943) highest hierarchy of needs, which is the search for transcendence, or self-actualisation. The indigo or dark blue colour becomes resonant. Patients often report experiencing an indigo-coloured beam of light around their brow. This may represent the release of *kundalini* energy. As we continue BART psychotherapy, the patient's imagination synthesises images, enabling target memories to be reprocessed. Intuition is developed at this stage in the treatment. An awareness of "all there is" may seep into consciousness. By developing mindfulness, the patient can become an outside observer, or witness, of events. This can enable the patient to enter a state of calm where they experience a world of recovery and triumph (Stage 5 BART psychotherapy).

Advocates of Taoist philosophy claim a connection to the electromagnetic heart field. The "third eye" of the sixth chakra reaches above the level of the personal ego, where transcendence can occur. Activation of the sixth chakra energy lays the foundation for discarding duality and enabling attunement with oneness. Further BART psychotherapy activates the collective unconsciousness represented by the seventh chakra.

Seventh (crown) chakra (Lotus Sahasrara)

This is known as the Spiritual Gateway centre and is seen as the seat of the soul. This centre is believed to filter soul energy, otherwise known as Prana. There are sixty outward petals, which lead to one thousand towards the centre. By activating this chakra, we are able to access the realms of the soul and cosmic consciousness (Table 7). It is necessary for the patient or client to reach a higher vibrationary plane to reach this level of conscious awareness.

The seventh chakra's perspective is one of knowledge acquisition at all the energy levels of the body. It involves getting in touch with your own unique purpose and path and/or direction. Patients start to experience a state of oneness instead of duality. This realisation of oneness can lead to a greater understanding of the role of humanity on earth.

Table 7. Seventh, or crown, chakra functions.

Mantra	None.
No. of petals	1000.
Physical functions	Vitalises cerebral hemispheres and integrates the spiritual and physical self.
Metaphysical functions	
Endocrine glands/organs	Pineal gland, central nervous system cortex and the right eye.
Symptoms if chakra is "out of balance"	Confusion, depression, alienation, and reduction in inspiration.
Lessons learnt once chakra is activated using BART psychotherapy	Higher self becomes linked to one's personality. Spiritual will, inspiration, unity, divine wisdom, understanding, continuity of consciousness and perception in higher dimensions.
Gemstones that crystallise this energy	Amethyst, diamond, quartz, crystal, celenite.
Element	None

During BART psychotherapy, one patient not only experienced purple healing light entering the third eye of the pineal gland (sixth chakra) but this was also followed by a band of white light penetrating through the crown chakra before washing over the rest of her body. This appeared to be a way in which she connected to the universal cosmic energy.

The dance of body, mind, and spirit may equate to the processing of gut-brain, heart-brain, and head-brain, as I have discussed earlier. Development of the patient's individual chakras' energies mirrors these processes. This can be achieved by gentle activation of the chakras through BART psychotherapy. Explanation of the functions of the chakras can help patients and clients understand how their body is processing information on these different levels.

Case example 2

A client had been through two years of difficult abdominal surgery. This had included removal of the gall bladder for acute cholecystitis.

The surgery was done the old-fashioned way and had left symptoms in terms of feeling bloated and wanting to retch. Now, several years later, the client was still complaining of abdominal discomfort.

During the BART session, the zappers were placed against the abdomen. Initially the left side felt bloated and the right side felt full of adhesions. The headphones were placed behind the mastoid process and the frequencies set to create entrainment between the cerebral hemispheres with the stimulation frequency greater in one hemisphere than the other. I encouraged the client to perform imaginary psychic surgery, cutting the adhesions away and removing the bloated feeling. This led to a reprocessing of the last memories of going under the anaesthetic and the first memories of waking up. These were successfully reprocessed. The client started to feel a headache and was able to use one of the zappers to lessen its effect. She started to rock back and forth, reliving the posture associated with recovery from the anaesthetic. She then spontaneously placed both zappers at the pingula and ida positions at the base of the spine. This is the point of activation of the kundalini energies, and a fundamental tenet of kundalini medicine and yoga is to activate these points. My client became aware of a warm sensation of heat over the sacrum where these points had been activated (Lotus Svadhisthana). The session concluded with my client standing upright and reporting that her abdominal contents felt more relaxed and the sensation of bloating was gone. I also used the zappers to activate the brainstem and shoulder where the gall bladder meridian was loosened. My client felt the whole process had been healing and integrative.

The soul star (transcendental) chakra

This is believed to filter divine light. It is the chalice of soul energy and facilitates access to the Akashic records, which are believed to hold the soul memories of our ancestors.

The soul chakra is also known as the Avatar of Synthesis. Its purpose is to integrate the patient or client with planet earth and raise their energy levels.

This is believed to be twenty centimetres above the crown chakra. It is a keystone for the other chakras and is believed to connect the patient or client to the source of all energy.

According to string theory, universal information comes from the eleven dimensions of a multi-universe world. The origin of the word universe is from the Latin *unus*, for one, and *versus*, to turn. One could hypothesise that when the space–time of the eleven dimensions becomes one, we have the singularity of the Big Bang. This again shows the links between ancient mythology and modern theoretical physics. As our knowledge expands, the worlds of myth and science appear to coalesce. My goal is to seek the common ground between the east and west and between ancient myth and modern scientific thought.

The stellar gateway (or transcendental) chakra

This is believed to be the centre of divine essence. It is seen as the light portal that connects the soul to the divine source. As such, it can be seen as the doorway into other worlds. The stellar gateway chakra is believed to be located above the divine star, where it links the patient or client to the sun and solar system. At the centre of this chakra is a black wormhole, which, according to string theory, gives us access to the multiverse and another eleven dimensions of possible existence. We have not yet evolved a capacity for interplanetary and intergalactic travel. There may be evidence from Sumerian cuneiform writing that there was advanced human civilisation 3,600 years ago. These assumptions in relation to the Nephilim and other civilisations, made by Zecharia Sitchin in his book, *The 12th Planet* (1976), have been refuted by Dr Michael Heiser, who has a PhD in Hebrew Bible and ancient Semitic languages and appears eminently qualified to dispel these myths.

Universal gateway chakra

Links to ancient civilisations on earth

On 19 October 2013, a correspondent for BBC news, Melissa Hogenboom, reported on an article by Professor David Lordkipanidze and his colleagues published on 18 October 2013 in *Science* magazine. This describes a complete skull from Dmanisi, Georgia and the evolutionary biology of early Homo. They write that the site has yielded remains consistent with the presence of the single human species Homo outside Africa around 1.8 million years ago. They describe the world's first completely preserved adult hominid skull from the early Pleistocene. This could range from 0.8 to 2.6 million years ago. The brain volume was 546 cc, compared with almost 1600 cc today. They conclude: "This implies the existence of a single evolving lineage of early Homo with phylogenetic continuity across continents".

Also, the earliest example of dyed flax was found in a cave in Georgia. It was dated to 34,000 years ago. This again provides evidence of human habitation dating to modern times.

Stringer (2012), from the Natural History Museum in London, stated that the large jawbone makes an excellent case for the single evolving lineage theory, but he was doubtful of a direct link to Homo erectus.

The Tiblisi team maintain:

1. Their hominids represent an early expansion of human ancestors outside Africa.
2. They are the most complete collection of Homo species from 1.8 million years ago to 300,000 BC.
3. They had human-like spines and limbs suited for long-distance upright travel.
4. The male was larger than the female.
5. They had brains thirty per cent the size of Homo sapiens. Their primitive limbs resembled Australopithecus, which is said to have existed two to four million years ago and is known as the southern ape.

The Happisburgh prints in Norfolk (Ghosh, 2014) are believed to be 850,000 years old and the oldest outside Africa. They are thought to have been left by a group of children and adults. At this time, it was possible to walk from Africa to Britain. These prints are the first direct evidence of people at the most northerly edge of habitation in Europe. Professor Stringer (a world authority on early humans) believes the Norfolk hominids were related to Homo antecessor, or pioneer man. They became extinct in Europe to be replaced by Homo heidelbergensis, then by Neanderthals around 400,000 years ago. The Neanderthals interbred with modern humans. Many of our inherited genetic diseases may have emerged from this interrelationship.

This is important in the context of BART psychotherapy, as, if confirmed, this places our ancestors on earth alongside the great apes for more than one million years. The process of brain evolution was more gradual than previously thought and lends further support to the Darwinian theory of natural selection.

The impact of BART psychotherapy will be strongest on the hard-wired parts of the human brain. This includes the brainstem, cerebellum, and limbic system, which are all parts of the early hominid's brain.

As the prefrontal cortex was the latest part of our brains to evolve, it is the most susceptible to traumatic stress (Gogtay, Giedd, Lusk, et al., 2004). It also explains why unmodified cognitive–behavioural therapy (CBT) is unlikely to reach the primitive reptilian parts of our central nervous system. This, I believe, has major implications for the initiative "Improving Access to Psychological Therapies" (IAPT) in the NHS. This tends to involve practitioners with limited training in CBT and does not include training in trauma-focused therapy such as BART psychotherapy.

The stellar gateway chakra is believed to exist far from the physical body. It is by activating this chakra that we gain energy and knowledge and any excess of energy cascades down into all the other chakras before revitalising the earth, the patient or client, and important others in their lives.

The ascending chakras can be equated to earth, water, fire, air, ether ajna, and the third eye. This is a different perspective from that of western medicine but can be accommodated within the framework of BART psychotherapy. The chakras are represented by different images with petals and colours, which match the spectrum of colours in a rainbow. The repeated figure of eight contains the first five chakras on their ascent to the brow and crown. This analogy is used to reflect the flow of information during BART psychotherapy reprocessing. This allows for the possibility of activating the high heart chakra, which is represented by the colour turquoise and the thymus gland. This chakra is most active in children and, as the thymus becomes vestigial in adulthood, can be assumed to merge with the heart chakra.

The Theosophical Society

Charles Webster Leadbetter (1847–1934) was a clairvoyant who wrote over thirty books on the spiritual life and the psychic nature of man. He was also one of the leaders of the Theosophical Society. In 1884, he went to India with Madame Blavatsky. He also joined her in Alexandria. In 1895, he began to examine the atomic structure of over sixty elements. He took the five vows of a Buddhist, although he was a loyal Christian. He moved to Australia, where he died in 1934.

His work is important because he brought the eastern ideas of the chakras as vortices of energy to a western audience for the first time. This was published in 1927 (reprinted in 2013) as *The Chakras*. Leadbetter illustrated what he termed "The streams of vitality", which originate from the sun, and the "Serpent-fire", which has its roots deep within the earth.

The kundalini energy is referred to with the activation of the lateral ida and pingula channels with the central sushuma rising in tandem. This is compared to the linga outside Hindu temples and comparisons are made with the peripheral nervous system.

The individual schools of yoga activate the chakras differently. Leadbetter has stressed the activation of the second, or splenic, centre. Stimulation of the third, fourth, and fifth chakras can enable the patient or client to awaken some of their astral planes.

The third eye chakra, when awakened, brings forth the image of the serpent projecting from the centre of the forehead. This was represented on the headdress of the Egyptian Pharaohs, who, as their country's chief priests, were believed to have occult powers. When the crown chakra was awakened, the patient or client is believed to be able to leave their body in full consciousness. Few except the most adept yogis have reported this level of conscious awareness. The arousing of the kundalini coincides with activation of the HPA axis and is represented in mythology by the caduceus symbol. Of interest, the rod of Asclepius has only one serpent coiled around the staff.

Leadbetter was able to divine the number of petals and colour of each chakra. These had slightly different locations shown in Figure 26, especially in relation to the sacral chakra, which he termed the splenic chakra. Of note, the chakras are divided into the following divisions: four, six, eight, twelve, sixteen, one hundred, and one thousand. The third eye and forehead chakra appear to merge as a combined sixth chakra.

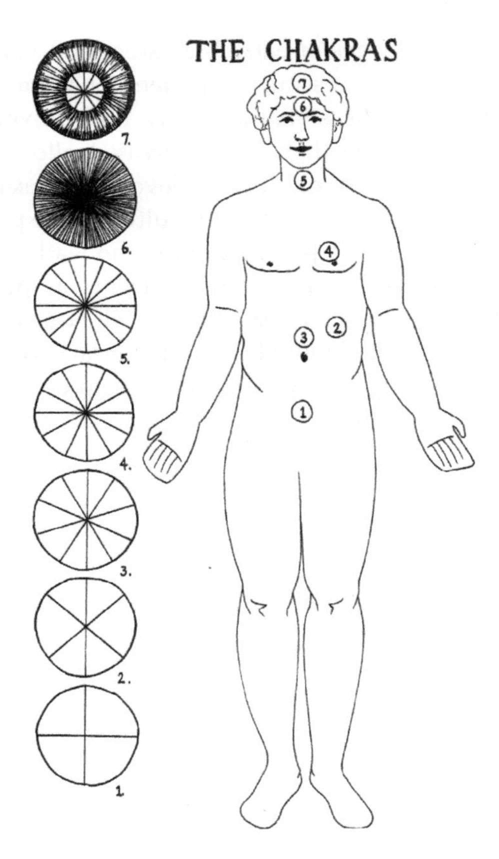

Figure 26. The chakras according to Leadbetter.

Summary

This chapter focuses on the nature of the chakra energies as understood by eastern traditions with a superimposition of western scientific thinking in terms of the endocrine organs they represent. There is also a proposed link to sacred geometry and intentional prayers. The chakras, in ascending order, are the earth star, root or spinal cord chakra, and sacral chakras. These are followed by the solar, heart, and throat chakras. I illustrate the reaction of the brain to fear and stress and how I explain the concepts of altered levels of arousal and dissociation experienced by the patient or client. This model introduces the Rapids, Waters, and Frozen concept into the literature. A case example shows how images of early brainstem and visual origins in fish can appear in the reprocessing of a patient. The remaining chakras are brow, crown, soul star, stellar gateway, and universal gateway. These are the energy centres that, when activated, allow the patient or client to access transcendent or elevated levels of consciousness. The use of the *bindi* symbol by many eastern cultures is explained. A case example showing how BART psychotherapy can lead to the release of kundalini energy following abdominal surgery is presented. The chakras according to Charles Leadbetter are illustrated. These show slight modification from the more traditional ones associated with the individual schools of yoga. A description is given of how the kundalini energy can be awakened.

CHAPTER THREE

Neurodevelopment of the head-brain, heart-brain, and gut-brain

Development of the embryo and clinical implications

The blastocyst forms soon after fertilisation and retains a memory of the circumstances of conception. There is debate about the moment that this group of cells shows signs of life. There is some evidence that, following two cell divisions (i.e., the eight-cell blastocyst stage), there is pluripotential for life. The question of when the soul enters the body remains open and is hotly debated between those who say there is no scientific evidence and others who have attempted to show that the body is lighter post mortem compared to ante mortem. The heart is often mentioned as the seat of the soul. It is of note that the first heartbeat occurs at eight weeks gestation.

The Ancient Egyptians believed that the soul had five parts:

1. Ren.
2. Ba.
3. Ka.
4. Sheut.
5. Ib.

The heart was seen as the seat of emotion, thought, will, and intention and was the key to the afterlife. Archaeological remains confirm that, in death, all the body organs were removed except for the Ancient Egyptian's heart. It was believed to be the key to a successful transition to the afterlife. If the heart was lighter than a feather, the person went to heaven. If it weighed more than the goddess Maat's feather, the monster Ammit consumed it. This might have given rise to today's expression, "with a heavy heart".

Maat personified truth and justice. Her blue ostrich feather represented truth. In Egyptian mythology, Maat bound the universe, world, state, and individual together.

The impact of violence during conception

When conception has been because of violence, such as rape, this has a profound impact on the mother's ability to accept the pregnancy. Often her feelings of loathing can be translated into dislike of self or be projected to the developing embryo. When the infant becomes an adult, this intrauterine stressful experience is triggered by any events that mimic, from a sensory point of view, the early months of pregnancy. Imagine a millimetre-sized embryo being transported down the fallopian tube before crash-landing during implantation as a foetus against the uterine wall. This journey is normally eventful. With the added influence of cortisol from the mother's umbilical cord on foetal development, you can imagine a terrifying ordeal for the developing embryo. If we fast-forward to when that baby becomes an adult, it is essential to explore their knowledge of their own conception, their attachment relationship with their parents, and how this history might impact on their current symptomatology. For example, they may be reluctant to travel in circumstances where they are unsafe and not in control. Classically, this involves flights over water, with the unconscious fear of a crash-landing. In addition, journeys in a coach may cause re-experiencing of that terrifying journey along the fallopian tube. In my experience, this provides completely new avenues to explore with patients and clients where the genesis of their phobias is from traumatic circumstances of conception.

Physiological evidence for the gut-brain and head-brain connection

According to Cryan and Dinan (2012b), there is a pathway of communication via the gut, heart, and brain axes that impinges on cortical functioning of brain regions such as the anterior cingulate cortex. These are affected by both chronic pain and chronic stress. Thus, disorders such as irritable bowel syndrome may be a brain-mediated disorder with associated deficits in cognitive functioning. The techniques I will describe in Chapter Thirteen, outlining how to conduct BART psychotherapy sessions, could benefit this cohort of patients. More work is needed in this developing field of research.

Synaptic potential of foetal brain during pregnancy and some clinical implications for infant development

The central nervous system starts to differentiate at ten weeks gestation. Sufficient organisation has occurred at twenty-four weeks to sustain independent life. However, most myelinisation and sensory development occurs in the final trimester, which is why nature has optimised forty weeks for human gestation. At birth, the foetal brain is fifty per cent of its adult size. This rises to ninety per cent by age five, provided the infant experiences normal developmental environment.

The environment the expectant mother is exposed to can directly influence the stress levels of the baby. This is being extensively investigated by the Predo pre-eclampsia project (Villa, Hamalainen, Maki, et al., 2013). Stress hormones produced by the mother end up in the foetus via the placenta. This project is attempting to identify the times in pregnancy when the foetus is most vulnerable to stress. The pregnancy experiences of 5,000 mothers are being collated to predict and prevent pre-eclampsia and intrauterine growth retardation. Evidence points to how exposure to prenatal stress can lead to both temperamental difficulties in children and paradoxically increased resilience. From studies of the famine experienced by people in the Netherlands during the winter of 1944–1945 (known as the "hunger winter") and the attack on the Twin Towers on September 11 2001, it is known that experiencing such traumatic events during pregnancy could have adverse effects on childhood development, with possible life-long consequences. Low birth weight may also give rise to diabetes, cardiovascular disease, attention deficit hyperactivity disorder (ADHD), depression, and even schizophrenia.

The development and expression of the six core emotional states in patients and clients

For face processing, we must be able to match the labelled emotion to the facial expression (Figure 27). We start processing faces moments after birth, as illustrated by the birth crawl reflex (www.breastcrawl.org). We become more sophisticated, recognising fear and disgust, with age. However, our ability to sense sadness and anger disimprove in comparison. This appears to be related to both hormonal development and maturation of the prefrontal cortex. It is recognised that there is a drop in performance in emotional recognition of ten per cent around puberty.

Figure 27. The six core emotional states and corresponding facial expressions.

In picture (a) an angry person is shaking her fist and, metaphorically, has steam coming out of her ears. The explicit message is keep away. Anyone approaching this person is likely to place him or herself in danger. Knowing when to approach someone and assess his or her readiness for therapy is essential if a therapeutic rapport is to be established.

Picture (b) shows "Disgust" (From Latin *dys* and *gustatory*, to taste), and the subject's revulsion is palpable. The downturned mouth coupled with frowning forehead conveys the subject's emotional state. This emotion links to potentially harmful foods or tastes. The reflex would be to spit out the food, thus warning others to be careful. This is a good example of gut, heart, and brain neurological connections.

This person depicted in picture (c) is pouting his lower lip and appears close to tears. The sense is of him welling up with the emotion of sadness. You might say he is burdened by a weight on his shoulders, or has a heavy heart. He also appears to have regressed to how infants are when they feel upset. The key goal of this emotion is to induce compassion in the other person and a sense of empathy for their suffering. It is this quality of compassion and caring for others in distress which is our essential human characteristic.

In picture (d), the brilliant smile of radiant white teeth helps to illuminate this expression. Not only is the person radiating warmth and the happiness of a contented internal state, but also is implicitly saying "approach me". This may also act as a preamble to attachment by sending out a bonding signal to a prospective partner.

This person in picture (e) shows the whites of her eyes in a wide-eyed expression, expressing fear. This is likely to move from the mobilised response to the point of frozen watchfulness associated with activation of the dorsal motor nucleus of the tenth cranial nerve, or vagus nerve. This has been most clearly elucidated by Porges (2001). This person may be close to collapse via the vasovagal response and must be dealt with sensitively to avoid a dissociative reaction. The fear response can also be associated with a state of high arousal. The person's heart is racing, but they are rooted to the spot.

The subject of picture (f) has experienced something unusual, which has led to a sharp intake of breath and an expression of surprise. This emotion is felt to be pivotal as a means towards resolving the emotions of disgust, anger, sadness, and fear. Thus, inducing curiosity or surprise during the therapeutic session is a key goal of BART psychotherapy.

Brain regions that are important for emotion states include the brainstem, amygdala, and prefrontal cortex; for the feeling of emotion, it is the insular and prefrontal cortex, and for level of consciousness, the frontal and parietal lobes. Other components of an emotion state and the content of consciousness are presumed to rely on more variable and distributed structures that would depend on the particular kind of emotion or conscious experience and, therefore, are not depicted here. The hypothalamus, amygdala, brainstem nuclei, including periaqueductal grey and parabrachial nuclei, orbitofrontal cortex, and anterior and posterior cingulate cortex are important for the expression of emotion. Intralaminar thalamus and the ascending reticular formation are necessary for the maintenance of arousal and wakefulness—that is, the level (state) of consciousness. The insular cortex is an important structure for the experience of emotion. Bilateral prefrontal and parietal cortices are broadly important for the level of consciousness. Other important central nervous system components of emotion include the rostral ventrolateral medulla (important for control of autonomic function) and components of the spinal cord itself, all of which contribute to substantial processing that is related to interoceptive and homeostatic information, and also parts of the nucleus accumbens and ventral pallidum that participate in reward and positive affect.

Development of head-brain, heart-brain, and gut-brain from birth onwards

Babies have one hundred billion neurones in their brain at birth but few are connected up into networks to form the connectome. Input and subsequent experience determine how these neural networks ultimately form into intelligences (Gardner, 1993). There is an initial overcapacity and additional synaptic pruning occurs.

There are one hundred million neurones in the enteric plexus, which is greater than the number of neurones in the spinal cord. These neurones and receptors develop at the same time as those of the cerebral cortex. This is because the neural crest divides in the embryo at ten weeks gestation to form both the head-brain and the gut-brain.

Professor David Paterson (Briggs, 2012), from the University of Oxford, has been studying how the brain and heart work together. Nerves from the brain directly affect the heart. The sympathetic nerves cause the heart to pump faster while the parasympathetic ones slow the heart. However, Paterson has discovered that there are 10,000 specialised neurones in the heart itself. These are integrated into the cardiac muscle of the right atrium. These neurones are known as the "heart's little brain". In the same way as the cerebellum is the brain's little brain, this could be termed the cardiacbellum. By electrically exciting these neurones, Professor Paterson has been able to show how much neural control is in the heart itself. His experiment was as follows: a rat's right atrium was suspended in a glass container containing nutrients and infused with oxygen. Although isolated from any other tissue, it was observed to be beating independently. The heart rate was at 200 beats per minute, but by electrically stimulating these neurones externally, messengers were released to slow the heart down to 100 beats per minute within a second. When the electrical activation was switched off, the contractions of the right atrium returned to their previous rate of 200 beats per minute. This experiment shows that there is a detailed neural network in the heart, which is independent of the brain's descending sympathetic and parasympathetic control. Hence, we can conclude that the heart can function independent of the brain or central nervous system. This provides scientific evidence for the Egyptian belief that the heart deals with truth. This means that the heart is important both scientifically and philosophically. This can be illustrated by some common sayings that are related to the role assumed by our hearts in society down the ages, some of which are mentioned in the following section.

The relationship between the heart and the head and how it can be expressed in language

The heart and the head are part of the mind–body continuum and live in a synergistic partnership with one dependent on the other, rather than subservient to each other. Over the centuries, poets and philosophers have referred to affairs of the heart in their literature. The following are some examples, with definitions where necessary.

> A generous heart, kind speech and a life of service and compassion are the things which renew humanity. (Buddha)

> A good head and a good heart are always a formidable combination. (Nelson Mandela, quoted in Meer's biography, 1990)

- "To wear your heart on your sleeve" means to be open with your emotions and express feelings openly.
- "The heart of the matter." This relates to the crucial or essential points.
- "Heartfelt feelings." This relates to being truthful and relates to the association with the goddess Maat discussed earlier.
- "To come straight from the heart." This means to say directly, without duplicity or deceit.
- "To do with all your heart." This means to put complete effort into something.
- "In your heart of hearts." This means your innermost, or soul, feelings. In some cultures, the soul is located at the inferior aspect of the heart. Cardiac surgeons have reported that during heart transplant surgery, this is the most difficult area in which to perform cardiac surgery.
- "From the bottom of my heart." The literal meaning is, with the full force of ventricular systole. The symbolic meaning is, with the greatest sincerity I can muster.
- "To have a change of heart." The literal meaning would be to have a heart transplant. The symbolic meaning would be to do things differently based on new feelings and a changed perspective on your life and values.

The heart can be in various positions in these idiomatic sayings, conveying different meanings:

- "In the right place"—activating the central chakra.
- "In your boots"—conveying a sense of depression.
- "In your mouth"—meaning an extreme state of excitement.
- "To pour one's heart out." This can mean to be emotionally overwhelmed.
- "To have your heart set on something." This conveys a sense of passion, drive, and commitment.

- "Take heart." This means to have courage (from French, *coeur*).
- "To trust with all your heart." This relates to our earliest attachments and feelings of security.
- "Heartthrob." Here, love signals its attractions as the heart speeds up or even "skips a beat", as in the lyrics of a song in the pop charts by Olly Murs.
- "My heart goes out to his family." This is a sign of empathy towards a bereaved or otherwise distressed family. This could be interpreted as allowing your heart's magnetic field to resonate with that of those around you
- "Eat your heart out." This has various meanings, but is generally used to draw attention to one's achievements in bettering someone else's.
- "Not for the faint-hearted." This means that you need strength or courage to complete this task.
- "The way to a man's heart is through his stomach." This means that by satisfying man's hunger, he will be able to feel love and affection. From a literal perspective, this was exploited by the Russians in their battle against German forces in the Second World War. In prolonging the conflict into winter, the Russians knew that the German supply lines would be nullified. Without provisions, the German soldiers would become demoralised and easier to defeat.
- "Cross one's heart and hope to die." Children usually said this when they wished very strongly for something to come true. There is a belief that this originated in the early twentieth century as a religious oath based on the signs of the cross. The four verses can be located at http://answers.yahoo.com/question/index?qid=20100901201717AAUQnEi (last accessed 13 April 2014).

The process of BART psychotherapy pays attention to all the patient's idiomatic use of language to better assess which part of their body is registering sensations, emotions, feelings, and thoughts. To quote Blaise Pascal:

> The heart has its reasons, which reason [i.e., the head-brain, or cerebral cortex] does not know. We feel it in a thousand things. I say that the heart naturally loves the Universal Being, and also itself naturally, according as it gives itself to them; and it hardens itself against one or

> the other at its will. You have rejected the one and kept the other; is it by reason that you love yourself? (Pascal, 1958, p. 78)

Thus, Pascal postulated that the heart was capable of reflective thought. This has not been fully accepted by western scientific thinking. It is often said that better decisions are made when the head rules the heart. However, in eastern philosophical traditions such as Confucianism and Buddhism, the true path to follow is that of the heart and mind. Indeed, the heart is seen as the governing organ of the brain.

The role of the heart in interpretation of facial expressions conveying emotion

The independent filmmaker, David Malone, underwent an experiment in which he received a brain MRI while rating the intensity of faces with a range of emotional expressions. Professor Sarah Garfinkel and colleagues (2013) from Brighton and Sussex Medical School designed this experiment. The key variable was whether the faces were shown in time with the heartbeat. When shown in synchrony with his heartbeat, David rated them as more intense. Particular faces, which displayed explicit fear, were registered in the amygdalae (the brain's threat appraisal centres). The conclusion from this experiment is that the heart helps you to connect with your emotional state. The heart is believed to be the main conduit, or channel, for emotional information such as compassion and concern for others and the capacity to share feelings such as joy, which help us to bond socially as a human species. In BART psychotherapy, I explain how the heart's intrinsic nervous system interacts with both the enteric plexus, or gut-brain, and cerebral cortex, or head-brain. These interpretations of our feelings and sensations are the emotional heart's gift to the rational mind. A couple of final quotes place things in perspective:

> I am certain of nothing but the holiness of the heart's affections and the truth of the imagination. (John Keats)

> A loving heart is the beginning of all knowledge. (Thomas Carlyle)

Lessons from mythology, language, and film in relation to neurodevelopment and symbolism of the brain, heart, and gut

In Egyptian mythology, one's life's deeds were measured by weighing the heart against a single feather. The more burdened or heavy the heart, the less likely was one to pass on to the next kingdom. Thus, the concept of "a true heart" anchors much of Egyptian philosophy. We know that the heart, which automatically tells the truth over the rational mind, mediates facial blushing due to embarrassment. It cannot help but give you away: "False face must hide what the false heart doth know" (Shakespeare, 1979).

The depiction by the Ancient Egyptians of the mythological Eye of Horus bears an uncanny resemblance to a sagittal section of cingulate cortex, thalamus, brainstem, and cerebellum. This suggests that the Ancient Egyptians were skilled in human dissection and understood functional neuroanatomy (Filler, 2007).

From this, we can surmise how knowledgeable the Egyptians were in their accurate representations of the brain. Might we assume that they also understood the impact of affective neuroscience on the developing brain?

Role played by body's autonomic nervous system in informing this historical legacy

Our organisational drives and behaviours are fuelled by instinct and emotion, with intellect providing direction. As described above, the amygdalae can easily hijack information processing in the prefrontal cortex. This can lead to a maladaptive reaction to complex trauma or "toxic" stress. The sports psychiatrist, Dr Steve Peters (2012), explores this concept further. He describes how all information comes first to the chimp brain, which is governed by its instinctual, drives, desires, and processes. It needs to be nurtured by the human brain's prefrontal cortex before it can exert control over it. This idea is explored further in the section on peak performance. The computer brain is a reference point for both the chimp and human brains. It processes information four times faster than the chimp brain and twenty times faster than the human prefrontal cortex. Dr Peters introduces readers to the metaphorical concepts of the computer brain functions as:

- autopilots, which are constructive, helpful automatic behaviours and beliefs;
- gremlins, which are destructive, unhelpful automatic programmed behaviours and beliefs which can be deleted;
- goblins, which are destructive, unhelpful behaviours and beliefs which are hard-wired or fixed;
- The Stone of Life, which contains the patient or client's life truths, values and life force or vitality;
- mindset, which is the patient or client's perceptions and influences their overall approach to life.

Improving heart, brain, and gut communication is an essential component of BART psychotherapy. The aim is overcome the instinctive gut reactions to incidents so that patients can be reconnected to their higher-order functioning in the prefrontal cortex. This can be achieved by having their gut, heart, and brain activate their respective chakras to vibrate at an increased frequency.

In the Chinese pictogram for listening, the symbols represent

- watching with your eye;
- listening with your ears;
- thinking with your mind;
- feeling with your heart;
- focusing with undivided attention.

In this oriental philosophy, the brain is linked to the heart and to our relation to authority within society. For thousands of years, the yellow heart symbol was seen as the centre of consciousness and represented both soul and spirit. Thus, the heart was the source of thoughts, feelings, and emotions. Integrating the functions of eyes, ears, heart, and the selfless act of undivided attention, using the mind captures the essence of listening. This implies activation of executive functions within the prefrontal cortex. It also symbolises the holistic approach to communication taken by the most populous nation on earth. I think this pictogram form of communication has some links to the hieroglyphics of the Ancient Egyptians and the wavelengths associated with the twenty-two letters of the Hebrew alphabet. The symbolism was an intrinsic part of the communicated message. All these pictogram and glyph scripts appear to have originated from African languages composed of click sounds. This shows that, as a species, we started with one hundred phonemes of sound. This reduced with migration: English has forty and Hawaiian only thirteen. This offers the possibility of changing the audible clicks in the bilateral headphone stimulation of BART to mimic the language of our ancient ancestors.

In Chinese mythology, Ma Gu is the goddess of longevity, and is represented in a late nineteenth-century mural in the Summer Palace's long corridor. She is depicted with cannabis plants and peaches.

Chinese alchemy comprises outer (*waidan*) and inner (*Neidan*). In traditional Chinese medicine, there are three treasures:

1. Jing, known as the essence of life. This is said to be in the adrenal glands.
2. Chi, which is the vital energy of life and is found in the lower dantian just below the umbilicus. This would correspond to the sacral chakra, the site of kundalini awakening.
3. Shen, which translates as spirit, or mind. This spiritual energy is located at the upper dantian. This is between the eyebrows and corresponds to the site of the pineal gland and the third eye. It might give rise to our western expression of advanced intellect being "highbrow".

Neurological representation of bottom-up and top-down processing

Figure 28 is a representation of the timeline for neuronal processing from unconscious neuroception to conscious awareness (500 ms), broken down as follows.

It takes from 40 ms for the onset of early processing of relevant sensory stimuli. Then, the subcortical route eventually feeds back to orbitofrontal cortex, via bottom-up processing, for eventual processing at the end stage of BART psychotherapy: onset is from 120 ms. Continuing the bottom-up process, the onset of detailed perception core processing through the amygdala and producing an emotional reaction including the body is from 170 ms. There is interaction between visual and somatosensory areas.

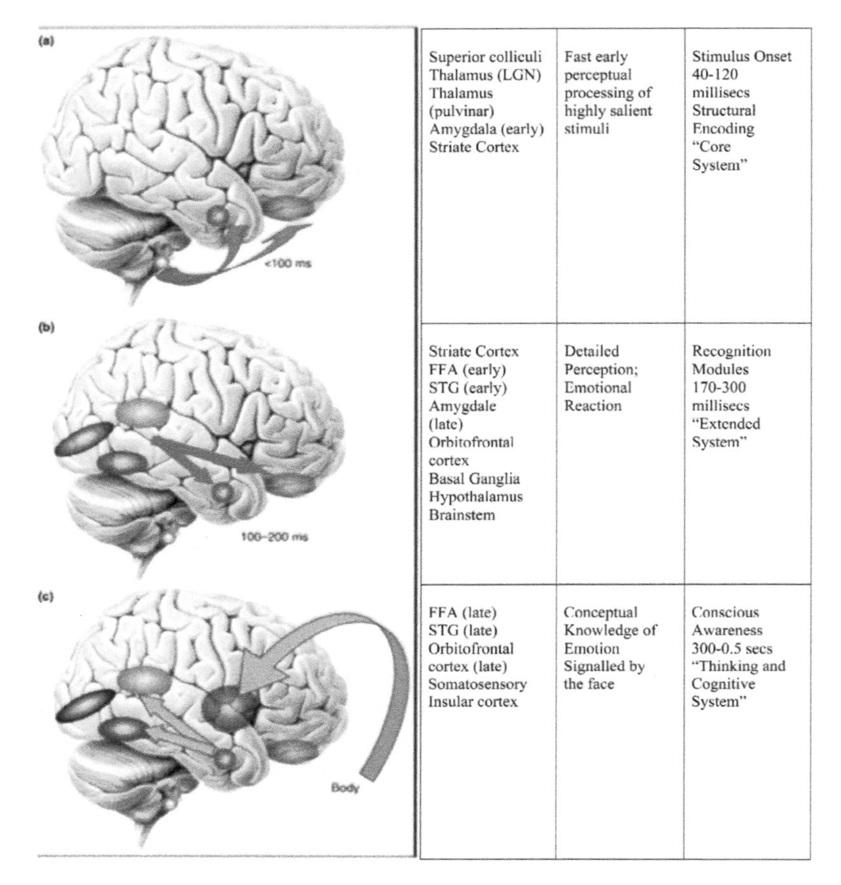

Superior colliculi Thalamus (LGN) Thalamus (pulvinar) Amygdala (early) Striate Cortex	Fast early perceptual processing of highly salient stimuli	Stimulus Onset 40-120 millisecs Structural Encoding "Core System"
Striate Cortex FFA (early) STG (early) Amygdale (late) Orbitofrontal cortex Basal Ganglia Hypothalamus Brainstem	Detailed Perception; Emotional Reaction	Recognition Modules 170-300 millisecs "Extended System"
FFA (late) STG (late) Orbitofrontal cortex (late) Somatosensory Insular cortex	Conceptual Knowledge of Emotion Signalled by the face	Conscious Awareness 300-0.5 secs "Thinking and Cognitive System"

Figure 28. Illustration of the timeline for neuronal processing. Adapted from Tsuchiya & Adolphs (2007) with permission from Professor Ralph Adolphs.

A top-down process involves recognition of faces and emotional processing (ventral vagus). Conscious awareness begins from 500 ms (cerebral hemispheres).

Symbolism of the film, The Wizard of Oz, *1939*

The Wizard of Oz film can be interpreted to support the basic tenets of BART psychotherapy in relation to how different body organs relate to intrinsic human characteristics.

The film was a collective effort of multiple directors and was an adaptation of the book, *The Wonderful Wizard of Oz*, by Frank Baum (1900). It has been interpreted in ways that reflect the cornerstones of my approach to patients in BART psychotherapy. Films are often inspired by dream states giving rise to archetypal images. Often, after BART psychotherapy sessions, patients will report profound dreams, which I see as continued reprocessing after the session.

The Wicked Witch of the West character represents that which seeks to dominate and control the patient's life, much as Adolf Hitler did in the 1930s and 1940s. The heroine, Dorothy, is on a spiritual journey towards self-actualisation, which is highest in Maslow's hierarchy of needs, the different pyramidal stages of which bear some relation to the chakras:

1. Root and sacral equate to physiological needs.
2. Solar and heart represent love and belonging needs.
3. Throat represents confidence and self-esteem needs.
4. Third eye, forehead, and crown can represent self-actualisation needs.

The development of an individualised optimum healing environment for each patient or client will allow Maslow's hierarchy of needs to be met. This will be comfortable and supportive, free from pain and anxiety. There will be an atmosphere of acceptance, hope, and optimism. The patient or client is able to relax, be honest, and feel free to be him- or herself. Restoring agency, that is, being an agent in one's own life, enables the patient to generate feelings of control necessary for recovery from trauma and allows the client to achieve their peak performance goals. Spiritual approaches, including encouraging mindfulness and meditation, can similarly help both patients and clients transcend their individual experiences.

In *The Wizard of Oz*, the dog, Toto, represents the inner intuitive, instinctual, animalistic part of us. BART psychotherapy allows venting of these gut instinctive reactions related to incidents at the onset of therapy. In the film, the Witch tries to capture Toto by putting him in a basket. He escapes, implying that our intuitive voice can sometimes be ignored, but not contained. Due to Toto's actions, Dorothy undergoes a transformation. In BART psychotherapy, the purpose is to notice our intuitive gut feelings. It is from these sensory fragments that reintegration occurs and our imagination can be unleashed.

The Tin Man needs a heart, but his love is already present, waiting to be connected up. There is a need to draw in the intellect represented by the Scarecrow's missing brain. This can occur when the Lion has received courage, *coeur*, or a heart. We find that he already has inner strength. The oiling of the Tin Man could represent a blood transplant. The blood metaphorically flows down to Dorothy's ruby-red slippers. By clicking her heels, she realises there is no place like home and she realises where her heart is. It was there all along.

The electromagnetic field around the heart helps to transit mechanical pressure waves along the blood vessels. The nerve plexi around the gut, heart, and brain are nourished with oxygen and become fully activated and integrated. Thus, in Dorothy's journey, the Tin Man, Lion, Scarecrow, and Toto represented aspects of herself that she needed to become aware of internally. This could only happen as she followed the yellow brick road, which, I believe, represents centring on the solar, or third, plexus. There are also parallels to the Chinese pictogram of the heart described above.

Knowledge of arterial and venous blood flow through capillaries can inform therapists as they help patients resolve their traumatic experiences during BART psychotherapy. In particular, the therapist can help the patient to tune into areas of heat or tension associated with the RAPIDS phase of dissociation, or areas where they feel numb, associated with the FROZEN phase of dissociation. The heart and lungs are central to the person's survival. The oil sought by the Tin Man might represent lubrication of his circulatory system so that he may perceive emotions. The heart of the Lion will also give him courage, while the Scarecrow, when he has a brain, will be able to rationally appraise the environment rather than instinctively reacting with fear. This symbolism shows that BART psychotherapy, by emphasising the reactions of gut, heart, and brain, will optimise the potential of the patient or client.

Embryonic development

In the human embryo, the heart starts beating at around eight weeks gestation. At around twelve weeks, the embryonic neural crest divides into tissue destined to form both the foetal brain and alimentary canal. This explains why so many serotonin or 5HT receptors are in the gastrointestinal tract, which is then responsible for the gastric side effects of psychotropic medication. It could also explain why drugs that are slowly metabolised by the liver's metabolic enzymes are associated with further adverse effects.

Role of anterior, medial, and posterior cingulate cortex in processing emotions

The anterior cingulate cortex (ACC) is the frontal part of the cingulated cortex. It acts as a clutch between the frontal cortex and the limbic system. The sagittal ACC is involved in the integration of sensations from the body's viscera. Figure 28 also shows the middle cingulate cortex (MCC) and the posterior cingulate cortex (PCC).

The ACC deals with emotions, while the region marked as sACC is responsible for integration of visceral sensations. The MCC deals with response selection, while the anterior and posterior parts deal with avoidance of fear and orientation of the skeleto-motor musculature. The PCC deals with personal orientation. Its dorsal and ventral aspects code for visuospatial orientation and assessment of the self. Finally, the retrosplenial (RSC) cortex is involved in memory access and formation.

The corpus callosum

The corpus callosum (from the Latin for "tough body") is a collection of three hundred to eight hundred million nerve fibres connecting similar areas in each cerebral hemisphere. This leaves ninety-eight per cent of cortical neurons unconnected. The majority of the remaining two per cent of cortical neurons are inhibitory via the GABA receptors, with the minority using the excitatory transmitter, glutamate. The ratio of the corpus callosum to the volume of the hemispheres has reduced over time. The main function of the corpus callosum (Figure 29) is to inhibit the other hemisphere.

The corpus callosum fibres continue to develop at least up to the age of thirty and perhaps throughout life. In a study of subjects with

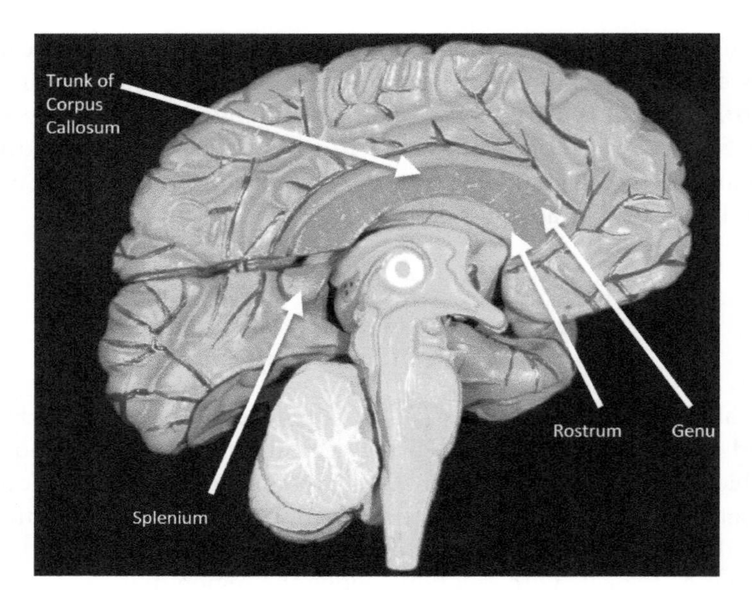

Figure 29. Schematic diagram of corpus callosum (CC).

high-functioning autism (Cherkassky, 2007), they had smaller parts of the relevant corpus callosum compared to controls. This suggests a deficit in their integration of information at both neural and cognitive levels. This might also relate to aberrant default network connectivity. It could also explain why they have difficulties with information processing.

This shows the small volume of fibres involved in interhemispheric communication. The corpus callosum contains 200–250 million white matter contralateral axonal projections. It only exists in placental mammals or eutherians. Myelination of callosal axons occurs rostro-caudally, that is, from back to frontal regions. It doubles in size from birth to age two, just like the cerebellum. It continues myelination throughout life. Axonal connections undergo pruning or synaptic refinement while the CC increases in area. These developmental processes may further functional specialisation of the cerebral hemispheres. Several studies show that the CC connecting the left cerebral and right cerebral cortex is larger in musicians. This is because the CC is activated by a motor task using both hands. The bilateral auditory and tactile stimulation of BART psychotherapy may replicate this stimulus. The band of fibres within the CC act to separate functions of the left and right hemispheres. The goal of BART psychotherapy is to help reunite these hemispheres so that they function as a coherent whole sphere.

The CC is divided up into the rostrum (named after its resemblance to a bird's beak), genu, or anterior part (or knee), trunk, and splenium (posterior part). It is the largest fibre tract pathway in the brain. These tracts are essential to the transfer of interhemispheric information. The pathway supports memory, learning, and sensory functions of the head-brain.

BART psychotherapy and peak performance is underpinned by Dr Iain McGilchrist's thesis, articulated in his book, *The Master and His Emissary* (2009). This is essential to understanding higher cortical functioning and to achieving stages four and five of BART psychotherapy and peak performance.

Summary

This chapter examines the interrelationship between the gut-brain, heart-brain, and head-brain by examining research on the brains' neurodevelopment. A new link has been proposed between chronic pain and stress and their negative impact on cognitive functioning. The synaptic potential of the baby's brain in pregnancy is illustrated, along with the patient or client's six core emotional states. The interrelationship of heart and head is described in terms of language and recent scientific experiments. The role of the heart in the interpretation of facial expressions conveying emotion is explained by the experimental observations of Professors Hugo Critchley and Sarah Garfinkel from Brighton and Sussex Medical School. Lessons can be learnt from mythology of the ancient Egyptians, the Chinese language, and *The Wizard of Oz* film from 1939. The autonomic nervous system of the body underpins this legacy and the concept of top-down and bottom-up processing is explained. The crucial roles of the cingulate cortex in integration, orientation, and memory formation and the corpus callosum in interhemispheric transfer of information are illustrated.

CHAPTER FOUR

Vibrational frequencies related to accelerated information processing in patients or clients

Development of vision from initial sensory input to the superior colliculus to movement of eyes scanning the natural environment

Ephrin ligands are a family of proteins that bind on to the ephrin receptors. They are involved in axon guidance, visual mapping from the retina to the superior colliculus. This is analogous to a computer keyboard and mapping in terms of the American Standard Code for Information Interchange, or ASCII, on screen characters. These ephrin molecules ensure that sets of neurons project and connect to other appropriate sets of neurons.

In mammals, seeing is mediated by projections to the thalamus and on to the cortex. The retina senses and transmits light to retinal ganglion cells (RGCs). There are more than twenty types of RGCs projecting from the retina to parts of the brain.

The most important area for eye movements is the superior colliculus. It mediates reflexive eye movements, head turns, and shifts in focus of attention. When RGC mutate and fail to make the appropriate connections, the patients may go on to develop autism, schizophrenia, Tourette's syndrome, and other neurodevelopmental disorders.

In the peripheral stimulation with zappers that is a central component of BART psychotherapy, the sensory stimulation reaches the superior colliculi on either side of the brainstem. This, in turn, sets up the cascade of protein binding that leads to visual mapping and scanning of the environment by the eyes. I first noticed this in 2007 when I was treating a teenager who was bedwetting at age seventeen. He was very motivated to change this behaviour, as he had signed up for the army cadets and was going on field trips. I used resource installation with visual imagery and drew a diagram showing neural control of the bladder. I got him to imagine responding to the bladder signalling him to wake up in the night to void urine. He visualised the image with his eyes closed while holding on to both zappers held against the contractile muscles of the bladder. I observed his eyes moving in saccades in time with the rhythmic pulses of the zappers. This was analogous to rapid eye movement and he was in a relaxed but fully conscious state. Since then, I never ask the patient or client to follow either a light bar or my fingers. I believe this is unnecessary to reprocessing trauma and might actually interfere with the natural pontine geniculate occipital waves, which are generated by stimulation of the brainstem, and also activate the mechanisms associated with REM sleep. This is a fundamental difference between this therapeutic approach and more traditional trauma-focused therapies such as EMDR, trauma-focused CBT, and sensorimotor psychotherapy.

Key reason for effectiveness of BART psychotherapy and peak performance

The heart has an intrinsic beat of sixty to eighty beats per minute. Its magnetic field is forty to sixty times stronger than that of the brain. BART psychotherapy taps into the internal commonality of sensory experience within each patient and client. The bilateral stimulation is optimised in intensity and amplitude. The resonance is experienced bilaterally at the level of the skull's mastoid processes. This enables the bilateral cerebellae to be activated. Over a ninety-minute therapeutic session, the patient experiences relaxation at the level of the cerebral cortex. The key to the success of BART psychotherapy is placing the auditory signal bilaterally over the area of maximal bone density. The evolutionary process of natural selection has strengthened this area of the skull to afford maximal protection to the cerebellum (little brain) and brainstem. Dr Seth Pollak (Bauer, Hanson, Pierson, et al., 2009) from the University of Illinois is one research scientist to have discovered the multiple functions of the cerebellum in terms of processing sensations, emotions, and feelings apart from solely movement impulses. The cerebellum has more neurons than the rest of the cerebral cortex put together. There are forty billion axons sent out from each cerebellum to the prefrontal cortex on the contra lateral side. Thus, the combination of auditory and aural bilateral resonating frequencies helps to quell brainstem instinctive reflexes. Also, the intuitive reflective capacities of the prefrontal cortices are enhanced. Patients frequently report to me that the cerebellar resonance often fades into the background as the session progresses. The regular background rhythm appears to maintain their attention, cognition, and memory while allowing them to reprocess their adverse life experience and the accompanying unwelcome body sensations. Thus, the mechanical input to the cerebellum is to help the patient pay attention to the bodily information that is being reprocessed during the session.

Functional anatomy of the cerebellum

The cerebellum has three divisions: spinocerebellum, cerebrocerebellum, and vestibulocerebellum, in relation to the brainstem. The spinocerebellum regulates muscle tone and contributes to voluntary movement. The cerebrocerebellum plans and modulates voluntary movement and is involved in storage of procedural memories. Finally, the vestibulocerebellum maintains balance and is involved in the control of eye movements. Together, the cerebellum plays a crucial role in the processing of thoughts feelings, and emotions. Bilateral activation of the cerebellum is an essential prerequisite for effective BART psychotherapy

Pollak and his colleagues (Bauer, Hanson, Pierson et al. 2009) have shown that there is a loss of cerebellar volume in children following institutionalisation. I believe the effects of this trauma can be effectively treated with early intervention using BART psychotherapy. This would need to be tested with longitudinal studies.

Figure 30 presents CT scans contrasting the volume of a normal three-year-old's brain with that of a child from an Eastern European

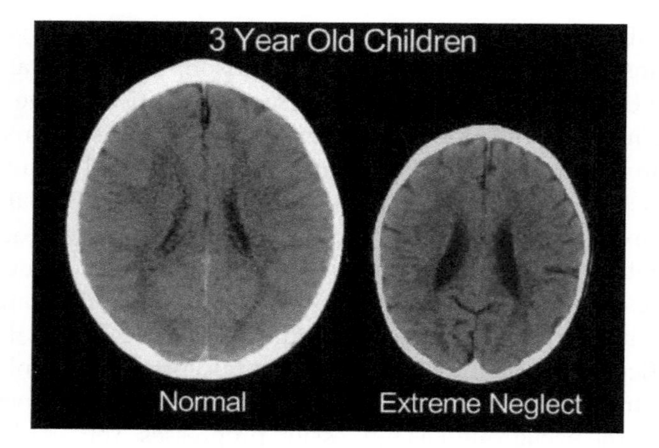

Figure 30. CT scans of a normal three-year-old and one exposed to extreme neglect. Image reprinted with permission from the Child Trauma Academy.

orphanage who was exposed to extreme neglect. The types of neglect included being allowed to cry and being left to feed from a bottle propped up with a towel. The brain shown has failed to grow from birth. The foramen ovale has closed and this skull will now prevent future outward brain growth. The gyri and sulci are now growing inwards and this will further compromise brain function and specialisation. This child is likely to grow into adulthood with severe disorganised attachments, inability to sustain meaningful relationships, and become a heavy user of adult mental health services. They often become revolving-door patients, resistant to effective treatment. This makes the case for investment in parental and infant mental health services which are currently not delivered by a substantial majority of the UK's current national health service trusts (National Health Service North West, 2011).

This contrasts the healthy neural network (enriched environment) with that of the child exposed to a deprived environment. Such deprived neurons experiencing fear are unable to reach out and synapse with their neighbours. This causes major physical and emotional ill health in future adult life. According to Dr Bruce Lipton (2011), cells exposed to fear are fed this information via their cell membrane. Its receptors are like human senses, but in microscopic form. Essentially, they are sentient beings and their growth mechanisms shut down when exposed to a fearful atmosphere. Dr Rupert

Sheldrake read of the work by Alex Gervage on the growth of mushrooms in 1920. He then proposed morphogenetic fields as a mechanism to explain how the environment could control the cell's genetic code or DNA. Thus, the normal child who has been exposed to a loving environment stimulates the neurons to grow and synapse, enhancing their ultimate potential.

Early child abuse has been shown to damage normal development of the corpus callosum, and the development of the brain as a whole (De Bellis, Baum, Birmaher, et al., 1999). Thus, neglect, abuse, and trauma can be "toxic to the developing brain".

Interaction of the autonomic nervous system with the social engagement system and historical perspectives on the ANS

In 1872, Darwin recognised the dynamic rural relationship between the heart and the brain:

> ... When the heart is affected, it reacts on the brain ... and the brain reacts through the vagus nerve on the heart so there will be mutual action and reaction between these two most important bodily organs. (p. 69)

In 1921, John Newport Langley wrote a book titled *The Autonomic Nervous System*. In it, he described a purely motor system, not linked to the brain. Then, in 1949, Walter Hess won the Nobel Prize for medicine/physiology. He described how the autonomic nervous system was a paired antagonism system of the internal visceral organs, involving sympathetic and parasympathetic innervations. This idea is based on the evolution of our nervous system over time.

Social behaviour was noted to be a uniquely mammalian feature and was linked to the distribution of nerves to the heart and muscles of facial expression. The heart also became recognised as an endocrine organ, producing both oxytocin and vasopressin. Reptiles, on the other hand, produce vasotocin (a combination of the previous two hormones). We have, therefore, evolved a complex integrated nervous system. This has a hierarchical response to challenges from the environment, involving four stages.

1. Changes have occurred through evolution which have involved endothelial heart regulation shifting from older unmyelinated nerve circuits to newer myelinated ones.
2. The quest for safety via regulation of metabolic output of the heart.
3. The social engagement system for safety became integrated over time.
4. A process of neuroception in the cerebral cortex that exhibited downward inhibitory control of the vagus nerve.

Introduction to the polyvagal theory developed by Dr Stephen Porges

This theory evolved during the 1990s, when Dr Stephen Porges was in discussion with neonatologists involved in caring for very premature infants (Porges, 1995, 2006, 2009; Porges & Doussard-Roosevelt, 1999). They were very susceptible to infection and often succumbed. Porges set out over the next few years to understand the multiple functions of the infant's vagal nerve.

Porges proposed the vagal paradox in 1992. This emphasised that respiratory sinus arrhythmia (RSA) represents the outflow from the vagus to the heart, otherwise known as cardiac vagal tone (CVT). Vagal mechanisms were found to mediate both the protective RSA and the potentially harmful bradycardia associated with the activation of the dorsal motor nucleus of the vagal nerve. The paradox existed only if a single central vagal source was assumed to be operating.

The concept of the social engagement system (SES) is part of Porges's polyvagal theory and involves myelinated vagal nerves, which inhibit sympathetic influences on the heart and dampen the hypothalamic pituitary adrenal (HPA) axis. This branch of the vagus nerve is involved in regulating heart rate and breathing, and is involved in self-soothing and calming behaviours. Only mammals have a myelinated vagus nerve. It originates in the nucleus ambiguus with preganglionic nicotinic and postganglionic muscarinic receptors. Under challenge, these are switched off by the sympathetic nervous system.

The polyvagal theory developed by Porges is based on the long wandering pathway and innervation of the tenth cranial, or vagus, nerve.

The old, unmyelinated vagus nerve is designed to preserve metabolic resources. Although initially protective, it can also kill you by causing panic and immobilisation. When Porges was working in a neonatal intensive care unit, he found that, in newborns, vagal tone was protective when associated with heart rate rhythmicity. A paediatrician wrote to him, stating that too much of a good thing can be bad. This led Porges to pursue his vagal paradox theory. He discovered that the phylogeny of the ANS was not well described. He proposed that, in the embryo, the vagus had two primary divisions:

1. The dorsal motor nucleus of the vagus nerve, which has its origin in the nucleus tractus solitarius.
2. The ventral motor nucleus of the vagus nerve, which has its origin in the nucleus ambiguus in the brainstem.

The ventral motor nucleus of the vagus nerve controls the striated muscles of the face and head, the larynx, the pharynx, and the common nuclei of the facial and trigeminal cranial nerves. Thus, the innervation of the heart goes with that of the head, as they are wired together from early embryonic development. This provides further scientific evidence for the theoretical underpinning of BART psychotherapy.

How does the body respond to environmental challenge?

The body's hierarchical response to an environmental challenge is initially regulated by the ventral nucleus of the vagus nerve in its control of the face and heart. Pre-term babies are vulnerable to this challenge, as their facial muscles do not fully work at birth. They exist in an unsafe state. The main mode of change is to involve neuro-regulation of the periphery by the brain. BART psychotherapy starts with stimulation of the peripheral nervous system at the level of the gut-brain and heart-brain, before reprocessing at a head-brain level.

Relationship between the Jacksonian theory of dissolution of the ANS and Dr Porges's polyvagal theory

When humans are in a safe environment, visceral homeostasis promotes growth and restoration. The myelinated vagus acts on the cardiac heart rate, slowing the heart and inhibiting the fight-or-flight mechanism of the sympathetic nervous system (SNS). It also reduces cortisol secretion from the hypothalamic–pituitary–adrenal axis and decreases immune mediated inflammation by decreasing circulating cytokines. Throughout the process of evolution and natural selection, the brain stem nuclei of the nucleus ambiguus merged with those the face and head. An integrated social engagement system then emerged.

To ensure survival in dangerous or life-threatening situations, further evolution of the nervous system was necessary. This involved progressive recruitment of the SNS and freeze or feigning death behaviour associated with activation of the dorsal motor nucleus of the vagus nerve (DMX). Normally, the vagus nerve acts as a brake on the heart rate. The resting heart rate is 70–85 beats per minute. If this vagal brake is released, for example, by being cut, the heart rate goes up to 100–110 beats per minute. In reality, this occurs every time we suddenly stand up and scan the environment. Our heart rate is, therefore, regulated by these distinct phylogenetic systems. For social engagement to occur, we must first assess risk in the environment and inhibit limbic control of our fight, flight, or freeze responses (Table 8). The nervous system is continuously evaluating risk via an unconscious process, which Porges has called neuroception. This helps us to distinguish safe, dangerous, or life-threatening situations from environmental cues. The key brain areas thought to be involved in this process are the temporal cortex, amygdala and periaqueductal grey. Together with activation of the SES, we are able to interpret voices, facial expression, and hand movements/gestures (Figure 31).

Via the sensory input from key cranial nerves, the brainstem, via the thalamus, feeds information into the cerebral cortex. From here, information is passed down to the motor component of the different cranial nerves. Thus, the muscles of mastication, middle ear, and face are activated. This represents the SES. Also activated are the bronchi of the lung to increase breathing if necessary and the heart rate, which varies according to the situation. Finally, we are innervated to speak (via the muscles of the larynx and pharynx) and simultaneously to turn our head to respond to any sign or sound of either danger or interest.

The dorsal vagus complex (DVC) includes sensory nuclei in the nucleus of the solitary tract (NTS), the area postrema, and motor nuclei in the dorsal motor nucleus of the vagus (DMX). When the indi-

Table 8. Illustration of the three stages of reaction predicted by the polyvagal theory of Dr Stephen Porges.

Dissolution following trauma	Evolved in brainstem (time in years)	Behavioural functions	Autonomic nervous system	Environmental stimulus
1st reaction	10,000	Social communication, self soothing, calming, inhibition of arousal (social engagement system)	Ventral vagal complex	Safe
2nd reaction	1 million	Mobilisation (fight, flight, fright, active avoidance)	Sympathetic nervous system	Dangerous
3rd reaction	100 million	Immobilisation (freeze, fall, feigning death, passive avoidance)	Dorsal vagal complex	Life threatening

vidual perceives the environment as safe, oxytocin is released from the hypothalamus (Figure 32).

It goes centrally to the sensory and motor portions of the DVC and systemically to the visceral organs as shown by the dashed arrow in Figure 32. Oxytocin helps to induce a calm or anti-stress state.

Figure 33 illustrates the activation of the amygdala and dorsal motor nucleus of the vagus nerve (DMX) when the patient or clients' cerebral cortex is exposed to an unsafe environment. When the patient perceives danger, they begin active mobilisation and arginine vasopressin (AVP) is released from the hypothalamus to both the NTS and the area postrema of the dorsal vagal complex (DVC). This changes the set point of several vagal reflexes, such as the baro receptor reflex. This activates the patient's SNS for fight or flight.

Figure 34 shows further activation of dorsal vagus nerve during exposure to a life-threatening environment. During life-threatening events, when fight or flight behaviours are not an option, immobilised

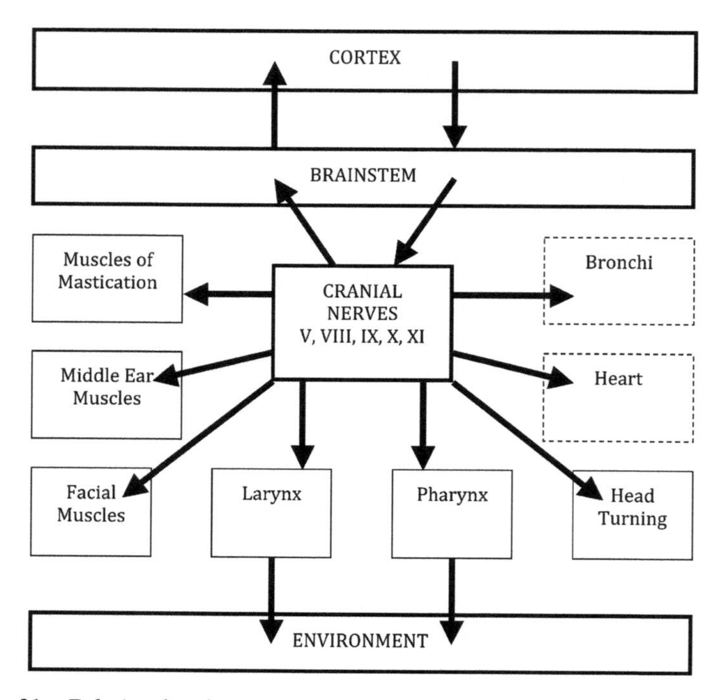

Figure 31. Relationship between the cortex, brainstem, cranial nerves, and the environment. Reprinted with permission from NYAS Porges, S., 24 Jan 2006, "Social engagement and attachment: a phylogenetic perspective". Doi10.1196/annals 1301.004 Figure 1, Social Engagement System.

fear responses are triggered. The DMX provides vagal input to the visceral organs, which are enhanced by systemic AVP. AVP stimulates visceral afferents via both the NTS and the area postrema of the DVC. This activates the most primitive unmyelinated fibres of the vagal tract.

The extent of the path of the vagal nerve in the body is illustrated in Figures 35 and 36. The word vagus means wanderer and reflects the tenth cranial nerve's journey from head to lung, heart, liver, stomach, spleen, kidney, small and large intestine, and bladder. The bilateral cerebellar auditory and tactile stimulation during BART psychotherapy activates the nerves and, hence, the feelings associated with each of these organs where relevant in either trauma resolution or peak performance.

According to Porges's polyvagal theory, the dorsal vagal unmyelinated fibres become activated when the patient or client is exposed to a life-threatening environment. This means that their reptilian brain-

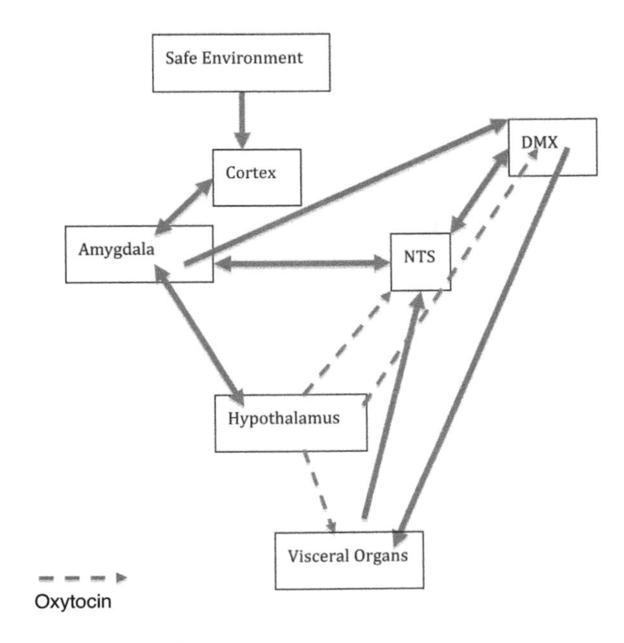

Figure 32. Regulation of the dorsal vagal complex in a safe environment (DVC).

stem processes all the incoming sensory information. Traumatic experiences can become locked in at this level of the brain. During BART psychotherapy, I often ask patients or clients to hold the tactile units on either side of their brainstem. This has the dual advantage of stimulating bilaterally the origins of several of the cranial nerves processing this traumatic sensory information. Also, this allows for activation of the reticular acting system and consequent production of pontine–occipital–geniculate waves. These are a precursor to REM, and towards the end of BART psychotherapy sessions, I have observed the majority of patients yawning as if about to enter a REM-like state.

Characteristics of the reptilian brain

Reptiles have no cortex, but well developed cerebellum and predominant olfactory lobe. They also have a predominant medulla oblongata. Thus, their behaviour is mediated at a brainstem level. This is the same response humans have in any life-threatening situation.

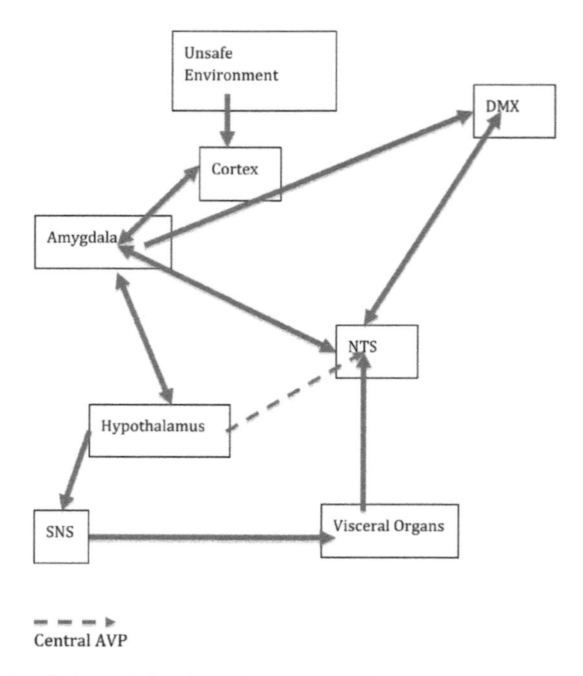

Figure 33. Regulation of the dorsal vagal complex in an unsafe environment.

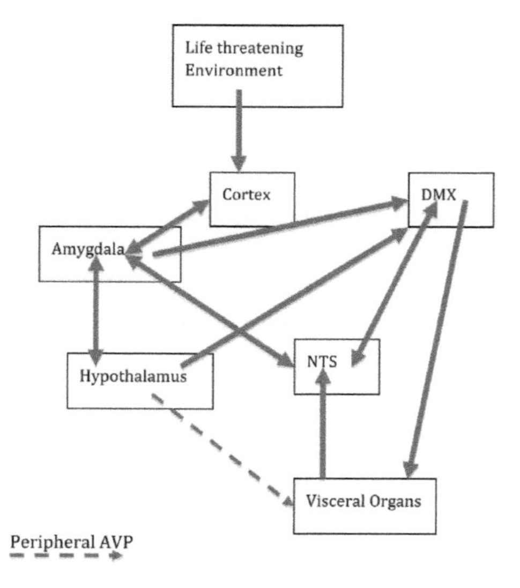

Figure 34. Regulation of the dorsal vagal complex in a life-threatening environment.

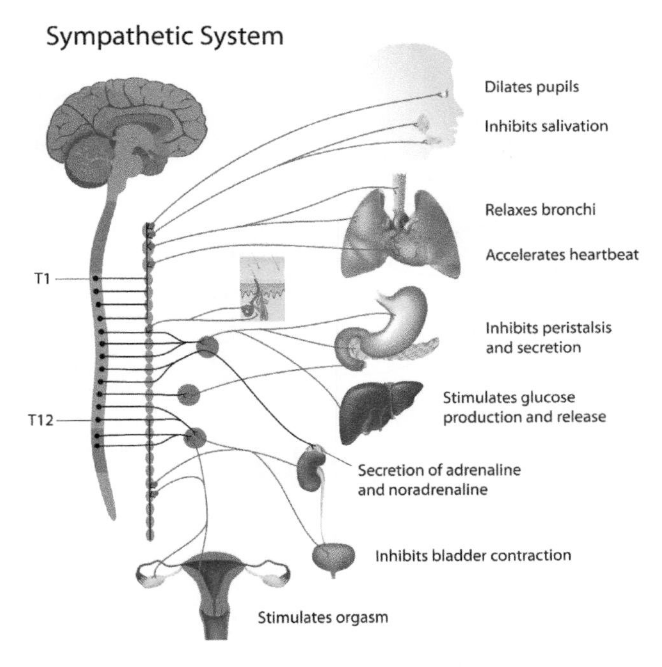

Figure 35. The connections of the sympathetic nervous system.

Our reptilian ancestors are natural predators with a strong survival instinct driven by their medulla oblongata, cerebellum, midbrain, forebrain, and olfactory lobe.

Dampening human brainstem reactions is a key goal of BART psychotherapy. The reticulating activating system in the centre of the brainstem plays a key role in this process. The inferior and superior colliculi process the inputs from the cranial nerves oculomotor, trochlear, and abducens. These act on the eye to perform all known eye movements. This explains why, during BART psychotherapy, bilateral stimulation induces eye movements naturally. They do not then have to be artificially activated, as in EMDR or brainspotting.

Role of the periaqueductal grey matter in mediating the patient's response to trauma and the client's optimisation of performance

The periaqueductal grey is an area of grey matter surrounding the third and forth ventricles. It plays a key role in mediating the brain's response to trauma.

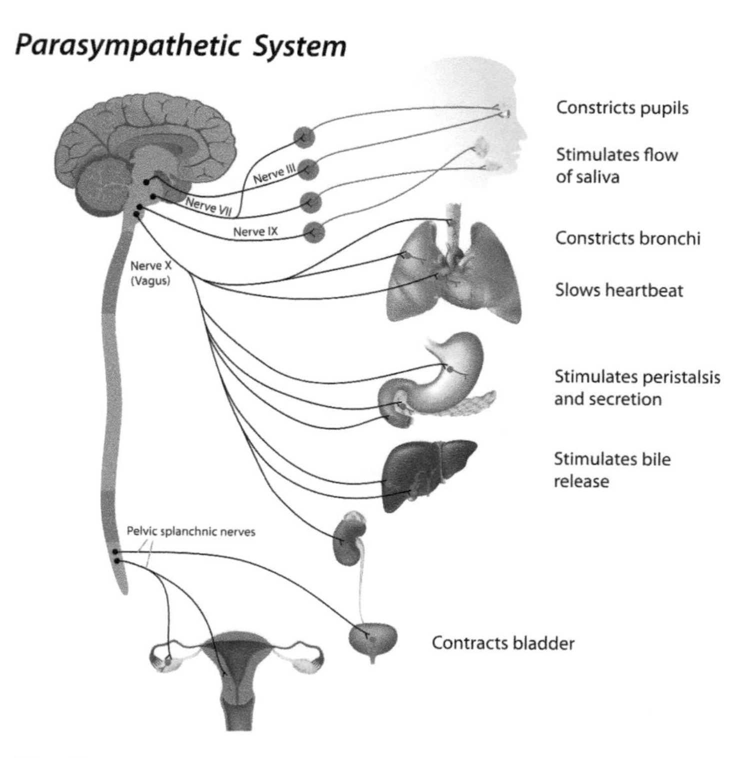

Figure 36. The connections of the parasympathetic system.

Neuroception has evolved below the level of consciousness. If the nervous system appraises the environment as dangerous when it is actually safe, an inappropriate response can occur. Table 9 illustrates the various responses to safe and dangerous situations.

For the SES to work, these instinctive responses and gestures must be switched off. This involves a level of top-down control from the prefrontal cortex to the bilateral almond-shaped amygdalae. When the risk is rated as high in the environment by a patient's neuroceptive processes, both amygdala and the PAG are activated. The PAG's dorsolateral, ventrolateral, lateral, rostral, and caudal nuclei trigger instinctive defensive responses (passive or active) or escape behaviours. I believe this has major implications for the evaluation of risk in the setting of patients' attending our mental health services.

Table 9. Outline of different stages of reactions of the autonomic nervous system dependent on sympathetic or parasympathetic activation.

Response	Level of arousal	Nervous system activated	Neuro-anatomy/ endocrine system
Fight	Increased (hyper)	Sympathetic	HPA axis Adrenaline
Flight	Increased (hyper)	Sympathetic	HPA axis Adrenaline
Fright	Increased (hyper)	Sympathetic	HPA axis Adrenaline
Freeze	Decreased (hypo)	Unmyelinated branch of vagus	Parasympathetic Acetylcholine
Faint (vaso–vagal syncope)	Decreased (hypo)	Unmyelinated branch of vagus	Parasympathetic Acetylcholine
Feigned death	Decreased (hypo)	Unmyelinated branch of vagus	Parasympathetic Acetylcholine

Assessment of risk for a patient in a clinical setting such as an inpatient or outpatient clinic

Neuroception in the patient or client is always evaluating threat or risk and triggering a cascade of viscera-motor and somato-motor reactions as an unconscious process in our patients and clients. If the nurse or therapist assumes these are conscious behaviours, then the level of intervention is likely to be unsuited to the patient's internal state. In order for the therapist to gauge the neurological level of risk, it is important that a detailed history of development both *in utero* and infancy is taken. The more traumatic the history, the more likely that the patient will have relied upon the primitive, or unmyelinated, vagal nerve responses as a defence against perceived threat.

Rate of myelinisation of nerve fibres

The level of myelination of nerve fibres occurs in a linear fashion from twenty-six to forty weeks of gestation. During the first three months of infancy, further rapid myelination occurs in preparation for bonding between the primary care-giver and the infant. From six months to three and a half years of age, attachment patterns are laid down. If the adult patient has had a sufficiently traumatic childhood (or was born with a pervasive developmental disorder), then opportunities for optimal SES development are minimal. The risk of self-harm and harm to others is increased because of this altered neuroception, leading to the misinterpretation of a safe environment as unsafe. The use of seclusion in such a patient might trigger aspects of their PAG. This could stimulate phylogenetically older responses of the dorsal vagal complex.

Aspects of early infant brain development

The first three years of brain development primarily involve the right cerebral hemisphere. It processes sensory information, positive affective information, and the adaptive expression of negative affect (e.g., Canli, Congdon, Constable, et al., 1998; Fox, 1991; Noesselt, Driver, Heinze, et al., 2005; Simon-Thomas, Role, & Knight, 2005). The right hemisphere also appears to have a primary role in regulating cardiac function, represented by cardiac vagal tone (CVT). This is the sum of the inhibiting influences on the heart of the myelinated vagal pathways, namely, the ventral vagal complex (VVC), originating in the nucleus ambiguus (NA) and the immobilising effects of the dorsal motor complex of the vagal nerve, originating in the nucleus tractus solitarius (NTS). The nucleus tractus solitarius is located at the origin of the vagal nerve and has evolved to mediate sensory information from the periphery. This relationship can be represented by the following equation:

$$\text{CVT} = \text{VVC (NA)} + \text{DMC (NTS)}$$

I believe that BART psychotherapy represents a unique opportunity to combine the high frequency of the ventral vagal complex with the low frequency bands associated with the dorsal motor complex. These become integrated with the gut- and head-brains, enabling the patient to resolve their traumatic experiences.

During the process of BART psychotherapy, attention is paid to heart rate variability, ensuring that neither the VVC nor DMC are overactivated and that the patient remains within his or her window of tolerance.

Afferent feedback from the viscera is emphasised in the early stages of BART psychotherapy by accessing and reprocessing gut reactions. The insular cortex is also thought to be involved by bringing integration of the diffuse visceral feedback and allowing cognitive awareness to emerge. This is the goal of the latter stages of BART psychotherapy.

Links between our unmyelinated vagus nerves and ancient reptilian ancestors

The unmyelinated branch of the vagus nerve is common to all those animals with a vertebral column, or spine. The integrated social engagement system links both the heart and head. If someone is then confined in a small space and is unable to escape—for example, through torture or ongoing trauma—the dorsal motor nucleus of the vagus nerve is triggered in this potentially life-threatening situation. The heart then slows and metabolic needs for oxygen and food supply are reduced. The gastrointestinal tract is stimulated to eliminate its contents so that scarce metabolic resources are not expended in digestion. We have evolved this survival technique from our reptilian ancestors, such as the Komodo dragon from Indonesia. They could survive anoxic conditions for hours because their brains were small and oxygen needs were limited.

Turtles are the oldest form of our reptilian ancestors and lived 210 million years ago in the age of the dinosaurs. The first probable mammal-like animal was known as lystrosaurus (the Therapsid missing link). It paved the way for the evolution of the Mesozoic mammals millions of years later.

The distinguishing features of these Mesozoic mammals are:

- milk-producing mammary glands to suckle young;
- hair or fur;
- warm blooded (endothermic metabolism);
- external ears with the presence of small bones in the inner ear.

In reptiles, these inner ear bones are part of the jawbone and therefore reptiles are unable to distinguish easily between low and high frequency sounds. Hence, we have a hierarchy to our response to environmental challenge. The neural feedback starts at the level of the visceral organs—which are sub diaphragmatic—before moving to the level of the heart. The sequences applied in BART psychotherapy enable this information to be activated towards the fifth (or throat) chakra before entering the brain at the level of the sixth chakra (or pineal gland). Ultimately, the goal is to raise consciousness by activating the seventh (or crown) chakra.

Evolution of the human brain from reptilian ancestors

As I have explained, the human brain has evolved from the primitive reptilian brain. While reptiles have no biological imperative towards socialisation, humans require interaction with other humans in order to survive. Humans reciprocally regulate each other's emotional and mental states through love, attachment, and intimacy. This can also occur maladaptively via bullying and oppositional behaviour. The human's neural pathways for social support and adaptive behaviour are the same as those stimulating health, growth, repair, and restoration. The governing principle in this neurological hierarchy is our quest for safety. Ideally, we achieve this in our interactions with others. This makes sense from a physiological perspective. By providing a safe haven to a sick or otherwise compromised individual, they then do not have to defend themselves from attack (conscious or unconscious). Hence, scarce metabolic resources are not used up. If this individual is frightened, they will not physically improve and his body might, indeed, shut down. Information coming from our nervous system helps us to feel calm through this human interaction. All humans are constantly monitoring the immediate environment to check whether it is safe or dangerous.

One of our earliest ancestors was the tortoise. When threatened, it would shut down neurologically by retracting its head into its shell. Its tenth cranial nerve (vagus nerve) was unmyelinated and it could stay in this state for long periods until the environment was safe again.

Comparing humans, who have a myelinated vagus nerve, this originates in the brainstem. Its nuclei send branches to the middle ear muscles, the larynx, and pharynx, along with branches to the muscles governing facial expression. As therapists, when listening to the voices of our clients (intonation and prosody) and monitoring their gaze, facial expression, and gestures, we are, in fact, tuning in to their physiological state. This includes motor impulses, bodily sensations, emotions, feelings, and instinctive reactions. Paying attention to, and processing, these aspects of our patients experience is integral to BART psychotherapy. If the patient's tone is flat, lacks prosody, is hard to understand, and their posture is slouched with minimal gestures, they may be experiencing stimulation via the dorsal motor nucleus of the vagus nerve.

For too long, clinicians have been told an event must be life threatening in order to diagnose PTSD. However, we are each wired up according to our own experiences from infancy and childhood to adulthood. The response of our nervous system to the event is of more critical importance to the eventual diagnosis than the event itself.

In setting up therapy, the client should be able to have a say in negotiating their proximity to the therapist. This will promote a shift in their physiological state towards safety. It is best to avoid loud environments with low frequency sounds, which might evoke a "threat" state, associated with a perceived predator nearby. Ideally, we should talk in a modulated way to our patients in order to trigger an appropriate neuroceptive response, filtering out low frequency and preferentially tuning into higher frequency sounds.

Summary

The relationship between the three parts of the cerebellum and its connections to the brainstem and frontal cortex are described and give rise to the unique technique of bilateral cerebellar stimulation, which is the foundation for BART psychotherapy. The historical descriptions of the autonomic nervous system have changed from John Langley to Walter Hess to Dr Stephen Porges. The latter's polyvagal theory is discussed in relation to safe, unsafe, and life-threatening environments (Buczynski & Porges, 2012). The wandering path of the vagal nerve is discussed, along with its ventral branch associated with the SES and the dorsal branch associated with the freeze response. The role of the periaqueductal grey matter in mediating the patient's response to trauma and the client's optimisation of performance is discussed. A new model for the assessment of risk for a patient in a clinical setting such as an inpatient or outpatient clinic, is proposed. This is based on an understanding of their neuroceptive responses to threat. This differs dramatically from the check list approach adopted by most NHS hospital trusts at present. It is my conviction that risk assessment based on an individual's neuroception and activation of their polyvagal complex will enable more appropriate targeted therapeutic interventions. There are links between our vagus nerve and that of our reptilian-brained ancestors. The evolution of the human brain from our reptilian ancestors is discussed.

CHAPTER FIVE

Proposals for BART psychotherapy with special populations and effects of abuse and neglect on the developing brains of the patient or client

Introduction to the information processing difficulties of children and adults with autism spectrum disorder

Play by children with autism stimulates their mobilisation responses. The fight or flight defensive reaction can be activated. Normally, by looking at one's playmate, these defensive behaviours are down regulated. If someone accidentally hits the other during play, then saying, "I'm sorry" normally diffuses the situation. Neurotypical children use their tone of voice and facial expression to communicate emotions. This prevents their playful behaviour from being interpreted in an aggressive manner by the nervous system of their playmate.

This moment-to-moment facial interaction is difficult for both children with autism and those who have grown up in an unsafe environment through trauma, neglect, or abuse. My clinical experience using BART psychotherapy with traumatised patients leads me to believe it will help patients with autism spectrum disorder (ASD). The goal here is: *B*ringing *A*ffective *R*egulation of *T*one.

In a safe play environment, children with autism would be mobilised and encouraged to develop behavioural reciprocity. This initial stage of interaction can progress to a "play-fighting" stage. The reciprocal behaviours are accompanied by face-to-face encounters so that each participant can maintain their playful engagement without straying into aggressiveness. In order to create this safe play environment, teachers must learn to understand the neurological impact of autism on the child. This will enable them to modify the child's environment and alter the intonation and prosody of their own voices when communicating with these children. A safe state of socialising, learning, and feeling good is then realised for these autistic children.

Dr Steven Porges set up a listening project for children with autism. He was able to determine which sounds pass into the middle ear via the eardrum and which simply bounce off it. The ideal situation is that the middle ear muscles contract. This allows the higher frequency sounds of the human voice through to the brain, once they have been processed by the auditory nerve. Porges found that as auditory sensitivity is reduced, children's language development improved. In the listening project, music was amplified to emphasise the tone and prosody of human voice. The vocal music was modified by computer algorithm so that it would wax and wane. Patients' auditory systems would strive to hear the sound as it faded, and as it started to come back, they would feel better. The aim of the project was to present high frequency sounds promoting safety, while excluding low frequency sounds, which can be interpreted to mean danger. When the child's nervous system is no longer hyper-vigilant, then the middle-ear muscles are able to adaptively modulate the ambient sounds. These muscle reactions are not dependent on voluntary control.

Auditory hypersensitivity is present in sixty per cent of patients with autism. They find it difficult to extract the human voice from other environmental sounds. Their social engagement system (SES) is compromised. They can pick out low-frequency sounds and they are often aware if someone is walking behind them. Usually, in potentially dangerous environments, for example, walking home late at night, people shift unconsciously from the SES to one associated with hypervigilance. Patients with autism remain in the hyper-vigilant state. They employ neural tone of the middle ear to hear low-frequency sounds, for example, footsteps, at the expense of hearing and understanding the human voice. Children with autism grow up in a sensory and auditory world where it is difficult to filter out low-frequency sounds. It is as if they are always aware of the possibility of danger with their heightened sensory awareness.

Treatment of autism spectrum disorder and traumatic stress disorders

By helping the patient to feel safe, they then enter that state physiologically. The neural connections of the heart, face, and head are accessed through regulation of the muscles of facial expression. This will inhibit the responses associated with hyper- and hypo-arousal. Ideally, the child with autism is then able to learn through play. They experience the environment as safe and their senses become less sensitive.

Porges found that the children with autism who were enrolled in the listening project were better able to hear their own voices. They did not have to talk as loudly or shout out and they were better able to engage in conversions with their families and at school. The treatment is simply passive listening to sounds, specially programmed to stimulate the child's nervous system. They tune in to voice intonation and prosody. The treatment comprises five one-hour sessions repeated daily, and Porges found that beneficial effects would occur by day three of the treatment. More research is necessary to test the repeatability of these results in the UK population of children with autism spectrum disorders and in those with quasi-autistic behaviours as a result of extreme neglect and abuse. The cohort of children brought to the UK from Romanian orphanages would be a good sample to study.

The response of the patient or client to stress

On exposure to extreme stress, many human bodily systems become "stuck" as stress hormones are secreted by the hypothalamic–pituitary–adrenal (HPA) axis. The human being continues to live in the world as if the trauma is still present. Often, a chronic pattern of hyper-arousal exists. In childhood trauma, the response is one of alternating hypo-arousal and hyper-arousal. The immune and perceptual systems are also affected by this exposure.

Memory is stored in both a verbal (or narrative) form and as somatic maps. The brain often becomes overwhelmed and the thalamus shuts down under the influence of traumatic stress. Hence, sensory fragments appear as flashbacks. The incident is not remembered as a story. Instead, it is stored at an organic level, for example, as a sense of fear with a lack of context. The patient might experience repeated nightmares due to unprocessed, non-REM sleep.

Implications for clinical practice and psychotherapists

Following trauma, information is encoded without its social context. The person's body organises itself as if the trauma is still present. Through BART psychotherapy, I enable the patient or client to tolerate traumatic emotions as they are experienced. The patient has often been changed by the trauma. The initial process involves shifting to experiencing the trauma at an internal bodily level. Talking can be a defence against feeling and may be a distraction from noticing the body's reactions. We know that different parts of the brain are activated when feelings are experienced, compared to when the patient is talking. Thus, in BART psychotherapy, the goal is to enable the patients to feel their feelings, notice bodily sensations, and allow a flow of information to occur within themselves. Initially, their bodies feel under threat. However, as clinician and patient notice together how these fearful sensations dissipate over time, the process continues and sensations and emotions become more tolerable.

Giving patients a degree of control over any procedure helps them to stay calm by engaging the observing or ego state of their mind. This ensures that there is less chance of them re-experiencing the traumatic event during the therapeutic session. BART psychotherapy provides verbal scaffolding enabling the patient to undergo the process of therapeutic change.

Effects of abuse and neglect on the developing brains of the patient or client

1. The functions of the prefrontal cortex are changed, with impaired ability to pay attention and focus.
2. Neglect and abuse can reduce the ability of the person to experience emotions appropriately.

3. IQ can be reduced by up to thirty per cent.
4. It interferes with the person's ability to engage with others.
5. Patients become less productive members of society.
6. Self-reflection, understanding, and caring for others do not develop adequately following neglect and abuse.

Another symptom is that the patient dissociates from the reality of neglect and abuse. In general, people want to believe that the world is a safe place. When trauma occurs, the dissociative defence emerges. For example, one dissociative identity may be able to learn and have friends, while the other can be the aspect of the personality that stores the traumatic event.

The level of brainstem arousal is related to heart rate variability. Mindfulness and posture are also interrelated. I believe activation of gut responses stimulates processing in the insular cortex. This is crucial in linking the gut- and heart-brains by tapping into the senses of both proprioception and body awareness. The aim of treatment with BART psychotherapy is reintegration of the whole body at the level of the gut, heart, and brain, to keep the patient within their window of affective tolerance and emotional regulation (see Figure 23, "Waters"). They remain fully alive in the present, having reprocessed their traumas. The patient or client should feel safe and powerful following treatment.

Implications of Dr Steven Porges's polyvagal theory for the treatment of trauma and autism

Stephen Porges discovered from his work on newborns the importance of the social engagement system (SES). Initially, babies are indiscriminate in their affections. Only at around six months of age do they become attuned to the sound of their primary carer's (usually the mother's) voice. This voice has a high frequency of approximately 900 Hz. The middle-ear muscles in the infant allow the frequency and intonation of these sounds to register acoustically when the infant is in a safe environment. However, children who have been abused, traumatised, or have autism are often afraid of their environment. This may include sudden noises or the low tone of their father's or male carer's voice. This is because it resonates with a low frequency and might be associated to their being held down or attacked by a predator. These events can activate the most primitive part of our reptilian brain: the dorsal (unmyelinated) branch of the tenth cranial, or vagus, nerve.

In 1902, it was noted by Wundt, "Respiratory movements are regularly accompanied by fluctuations of the pulse, whose rapidity increases in inspiration and decreases in expiration" (p. 247).

In 1910, Hering reported, "It is known with breathing that a . . . lowering of heart rate . . . is a function of the vagal nerves" (p. 1931).

Back then, we can see that there was a connection between breathing and heart rate. With the polyvagal theory there is a common cardiopulmonary oscillator, autonomic function governs primary emotions, and there is a link between vagal control of the heart and neural control of the face and head muscles (Table 10).

In a safe environment, the patient is in a state of visceral homeostasis, allowing growth and restoration. The heart rate slows and the production of cortisol and cytokine is decreased, resulting in a decrease in immune mediated inflammation and an inhibited flight/flight response. Brainstem nuclei integrate these responses with muscles regulating eye gaze, facial expression, listening, and prosody.

However, humans have evolved to avoid dangerous and life-threatening situations. The modulating response of the integrated brainstem nuclei promotes social engagement and reciprocal communication. The faster reacting bottom-up and phylo-genetically older

Table 10. Anatomical divisions of the autonomic nervous system.

	Component	Behavioural function	Lower motor neurons
III	The myelinated vagus (ventral vagal complex)	Social communication, self-soothing, calming	Nucleus ambiguus
II	Sympathetic–adrenal system	Active avoidance (mobilisation)	Spinal cord
I	Unmyelinated vagus (dorsal vagal complex)	Immobilisation (feigning death or passive avoidance), vaso-vagal syncope (fainting), bodily shutdown (potential death)	Dorsal motor nucleus of the vagus

circuits kick in when our survival is endangered. These occur in sequence via the dorsal vagal complex and the endocrine system. Conversely, the newer myelinated vagus inhibits both the sympathetic nervous system and dampens HPA axis activity.

Importance of myelination in utero *and early neuro development*

Developmentally, myelination occurs rapidly in the last trimester of pregnancy. There is a linear increase in the rate of myelination, equivalent to that present in adolescence. During the first three months after birth, further myelination prepares the infant for bonding. The ventral vagus complex, from six months until approximately 3.5 years, lays down attachment patterns. An adult who experienced abuse, neglect, or trauma in childhood, or who developed a pervasive language or developmental disorder, will have sub-optimal SES development. They will be at an increased risk to self, others, and property in any environment appraised as unsafe by their unconscious neuroception.

Social engagement in newborns to the infant stage of development depends on the regulation of their visceral state (or gut feelings) by the myelinated fibres of the tenth cranial nerve, which act as a "vagal brake". If the environment of the infant is one of stress and threat, then defensive behaviours are activated. These are preferentially initiated by the infant's endocrine system via the spinal cord and by the unmyelinated fibres via the dorsal vagus complex. Myelination and, hence, social engagement are not prioritised and this might have crucial implications for the genesis of attachment disorders, autism, schizophrenia, and personality disorders in later life.

These myelinated pathways connect to the heart's sino-atrial node, or pacemaker. This ensures that the resting heart rate is lower than the intrinsic pacemaker rate. The heart rate occurs at the frequency of spontaneous breathing. This respiratory sinus arrhythmia (RSA) provides a connection to the brain, heart, and gut via diaphragmatic breathing. However, the rapid breathing of a panic attack is initiated by brainstem nuclei activation.

The mechanisms that enable humans to engage facially (i.e., through facial expression and eye gaze) are shared with those needed to listen to the human voice. Problems in these areas are a feature in many psychiatric conditions, such as autism and pervasive developmental disorders. An integrated activation of these pathways will reduce heart rate and blood pressure and levels of autonomic arousal. This will promote social engagement and enable patients to reprocess feelings, sensations, and thoughts in their window of affect tolerance and emotional regulation (cf. Figure 23).

The frontal cortex influences the inhibition of heart rate, blood pressure, and autonomic arousal via descending corticobulbar pathways. The SES links the HPA axis and social-neuropeptides (oxytocin) to the patient's immune system. It is believed that exposure to chronic stress interferes with immune system function, thereby weakening patients' resistance to infection. It is likely that a compromised antigenic response to viral inflammation is a component of chronic fatigue, fibromyalgia, and other immune system related disorders. These conditions often appear many years after the initial traumatic events: for example, soldiers from the first Gulf War in 1990 exhibited such symptoms by the year 2000. There are clear neuro-physiological links to the somato-motor system in patients with ASD. Deficits in eye gaze, minimal facial expression of emotions, monotonous intonation, lack of prosody, and difficulty eating are all linked to immature somatomotor development. Lung, heart, and digestive problems are secondary to impaired viscera-motor regulation. Both somato-motor and viscera-motor dysfunction lead to a deterioration of the myelinated fibres' ability to activate the SES. Consequentially, spontaneity, social skills, detection, and expression of emotions, language prosody, and intonation are weakened.

Treatment aimed at neurological regulation of the SES would enhance appropriate spontaneous behaviour, expression of affect, prosody in expressive speech, and the ability to extract the human voice from ambient background noise. This would improve the triad of impairments associated with autism: that is, communication, reciprocal social interaction, and stereotypical behaviours. The hearing and understanding of language is dependent on filtering out low-frequency sounds (associated with shouting and aggression) in favour of high-frequency sounds (900 Hz) consistent with a soothing human voice. This explains the calming effect of a lilting lullaby on a newborn's state of affective regulation. Preferential filtration of high-frequency sounds depends on appropriate innervation of the middle-ear muscles. These are the stapedius muscle, innervated by a branch of the facial nerve, and the tensor tympani muscle, innervated by a branch of the trigeminal nerve. These nerves are impaired in children with language delay, learning disabilities, and autism. Repeated middle-ear infection related to otitis media may also delay language development. Early detection and restoration of function of both these nerves will improve the patient's SES.

The role of experience-dependent plasticity on the development of the cerebellum, or little brain

In 2006, Schutter and van Honk reported an electrophysiological link between the cerebellum, cognition, and emotion. Frontal theta EEG activity was recorded in response to single-pulse cerebellar transcranial magnetic stimulation (TMS). Dr Pollak (2012) estimates that forty per cent of cerebellar connections are with the prefrontal cortex. These occur via the dentate nucleus of the cerebellum and correlate with complex cognitive processes. The neocortex and cerebellar hemispheres develop experientially. Cerebellar neurogenesis continues until the age of two. Children abused through neglect or trauma have smaller cerebellar volumes. This has major implications for their future emotional, physical, psychosocial, and intellectual development. Dr Pollak reported on children adopted into an enriched family from institutionalised care. In the group comparison of cerebellar regional volumes, there were smaller volumes, bilaterally, in the right and left superior–posterior lobes in institutionalised children compared to controls. The left superior–posterior lobe of the cerebellum was associated with visuo-spatial memory and the right superior–posterior lobe was correlated with planning and executive function. We can conclude that cerebellar function is dependent on neuroplasticity from these results.

Dr Pollak further concluded that physiological and social deprivation impacts negatively on cerebellar development. Environmental distress can lead to limited neural activity between the cerebellum and the cortex, especially during the first two years of life. It might only be in adolescence, with renewed brain development, that this "faulty wiring" manifests in behaviours linked to psychiatric disorders.

When I read an article by Hanson, Suh, Nacewicz, and colleagues (2009), I became interested in the role of the cerebellum in emotional development. I attended a neural developmental seminar given by Dr Pollak at the University of Manchester, where he discussed his research on this topic (Pollak, 2012). Until then, I had been using bilateral auditory stimulation, using the standard BOKA-9 machine, built by Dr Gerhard Karl (of Karlware). As my BART psychotherapy involved a lot of therapeutic feedback with re-framing of somatosensory and viscero-motor client experiences, I found that placing the headphones directly over the ears interfered with the therapeutic alliance. I hypothesised that if the auditory tones were applied bilaterally, directly over the mastoid processes, there would be maximal resonance via bone conduction within the patient's posterior fossae. The posterior fossae contain both cerebellae and brainstem. Since then, I have used this technique during sessions lasting 90–120 minutes. It appears that exposure to bilateral auditory tones, placed at the level of the level of the mastoid processes, inhibits brainstem responses and strengthens connections to the prefrontal cortex.

Inhibition of instinctive brainstem responses helps to modulate primitive gut reactions, including abdominally registered feelings of anger and anxiety. Levels of arousal in the aftermath of traumatic experiences are contained within the patient's window of affect tolerance, emotional regulation, and safety (WATERS). Information then flows at a higher level of organisation within the body, that is, from the cardiac plexus to the insular cortex and from the cerebellum to the prefrontal cortex, bilaterally. The patient is left with both time and space to reflect on their traumatic experiences in a calm and safe state. Through this reflection, they can learn from their experiences to help them in the future.

Adolescents have a greater capacity for self-reflection than younger children. Experiments in the 1970s and 1980s confirmed that adolescence was a time of structural change in the prefrontal cortex. Glial cells produce myelin, which then enveloped brain axons, thereby increasing their rate of transmission 100 times. This process continues throughout childhood and adolescence. In the prefrontal cortex, the brain axons are the last to be fully myelinated, and this may not be completed until the patient is between the ages of twenty-five and thirty.

The sensory pathways (i.e., vision, hearing, taste, touch, and smell), as represented by synapse formation, are entirely dependent on the child's early experiences. Typically, they start to develop at twenty-four weeks gestation, peak at four months, and complete their development by age seven. Thus, the vision and hearing of a premature baby will be significantly delayed. Language development starts at thirty-two weeks gestation, peaks at nine months, and reaches maturity at seven. Finally, higher cognitive functions start to develop before birth, peak between one and two years of age, and complete their development around thirty.

There are approximately one hundred billion neurons, both at birth and in the adult brain. In the months after birth, new synapses form, that is, synapto-genesis, thus increasing the density of synapses in the infant brain compared to the adult brain. The frequently stimulated synaptic connections are strengthened while infrequently stimulated ones atrophy (i.e., synaptic pruning). The initial period of rapid brain growth is dependent on the infant's environmental experiences and lasts for approximately three to four years, before synaptic density is reduced to adult levels.

In the prefrontal cortex, synapto-genesis occurs in the sub-granular layers during both childhood and adolescence. Following puberty, new synaptic growth plateaus, leading to elimination and reorganisation of the synapses (Zecevic & Rakic, 2001). This synaptic pruning in adolescence decreases synaptic density in the frontal lobes. This has implications for learning and teaching. The superior anterior cingulated cortex is involved in the integration of sensations from the body's viscera.

Why is synaptic pruning an essential component of development of the prefrontal cortex in adolescents?

In adolescence, neural networks become more efficient and sound categorisation occurs. There are increased connections between Wernicke's receptive and Broca's expressive areas of the left cerebral hemisphere. In 1993, Pujol, Vendrell, Junqué, and colleagues observed that the fibres of the corpus callosum continue to grow until the patient is in his late twenties. This facilitates inter-hemispheric communication.

The volume of grey matter in the frontal lobe peaks at twelve in males and eleven in females, before declining in adolescence. The peak volume may equate to the wave of synapto-genesis, which occurs before the onset of pruning. This excess of grey matter at the beginning of puberty allows for the processing of information.

The volume of white matter in the temporal lobe peaks at seventeen for both males and females. As grey matter reduces in the frontal cortex, during adolescence, the myelinated white matter increases in volume. As children develop, their sensory and motor regions mature first, followed by the cerebral cortex in a back-to-front manner. The phylo-genetically older parts of the brain develop before the newer areas, such as the prefrontal cortex. The prefrontal cortex is a recent evolutionary development and has been present for about 10,000 years. In comparison, the reptilian parts of the brain have evolved over the past two hundred million years. This means the reptilian brain is more hard-wired than the neuroplastic prefrontal cortex.

The peak of grey matter development, at the onset of puberty, is due to a new wave of synaptic proliferation. Refinement then occurs, pruning out or eliminating the least used synapses. This prepares the adolescent brain for more controlled sensorimotor, emotional, and cognitive processing. Testosterone levels in boys may slow down synaptic pruning, making boys clumsier at this stage. Gender differences remain to be fully explained. Some studies suggest grey matter in the frontal cortex continues to be lost until the age of thirty. Others suggest until the age of sixty or longer. There is now felt to be a linear increase in myelinated white matter throughout life, increasing the potential for lifelong learning.

Development of executive functions in the brains of patients and clients

The term "executive function" means coordination of thoughts, feelings, and behaviour. It includes selective attention, working memory, and problem solving, which all improve during adolescence. Multitasking is believed to be a test of perception. This is the ability to hold in mind an intention to carry out an action at a future time (Ellis, Brandimonte, Einstein et al., 1996). This was tested in children between the ages of six and fourteen and in adults. An improvement was found between the ages of six and ten, which tailed off between the ages of ten and fourteen. It is possible that the lack of improvement in performance for children aged between ten and fourteen was related to their pubertal status. In the matching-face-and-word task the results revealed that between the ages eleven and twelve performance declined, compared to the younger children. Reaction time increased by up to twenty per cent on the match-to-sample task in girls aged ten to eleven and boys aged eleven to twelve, compared to the nine to ten and ten to eleven age groups, respectively. Performance gradually improved from age thirteen to fourteen, reaching pre-pubescent levels by age sixteen to seventeen. This may explain why adolescents are clumsy during this period of new synaptic development (McGivern, Andersen, Byrd, et al., 2002). These new synapses are not fully pruned or connected up, making the pubertal frontal cortex less efficient. Only at the end of puberty are these synapses pruned in specialised, efficient networks, allowing performances in general to improve.

Social cognition development

The development of social cognition is influenced by the person's social experiences consequent to entering a new school. On entering secondary school, both social cognition and self-consciousness are affected. The child's theory of mind, the understanding of others' desires, intentions, and beliefs, is challenged.

Social communication skills are dependent on the perspective of the individual and their understanding of another's perspective. When an action is observed and then performed by an individual, mirror neurons fire (Rizzolatti, Forgassi, & Gallese, 2001, for review). With regard to face processing of the six Ekman emotions (2003), it was noticed that recognition of fear and disgust improve most with age. There was no improvement in the recognition of sad and angry expressions between the ages of six and sixteen. These findings suggest that puberty interrupts the developmental course of facial recognition (Carey, Diamond, & Woods, 1980). Recovery in recognition of these basic emotions occurs from ages fourteen to sixteen. Future research could involve working with endocrinologists to take saliva swabs of pubertal hormonal levels. This would give a more accurate measure of pubertal status when testing other cognitive and emotional functions.

Risk taking in adolescents

Adolescents find it difficult to recruit circuits in the brain that are associated with motivation. This means that more extreme incentives are sought by adolescents to compensate. This might include behaviours such as deliberate self-harm, joy-riding, alcohol and drug misuse. By attempting to activate the dorsolateral prefrontal cortex (motivational circuit), more effort is required, as these circuits have not yet matured in the adolescent brain.

When confronted with risk, adults link their gut response to the associated visual image. This is the somatic motor hypothesis (Damasio, 1996). Adolescents try to directly engage their prefrontal cortex, which requires more effort. By helping adolescents to understand this propensity, we might help to minimise their risk-taking behaviour. Based on my clinical experience of dealing with adolescents affected by traumatic events, BART psychotherapy can limit their risk-taking behaviours. Girls may have an increased ability to both regulate and contextualise their emotions due to an earlier maturation of their prefrontal cortex. In 2005, Nelson, Leibenluft, McClure, and Pine developed the social information processing network model (SIPNM). A group of young people aged seven to seventeen and a group of adults aged twenty-five to thirty-six viewed faces showing different emotional expressions. The young people showed greater activation of the amygdala, orbitofrontal cortex and anterior cingulate than their adult counterparts. However, when asked to switch their attention from the emotional expression to a non-emotional property, only the adults were able solely to engage and disengage the orbitofrontal cortex. This suggests that the adults had further development of their emotional processing and cognitive appraisal system compared to the group of young people.

Implications for learning by, and teaching of, adolescents

Executive function and social cognition are fundamental prerequisites for optimal learning by, and teaching of, adolescents in our secondary schools. Can the curriculum be modified to adapt to key changes in the pubertal brain that reflect this crucial period of neuroplasticity?

How do the processes of axonal myelination, synaptogenesis, and pruning influence learning of subjects such as languages, maths, science, and creativity?

How does the school's physical environment and teachers' knowledge of central nervous system development in their pupils influence the learning process?

The development of social and communication skills from age eight to twelve (known as the skill-hungry years) is a key life stage but is currently mapped against Key Stages Two and Three in settings of two different schools (primary and secondary). Integrating the learning of these years is a challenge in our current educational system, but offers the prospect of tackling both antisocial behaviour and lack of engagement in the learning process (Figure 37).

This will not only address the intellectual, physical, and participatory aspects of the curriculum, but also foster emotional development and resilience. Teachers having knowledge of the art and science underlying BART psychotherapy will be in a strong position to foster the integration and optimisation of these attributes.

During the past ten years, Dr Neil Mercer, Professor of Education and Educational Psychologist at the University of Cambridge, has explored collaborative learning in the classroom.

When children think together, they solve problems with better reasoning. By airing ideas openly and allowing criticism to be non-judgemental, teachers found that the best results were achieved when the classroom sought agreement.

LEARNER PROFILE

Academically capable, qualified, and multi-skilled; slef-reliant and rounded; morally responsible and happy

INTELLECTUAL

Versatile

Skilled

Knowledgeable

Inquisitive

Committed

PHYSICAL

Fit and active

Health conscious

Presentable

Practical

EMOTIONAL

Responsible and mature

Confident, positive and ambitious

Self reflective and empathetic

Cooperative and collaborative

Disciplined and resilient

Culturally and globally aware

PARTICIPATORY

Performing arts

Sport

Outdoor activities

Public service & charities

Figure 37. An ideal learner profile for children in secondary school. Student Learner Profile concept courtesy of Steve Pagan, Deputy Head (Academic) and the Thinking Skills Curriculum Team at Cheadle Hulme School.

Conversely, an emphasis on individual acquisition of knowledge and on purely analytical reasoning, as is most commonly practised in schools, tended to confirm children's pre-existing biases and prejudices.

Exploratory talk was used to stress sharing relevant knowledge with reasoning and a commitment to collaboration. Teachers agreed the ground rules for talking with the class in advance. Children were divided into groups of three to work on the scheduled task. In evaluating this approach, Professor Mercer (Littleton & Mercer, 2013) noticed the following:

1. Improved quality of work of the whole class.
2. More improved reasoning when solving problems.
3. Improved individual attainment, surprisingly.
4. Children showed synergistic social and psychological development.

A future goal for BART psychotherapy is to apply the multi-user BOKA machine to a group of ten to twelve teachers to induce them to adopt this approach by overcoming their natural fear of change and conception that a previous didactic approach was the only route towards achieving high grades for their pupils.

The process builds on the concept that integration of information at the level of the cerebral hemispheres is aided by the concept of three brains in one, explained below.

We can conceive of three brains in one within the human brain. This is a refined hypothesis of the gut- and heart- and head-brain plexi being reflected within the insular cortex and limbic system. The initial information processing occurs at the level of the splanchnic nerves of the gut nervous system. This gut instinct is referred up to the heart, where the cardiac nervous system processes heartfelt emotions and sensations (e.g., tugging at your heartstrings). From here, information is filtered via the sensory thalamus. Depending on the patient or client's level of arousal, further processing occurs at a conscious or thinking level. This gives further impetus to the theory of cerebellar reprocessing with the patient or client during BART psychotherapy.

Summary

An introduction is given to the information processing difficulties of children and adults with autism spectrum disorders and traumatic stress disorders. The response of the patient or client to stress in general is discussed along with the implications for clinical practice and psychotherapists. The developing brain is affected by neglect and abuse. This is related to the polyvagal theory first postulated by Dr Stephen Porges. The relationship between myelination of nerve fibres and the social engagement system is highlighted. This is also related to the development of the cerebellum in the first few years of life. The stages of adolescent brain development are further described, with particular attention to the role of pruning in the formation of executive functions. The development of social communication skills is a consequence of this pruning and it is related to risk-taking in adolescents. The implications for learning by, and teaching of, adolescents are discussed with an outline learner profile for a child in high school. The role of collaborative learning in the classroom is outlined. This is tied in with the concepts of the gut-brain, heart-brain, and head-brain, as represented within the cerebral cortex.

CHAPTER SIX

The mystery of consciousness

In his book, *Self Comes to Mind: Constructing the Conscious Brain* (2010), Antonio Damasio discusses this mystery. According to Damasio, when the self meets the mind we experience consciousness. He describes the mind as a flow of images and a conscious mind as one containing a self. The self introduces a mental subjective perspective. We become fully conscious when the self comes to mind.

The unison of mind and self creates auditory, skin, and neural "maps". The mental experience is closely related to the firing of retinal neurons. Islands of image-making perception provide signals to the association cortex, or memory-holding regions, of the brain, before sending images back for perception. The self is more elusive. Our brains generate "maps" of the body internally that are used as the reference for all other neural "maps". The "I" in our processing must be stable, so that the reference point is one body. The internal milieu must be maintained in a state of homeostasis, otherwise sickness or death occurs. The brain and body are tightly coupled and the brainstem governs breathing, heart rate, and blood pressure. The brainstem nuclei provide neural "maps" allowing the grounding of self to occur, in terms of primordial feelings. There is a wealth of cognitive and emotional content stored in the cortex.

The self is built in three stages. The first stage, or protoself, is a neural description of relatively stable aspects of the organism. The main product of the protoself is the living body's spontaneous feelings (primordial feelings). In the second stage, a pulse of the core self is generated when the protoself is modified. This modification is due to an interaction between the person and the object, which results in alteration of the object also. The modified images of both person and object become momentarily linked. The resultant coherent pattern between the person and the object becomes a sequence of images, some of which are also feelings. In the third stage, or autobiographical self, objects in the person's life story activate the second stage. The second and third stages are subsequently linked in a logical manner.

Searl (1990), in his review of Damasio's book, quotes the following:

> . . . The distinctive feature of brains . . . is their ability to create maps. Minds emerge when the activity of small neuronal circuits is organised across large networks . . . to compose momentary patterns (which represent events located outside the brain).

The decisive step in the making of consciousness is not the image making that is at the basis of our mind, but in making the images unique to us.

The protoself is an integrated collection of separate neural patterns, mapping moment by moment the most stable aspects of our body. It produces primordial feelings, which are acknowledged and reprocessed in Stage 1 of BART psychotherapy.

The core self involves images modifying the protoself that become conscious through the person's actions.

Finally, the autobiographical self contains our sense of person and social identity. It contains a tapestry of life's memories. This analysis adds to the ongoing debate in relation to defining and distinguishing the concepts of the mind, self, and consciousness.

The Master and His Emissary *(McGilchrist, 2009)*

The ratio of the corpus callosum to the volume of the hemispheres has become smaller from Homo erectus to Neanderthals to Homo sapiens. It has been surmised that this is due to the specification of language in the left hemisphere.

People who lose the function of their right hemisphere have a pathological narrowing of the window of attention. In extreme cases, they fail to acknowledge the existence of the left half of their body.

Functions of right and left hemispheres

In reality, both hemispheres work together and communicate via the band of fibres known as the corpus callosum

As humans have evolved, the ratio of corpus callosum to volume of hemispheres has decreased. This has led to different functions between the right and left hemispheres (Figure 38). In conditions such as autism, there is less potential for hemispheric integration. This shows the consequences for mankind in relation to individual functional tendencies in terms of the LH and RH. The static fixed and

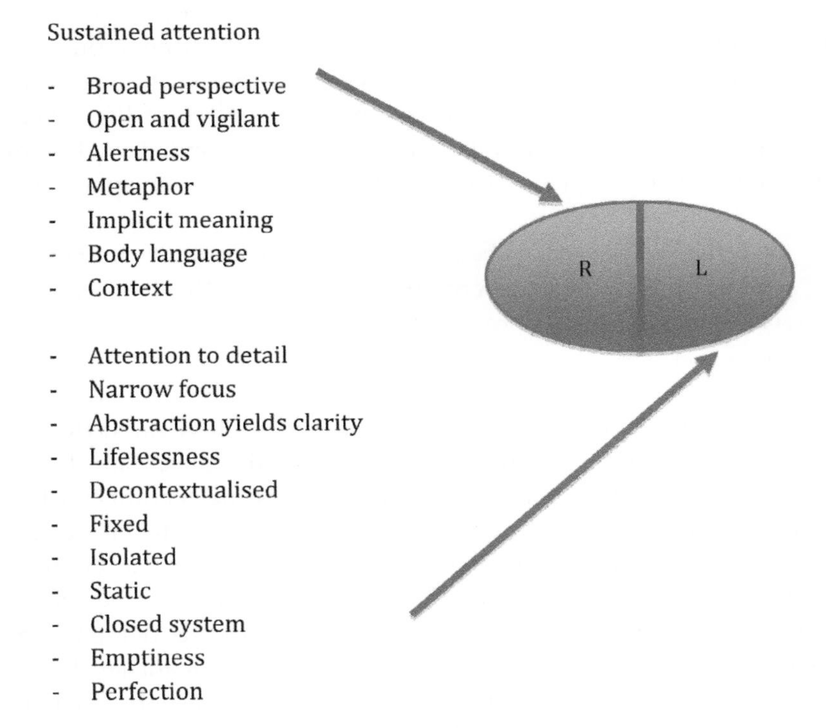

Figure 38. Different functions of left and right hemispheres.

isolated functions of the LH are contrasted with the changing evolving and interconnected world of the RH.

The right hemisphere yields a world of the individual. This is changing, evolving, interconnected, implicit, and incarnate. Living beings are represented in the context of their lived world, yet are never perfectly known.

The world of the left hemisphere involves a network of small complicated rules. It is vocal of its own accord. I hypothesise that BART psychotherapy, by accelerating interhemispheric neural networks and proliferation of synaptic connections in the patient or client's connectome, can help reverse the trend of separate hemispheric function.

Thus, two versions of the world, which are combined in different ways, exist inside our head. In the early part of the sixth century, the hemispheres were more balanced. However, in the fifteenth and sixteenth centuries, the left hemisphere came to dominate, and the more we tended to pursue happiness, the more we were left feeling resentful. This led to an explosion of mental illness. As civilisation pursued freedom, De Tocqueville stated how this was "strangled" by a network of small complicated rules that covered the surface of life. There were limits to rationality, as rationality itself was grounded in a leap of intuition and, according to McGilchrist (2009), the left hemisphere is

> the Berlusconi of the brain because it controls the media, it's the one with which we . . . it's very vocal on its own behalf. The right hemisphere doesn't have a voice and it can't construct these same arguments.

Einstein (Calaprice, 2011) declared that the intuitive mind (RH) is a sacred gift and the rational mind (LH) is a faithful servant. In his world (1888–1955), he felt that society honours the servant but has forgotten the gift. McGilchrist suggests that a fundamental bi-cameral difference is that the left hemisphere rationalises (the "what" from its narrow perspective) while the right hemisphere "intuits" (the "how" from its much broader perspective). I believe that BART psychotherapy can help to redress the tendency of a dominant left hemisphere and restore the primary function of the RH in its intuitive role, as mentioned on page 1 of this book.

The role of asymmetry in the human brain

The divided brain gives us two different, but ultimately complementary, views of the world. The hemispheres are in a power struggle to bring us their own unique experience of the world. As I will explain later, this is influenced by eastern and western cultures.

The structure of the brain reflects its history. Each part evolves from, and in response to, an adjacent part. From the sub-cortical structures, responsible for unconscious biological regulation, evolved the outer cortex. The frontal cortex further evolved from the neocortex. The prefrontal cortex has evolved in the past 10,000 years and now comprises forty per cent of the frontal cortex. Our planning abilities, perspective taking, decision making, and consequential thinking arise from here. This may give rise to our quintessential human personality characteristics.

The key components of the peripheral and central nervous systems are:

- spinal cord with connections to the periphery;
- brainstem with origin of cranial nerves;
- cerebellum with links to prefrontal cortex and brainstem;
- limbic system with amygdala, basal ganglia, and hippocampus;
- neocortex with occipital, parietal, temporal, and frontal lobes.

The neocortex is further divided into the allocortex, which comprises paleocortex and archicortex. These are the cortical parts of the limbic system and have four or five and three layers of neuronal cell bodies, respectively. The number of cell body layers relates to the information-processing capacity. Thus, the neocortex does the greatest amount of information processing.

Sherrington (1906) described "opponent processors" in the brain, which controlled the sensorimotor system. Kinsbourne (1988) described three pairings within the head-brain:

1. "Up/down": the cortex exerts downward inhibition of the automatic subcortical responses.
2. "Front/back": the frontal cortex inhibits the posterior cortex.
3. "Right/left": the interrelationship between RH and LH via the corpus callosum, which is discussed in detail in Chapter Seven.

The embryological development of the foetal brain

The forebrain is the forward, or rostral, part of the brain. The prosencephalon, or forebrain, divides into the telencephalon and diencephalon. The telencephalon, or cerebrum, contains the cerebral cortex. The diencephalon consists of thalamus, hypothalamus, subthalamus, and epithalamus. The mesencephalon forms the midbrain. Finally, the rhomboencephalon, or hindbrain, forms the metencephalon and myelencephalon. The descending neural tracts aggregate as the spinal cord.

At eight weeks gestation, the heart starts to beat. At ten weeks gestation, the neural crest divides into tissue that will form both the brain and the gastrointestinal tract (GIT). Therefore, the GIT has similar neurotransmitter receptors to the brain. This explains why drugs acting on the CNS also exhibit side effects on the GIT. Good examples are the antidepressant drugs known as selective serotonin reuptake inhibitors (SSRI). While it takes up to three weeks for these drugs to show a therapeutic effect, the adverse effects on the GIT (nausea and vomiting) are more immediate.

Frontal lobes of the brain

The frontal lobes have expanded rapidly since they first evolved. Although the latest region of the brain to "come online", they are also the first to shut down at the onset of traumatic stress. Currently, they represent forty per cent of total brain volume. They contain more myelinated white matter for faster neuronal transmission. Under the effect of toxic or traumatic stress, the brain is, therefore, forty per cent less efficient in processing information. The frontal cortex comprises forty per cent of the neocortex and is engaged in the following functions: planning, organising, problem solving, memory, impulse control, decision making, selective attention, and controlling our behaviour and emotions.

Frontal lobe injury may affect emotions, impulse control, language memory, and social and sexual behaviour. The left frontal lobe contains Wernicke's and Broca's areas and is responsible for receptive and expressive language.

The frontal lobes help to inhibit the limbic system, or emotional brain, and help us to read other people's minds and intentions. By seeing the other person's perspective, we are able to allow empathy to occur. This is known as "theory of mind" and is crucial for communication and reciprocal social interaction to develop.

At the onset of trauma, blood flow is diverted away from the frontal lobes towards the brainstem. This ensures that breathing, heart rate, and other functions essential to our survival are maintained. Thinking processes are temporarily shut down as they could hamper our instinctive survival reflexes. This blood flow is gradually reversed, as confirmed by feedback from patients during BART psychotherapy. They describe a tingling sensation moving from the back of their head to their forehead, which is accompanied by a gradual return to homeostasis. This is often accompanied by a release of light energy from the area of the forehead associated with the sixth chakra and pineal gland. The significance of the pineal gland in processing emotion has been known to cultures as diverse as the Egyptians, Romans, Hindus, and philosophers of Ancient Greece.

Yakovlevian torque (Toga & Thompson, 2003) means there is bilateral asymmetry with reference to the mid-sagittal plane of the brain. This might relate to the evolution of language dominance in the left cerebral hemisphere. I would suggest that this bilateral asymmetry provides theoretical support for the use of continuous bilateral cerebellar auditory stimulation during BART psychotherapy sessions. The right hemisphere directs its attention to whatever is going on in the outside world. The left hemisphere focuses narrow attention directed by our immediate needs. The left hemisphere prefers what it knows and is led by its expectations. The right hemisphere sees things as a whole and in their context, while the left hemisphere sees things broken up, from which it reconstructs a whole perspective. The brain, therefore, attends to the world in two distinct ways. In one reality (RH), we directly experience the "live" version. In the other (LH), we experience a re-presented version of reality. Working together, the two hemispheres allow us to know, learn, and make things. In essence, we become powerful and authoritative.

What are the functions of the individual hemispheres?

The hemispheres can distinguish five types of attention:

- vigilance;
- sustained;

- alertness;
- focused;
- divided.

The intensity axis of attention is a function of the right hemisphere and the selectivity axis of attention is a function of the left hemisphere. Thus, globally, attention is served by both cerebral hemispheres.

Development of ideas on the theory of mind

The right hemisphere explores the environment for attentional intensity. When the right hemisphere prioritises something, this orientates the left hemisphere to focus on it. It grasps the salient features with input from the right half of the body, to which it is connected.

The right hemisphere is involved in the person's theory of mind. This is the capacity to "put oneself in another's shoes" and imagine what their feelings, ideas, beliefs, and motivations are. The right hemisphere understands emotions and mediates social behaviour.

The pars opercularis of Broca's area contains mirror neurons for imitating finger movements. The right frontal pole regulates the HPA axis. The right frontotemporal cortex helps to dampen emotional hyperarousal. The right superior temporal sulcus recognises emotion in faces. Focal intonation (prosody) and gesture are both interpreted by the right hemisphere. The left hemisphere reads blunt emotions by examining the mouth, for example, to determine whether friend or foe. The right hemisphere, on the other hand, can interpret tertiary theory of mind from the eyes alone. All emotions, apart from anger, are connected to the right frontal lobe. The second order theory of mind can be assessed using the Sally Anne test.

This false belief task was developed by Wimmer and Perner (1983). Anne has a box and Sally has a basket. Sally puts a marble into her basket and goes outside for a walk. Then Anne mischievously takes the marble from Sally's basket and puts it in her own box. When Sally comes back, she wants to play with her marble. Where does Sally think the marble is? Most four-year-old children say that Sally will look inside her basket, as that is where she thinks the marble is. Younger children, and those with autism, often point to the box, showing that they believe Sally will look where the marble is actually located. They have not yet developed a second-order theory of mind. This ability is independent of intellect. Thus, children with Down's syndrome have a normally developed theory of mind, whereas many patients with high-functioning autism will have an abnormally developed theory of mind. It appears that this ability is genetically hard-wired in the brain. It remains to be seen whether BART psychotherapy could reverse this process in some patients with high-functioning autism.

Baron-Cohen and Wheelwright (2001) have devised the "revised mind's eye tests" as a pure test of theory of mind (TOM). There are thirty-six pictures of eyes in total. Each set of eyes is accompanied by four words describing feeling states. Only one is correct. Examples include playful, upset, and desire. Patients with autism are unable to read these facial expressions, as they tend to avoid eye contact, which is a traumatic experience for them. BART psychotherapy has the potential to help them overcome this trauma and learn how to process and make sense of this visual information.

In autism, the functions of the right frontal cortex are impaired. These patients have problems with social language, irony, metaphor, empathy, prosody, and the ability to convey meaning and feeling through vocal intonation and inflection. Initial results with BART psychotherapy suggest that it helps to integrate cerebellar function and improve impaired frontal cortex function.

Professor Colwyn Trevarthen at the University of Edinburgh first studied the interaction between mothers and infants (Figure 39). His pioneering work shed light on the incredible interactive abilities of the newborn and infant in terms of their functional ability to engage all their senses to enhance the mother–infant interaction (Figure 40).

There is a dynamic evolving interaction between mother and infant, which dramatically grows the infant brain from fifty to ninety per cent of adult size in the first four years.

Infants are normally cradled to the left and, therefore, come to attune to their primary care-giver's right hemisphere. This controls the emotionally expressive left side of the adult's face. Close exposure to the left hemiface of the mother puts the baby in touch with emotions and aware of the impact of touch. The first three years of the child's life allow the mother's expressed emotions to be actively perceived. During this time, it is primarily the right hemisphere of the baby that experiences connectome development from the process of synaptogenesis (Blakemore & Choudhury, 2006).

Primary intersubjectivity

Mother watches and listens, intuitively anticipating the baby's expressions. She replies playfully with touches, motherese speech, and face and hand expressions.

The baby, attracted to the sound of mother's voice, facial expressions, and hand gestures, replies playfully, with affection, imitation, and provoking imitations.

Figure 39. Example of mother–infant interaction.

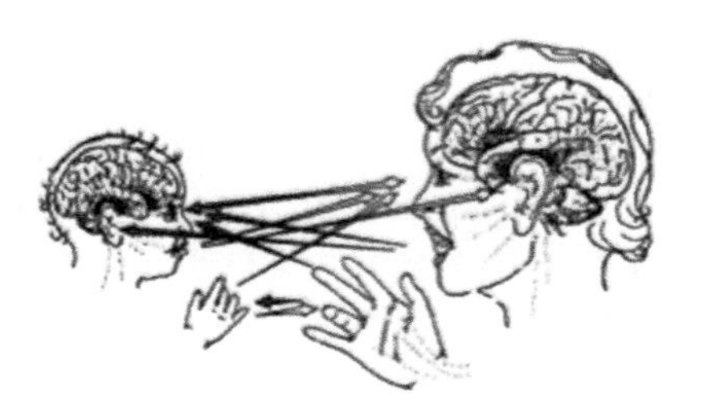

Emotions expressed and actively perceived
Protoconversation
Rhythmic turn-taking of expressive acts.

Figure 40. Primary intersubjectivity of mother and infant (reprinted with the permission of Professor Colwyn Trevarthen).

The baby is attracted to the mother's voice in tone and rhythm. Facial expressions of warmth and positive emotion and hand gestures from the mother elicit playfulness, affection, and reciprocal imitation from the infant. As the mother watches and listens, she intuitively anticipates the baby's expressions. The mother mirrors the infant's vocalisations with "motherese" speech, touch, facial expressions, and hand gestures. A protoconversation is initiated with this rhythmic turn-taking of expressive acts. As positive emotions are processed, the baby expresses joy freely. A happy, responsive mother matches her infant's arousal. The mutual delight evoked via turn-taking promotes resilience and attunement. However, in these early years, the infant must be allowed to express negative emotions such as moodiness. A mother who can tolerate anger, sadness, and fear in herself and her infant will encourage interactive repair and mutual attunement. If the baby–mother interaction becomes stressed, there may be minimal mother–infant play. The interactive levels of arousal become mistuned and the mother and/or infant can become overwhelmed. Another type of stressful interaction involves the baby withdrawing or becoming non-responsive. This induces negative feelings in the mother, which she is unable to tolerate. The result is mutual frustration and, if prolonged, can lead to developmental delay. The earlier CT scans of a healthy three-year-old and a neglected one demonstrate the profound deleterious effects on growth of the infant brain that deprivation can have. This was recently brought to media attention in the UK. A child aged four was discovered under a pile of blankets in his cot, having been dead for over two years. His emaciated, shrunken frame was estimated to be the size of a six-month-old baby. The mother was sent to prison, having been convicted of starving him to death.

When the mother and infant are in a state of interactive regulation, the infant seeks out the mother for cooperative regulation and learns self-soothing behaviours. The mother then seeks to regulate her infant's inner state of being. This assists the infant's auto regulation. With both interactive attunement and frequent play, both become calm, interactive beings.

> Human relationships and the effect of relationships on relationships are the building blocks of healthy development. From the moment of conception to the finality of death, intimate and caring relationships are the fundamental mediators of successful human adaptation. . . . (Shankoff & Phillips, 2000, p. 27)

> These important relationships during the first years of life form the foundation and scaffold on which cognitive, linguistic, emotional, social and moral development unfold. (Shankoff & Phillips, 2000, p. 349)

When the right hemisphere:right hemisphere relationship is dysregulated, the infant averts his eye gaze, disconnects from the mother, is easily startled, and feels unsafe. The mother is angry and hostile and averts her gaze from the baby. If she suffers with postnatal depression, her still or unresponsive face fails to react to the inner distress of the infant. The infant starts to autodysregulate by crying, arching, and then displaying a blank stare and becoming motionless. The baby is exposed to a chronic state of threat with no sense of safety. The mother can be threatening to her baby if the depression becomes delusional. She might be intrusive, unresponsive, or even dissociative to her infant's stimuli. The result is that the mother's confidence as a "good enough mother" is shattered and both she and her infant can become agitated or withdrawn with little capacity for affect regulation.

The corollaries are an impaired window of tolerance in later life and this shows the necessity to develop capacity within national health systems for perinatal and infant mental services. This would lay a firm foundation for identifying those at risk of mental health problems in later life. Along with several colleagues, I was trained in the "watch, wait and wonder" (Muir, Lojkasek, & Cohen, 1999) parent–infant dyadic psychotherapy technique. This involves the mother and infant being together on a mat on the floor surrounded by age-appropriate toys. For the first twenty or thirty minutes, the mother is encouraged to watch her infant and stay in close proximity. She then waits for the infant to take the lead in initiating contact. This might prove very difficult for the mother, and the therapist's role is to be supportive at this stage. For the last half an hour of the weekly session, the mother is asked to reflect or wonder what the experience was like, both for herself and for her infant. There is the opportunity to put in place repair of any damage to mother–infant bonding both by practice of the techniques at home and addressing any unresolved trauma issues for the mother. In our use of this technique in an adult inpatient setting, we found that all of the mothers had experienced traumatic stress. This was because of abuse in their own childhoods, trauma at the infant's birth, or from postnatal depression or psychosis. This meant that significant direct trauma-focused therapy was needed by the mothers before they could benefit from the "watch, wait and wonder" therapy.

Further brain development in the infant brain

In later years, the right anterior superior temporal gyrus is activated when the child starts to speak and count. The precuneus exist bilaterally in the parietal lobes. They are activated when we are able to relate to a first-person perspective and episodic memory has been established. The right ventromedial prefrontal cortex links emotion and feeling with cognitions and meaning. This is activated by bilateral auditory stimulation during both EMDR and BART psychotherapy, due to the use of continuous bilateral cerebellar activation. The RH, which is embodied with the self, produces body language and tone of voice. The right parietal lobe senses, feels, and images the body, whereas the LH builds up an image from its component parts. Body dysphoria and anorexia combine body image disturbance with significant affective distress. BART psychotherapy can help to relieve emotional dysregulation associated with these disorders.

The RH regulates the sympathetic nervous system; the parasympathetic nervous system is more under LH control. The former regulates heart rate and blood pressure, the latter boosts body relaxation. The RH pays attention to whatever exists apart from us while the LH attends to its created virtual world. Both hemispheres are involved in all brain functions, despite their lateral specificity. This explains why integration of cerebral hemispheric function would be enhanced during BART psychotherapy.

Development of language in the left cerebral hemisphere

The RH is engaged processing new experiences. Once this is familiar or routine, this information is embedded in the LH. We then have knowledge of someone in the sense of a feel for what is distinctive about him or her. This is the kind of knowledge we first think of when talking about the living. A second type of knowledge is facts. Factual knowledge is general, impersonal, fixed, certain, disengaged, put together from individual bits and mostly associated with the LH.

Languages other than English refer to these types of knowledge with different words. In Latin, *cognoscere* is used, in French, *connaître*, and in German, *kennen*. Another Latin example is *sapere*, in French, *savoir*, and in German, *wissen*. Jung said "all cognition is akin to recognition" (1964). This means we come to know or cognise/*wissen* something only by recognising (*erkennen*) something we already know (*kennen*) (McGilchrist, 2009). The RH apprehends things when new. The LH takes over when things become more familiar. Thus, initial holistic knowledge becomes fragmented. Knowledge perception and experience exist in the differences between things. Our senses quickly acclimatise to constant input (e.g., bilateral auditory cerebellar stimulation). From the age of three, language in the form of sentences tends to emerge.

The neuroplasticity of the brain is such that, in the first eighteen months, infants have synaptic development of Wernicke's area to such an extent that they can fully comprehend any languages they hear consistently. By the age of two, Broca's area for spoken language has lagged behind in its development. This explains the frustration of the toddler–parent dyad known as the terrible twos. It takes about one year for the expressive and receptive parts of the cortex to make sufficient connections for the infant to express their wants and desires. Vulnerable mothers need to be supported during this critical stage of language development.

The BOKA machine used for BART psychotherapy can be conceptualised as a "body of knowledge activator". For half a million years, our nearest ancestors had the capacity for some form of communication. The Homo erectus species appears around 200,000 years ago. Spoken language appears to have evolved around 60,000 years ago. Children use intonation, phrasing, and rhythm as a precursor to syntax and vocabulary. Newborn babies enjoy motherese, which is the music of speech. They have a sense of prosody and rhythm from birth even if born completely deaf. They do this via right hemispheric holistic processing.

Music was built upon the prosodic mechanisms of the right hemisphere that allow us affective emotional communications through vocal intonations (Panksepp & Bernatsky, 2002, p. 136).

Music helps to communicate emotion, which came before language both phylo- and ontogenetically. Human language may have developed from the gestures of the ogham language, for example. The metaphor "to grasp" has roots in the description of thinking in different languages. In Latin, *com-prehendere,* in German, *be-greifen* or *handeln* describe meaningful, goal-directed human activity (McGilchrist, 2009). Derivations of the Latin word *tendere* mean to reach out with the hand. This shows the link between gestures and the development of language (McGilchrist, 2009)

Metaphor links language to life experience and is a function of the RH. Its Greek roots are "meta", across, and "pherein", to carry. This enables purposeful thought via embodiment and placing it within a living context (McGilchrist, 2009). In practising BART psychotherapy, I am constantly drawing the attention of the patient to their statements using metaphor. McGilchrist argues that thought structure and content has an earlier bodily existence before being processed in Broca's area of the LH as speech. Language is seen as an extension of life. As Wittgenstein stated,

> Our language can be seen as an ancient city: a maze of little streets and squares and of houses with additions from various periods and this surrounded by a multitude of new boroughs with straight regular streets and uniform houses. . . . And to imagine a language means to imagine a form of life. (Wittgenstein, 1967, p. 241)

Language is an embodiment of emotion. It has origins in music and rhythm (e.g., drumbeat) and is registered via the anterior cingulate cortex before cerebral reprocessing. Music is beneficial to the group rather than the individual, and both dolphins and whales have comparatively enlarged anterior cingulate cortices, which facilitate their ability to communicate across large distances. Indeed, the brains of dolphins and humans are of equal size, despite their diverse evolutionary habitat.

Evolution of the infant brain into functioning adult right and left hemispheres

During infancy, the RH matures first, followed by the LH from the third year onwards as speech and language areas become myelinated and activated. By years five and six, the RH starts to evolve the capacity for emotionality and prosody of language. The right frontal lobe serves functions such as empathy, humour, irony, imagination, creativity, capacity for awe, music, dance, poetry, art, love of nature, moral sense, ability to conceptualise, to think consequentially, and how to change your mind. My experience of using BART psychotherapy is that patients experience new sensations in their frontal lobes at the final stage of reprocessing. At this point, it can be postulated that both frontal lobes are benefiting from activation by continuous bilateral cerebellar stimulation. Consequentially, these functions may be enhanced. According to McGilchrist, the RH reaches out while the LH has an end in mind, as if directed by conscious will. The RH tends to seek out hemispherical coherence while the LH is its master's valued emissary. The LH is purposeful while the RH attends to what is out there. Thus, the brain evolves a dual perspective according to the perspectives of both hemispheres. The LH might initially be unaware of the primary awareness of the RH. Which version of the "truth" are we to believe? On the one hand, there is broad vigilant attention and wholeness of the RH worldview, whereas, on the other hand, transformation and re-presentation by the LH occurs using its functions of separation, division, and analysis. The LH makes the implicit explicit and is directed by conscious will. In its turn, the RH delivers an experience to the LH, which is bound by context and incorporates affective awareness. According to Panksepp (1988), this affective awareness is the prerequisite for perception and cognition.

BART psychotherapy focuses on the primacy of our *affective* experience. Descartes opined, "cognito ergo sum" (I think, therefore I am) and led the movement for mind–body dualism. In the twenty-first century, we are entering an era of reintegration of mind and body. I believe a more prescient axiom is "affectio ergo sum" becoming "sum ergo sum". Feeling (from Latin *affectio*) is at the heart of our being and from emotion humankind has developed logic and reasoning. This is a significant shift from Cartesian dualism. Damasio states, in *Descartes' Error* (2006), "Nature appears to have built the apparatus of rationality not just on top of the apparatus of biological regulation but also from it and with it" (p. 128).

Achieving affective regulation for the patient is a key function of BART psychotherapy along with the parallel integration of the influences of nature and nurture.

Summary

The work of Antonio Damasio in his book, *Self Comes to Mind: Constructing the Conscious Brain*, is discussed, illustrating the mental maps in the brain. He described three stages of development: the protoself, core self, and autobiographical self. The relationship of these self-stages to BART psychotherapy is compared. Dr Iain Mc Gilchrist has written a classic text, *The Master and His Emissary* (2009), outlining the respective roles of the right and left hemispheres. A YouTube video presentation highlights the significant differences in function between the hemispheres. As the volume of the corpus callosum has decreased over time, so specialisation between hemispheres has increased. The role of asymmetry in the human brain is discussed, along with its embryological development. The concepts of theory of mind are explained alongside its facilitation by appropriate attunement of mother and infant. The early development of the infant brain is explained, including the development of language. A potential way forward for perinatal and infant mental health services is described, using the "watch, wait and wonder" psychotherapeutic approach. This links to the ancient origins of language, music, and communication between animal species such as birds, whales, and dolphins. The evolution of the infant brain into adult right and left hemispheres is dependent on experience. BART psychotherapy can play a role in optimising this process and focuses on the primacy of affective, compared to cognitive, experience. Hence, I make the case for it being an effective, if not essential, precursor to cognitive–behavioural therapy. Until the affective component of trauma has been activated and reprocessed, it has not registered in the prefrontal cortex for cognitive reappraisal. Hence, CBT initiated before this stage is more likely to prove ineffective. This has implications for the effectiveness of trauma-focused therapy within the mental health service.

CHAPTER SEVEN

Development of thought and the role of BART psychotherapy and peak performance in reprocessing thoughts

Conscious thought accounts for about five per cent of brain activity. The first manifestation of thought is its global synthetic form generated by the right hemisphere. Hand and other gestures become integrated with speech production once the LH becomes activated. The words generated from thought patterns are segmented linearly and hierarchically as both hemispheres and gestures combine. These influences reverberate reciprocally in the forebrain. The thought processes that begin in the RH are sent to the LH for processing and re-presentation. This is recycled to the RH, becoming a new synthesis of the original recalled experience. This helps to explain why bilateral cerebellar activation in BART psychotherapy facilitates patient's reprocessing. I would argue that all forms of psychotherapy would benefit from this augmented form of interhemispheric communication. It promotes unification between the left hemispheric division of information and the right hemispheric tendency towards wholeness. In other words, thesis and antithesis are combined as a synthesis. The role of individuation from the LH is integrated with that of coherence from the RH. The rationality of the LH is subject to the intuitive wisdom of the RH. Knowledge of the five stages of BART psychotherapy and of peak performance helps to bring these perspectives together. Also, as the therapist seeks to identify and locate anatomically points of maximum distress, this can highlight areas resistant to information reprocessing. They can use this knowledge to hypothesise which hemispheric functions are most compromised and need to be accentuated.

The origin of consciousness

Panksepp (1988) believes it starts at the periaqueductal grey matter in the midbrain before migrating through the cingulate, temporal, and frontal regions of the cortex. An analogy is made of a forest canopy being akin to a cerebral canopy. This is like a tree growing upwards from roots deep within us. The primacy of affect in generating consciousness is the approach of this neuroscientist. As our cerebral canopy has evolved, we are aware of greater empathy with the world at large and also develop the capacity for abstraction.

The rise of drama in Ancient Greece initially objectifies the thoughts and feelings of others and us. Through ownership of these thoughts and feelings, we gain insight. Crucially, we achieve the capacity for empathy and objectivity. These concepts have been recognised in different ways through both culture and language. Initially, words for thinking and seeing are similar. Then the word "theorein" is added to the lexicon and relates to theory and "noein" or "noos" related to reflection, generation of ideas, and images. In the sixth century BC, "apeiron" means indefinite or ill defined, but later becomes the essence of "sophia", or wisdom. "Thymos" becomes instinct and couples motion and emotion (McGilchrist, 2009). This gives us our current nosology for mood disorders and the word euthymic. The latter can be translated as having normal instinctual drives and impulses.

The connectome

This refers to the title of Seung's recent book (2012). In it, he discusses how the wiring of the brain is the main factor driving our individual personalities. It took twelve years to map the connectome of the worm C. elegans, which has 300 neurons. We have 86 billion neurons, as estimated by Azevedo, Carvalho, Grinberg and colleagues (2009), each with millions of connections, emphasising the mammoth task involved in mapping the human connectome.

Neurons are influenced by four main factors:

1. They adjust or *reweight* strengthening or weakening connections according to experience.
2. They *reconnect* through new growth or pruning of synapses during periods of neuroplasticity.
3. They *rewire* when firing action potentials, which stimulates branches to both grow and retract.
4. They *regenerate*, depending on epigenetic influences and where in the forest of the neuronal brain's synaptogenesis occurs. Alongside regeneration, apoptosis occurs where existing neurons shrivel, degenerate, and die off, like leaves falling from the tree.

According to Seung (2012), "You are more than your genes. You are your connectome".

Also as the maxim goes, if you do not use it (neural synapse and corresponding muscle reflex), you lose it.

This has major implications for the rehabilitation of stroke patients and those with major limb or spinal injury. The body and brains can reshape and remould, gaining lost function, especially when the injury occurs in childhood. However, the holy grail of those working in rehabilitation technologies is to apply the research from biomechanical engineering to the neural maps of Hebbian learning to effectively regain lost muscle and nerve function.

Brain size is not related to the functions of the conscious mind. Both Anatole France, the celebrated writer and anatomist, and Albert Einstein had brain sizes smaller than average Seung (2012). What does appear to be important is the way neurons intricately cooperate to perform mental tasks. The cerebral cortex can remap following injury, showing that the Brodmann areas are not rigidly defined. Each functional brain area may contain over one hundred million neurons. Seung (2012) hypothesises that the different brain functions are heavily dependent on how these neurons are connected.

These famous words were written by John Donne in 1624, from Donne (1987):

XVII. Nunc Lento Sonitu Dicunt, Morieris

Now, this bell tolling softly for another, says to me: Thou must die.

XVII. MEDITATION.

> No man is an island, entire of itself; every man is a piece of the continent, a part of the main; if a clod be washed away by the sea, Europe is the less, as well as if a promontory were, as well as if a manor of thy friend's or of thine own were; any man's death diminishes me, because I am involved in mankind, and therefore never send to know for whom the bell tolls; it tolls for thee . . .

For man, we can substitute the word neuron. By means of mechanisms yet uncertain, these neurons form a body-wide web of interconnectivity. This results in our ability to sense, feel, perceive, think, and generate the remarkable capabilities of our mind.

In the same way that we expectorate, sweat, and urinate, so it is the function of the gut-brain, heart-brain, and head-brain to secrete thoughts and feelings.

There are more than one million synapses per cubic millimetre in the head-brain. Each connection may have many synapses. The influence may be chemical, electrical, or mechanical. It is unidirectional and passed on when neurotransmitter (key) meets receptor (lock). These neurotransmitters may be excitatory or inhibitory and the resulting synapse may strengthen or weaken the neuronal connection. All these interactions take place in a timeframe of 40–500 milliseconds.

In 2005, the Royal Society in England voted Isaac Newton an even greater genius than Albert Einstein (Seung, 2012, p. 64). Newton (1675), stated in his reply by letter to Robert Hooke,

> What Descartes did was a good step. You have added much several ways and especially in considering the colours of thin plates. If I have seen further it is only by standing on the shoulders of giants . . . your humble servant,
>
> "IS. NEWTON."

If we say there is nothing new under the sun, then all ideas preexist in some form or another. Many discoveries are spontaneous, seemingly unconnected and simultaneous. Examples include Newton and Leibnitz's discovery of calculus (Seung, 2012, p. 64) and the work on AC and DC electricity generation by Nicola Tesla and Thomas Edison. Similarly, if one neuron is able to make stronger connections, it is because a longer, taller, and thicker trunk in the interconnected neural network, or connectome, has supported it.

Each neuron lower down the neural hierarchy sends excitatory synapses to higher up neurons that can detect the whole sum of its individually detected parts. According to Seung (2012, p. 50): "The function of a neuron is defined chiefly by its connections with other neurons".

This is defined as connectionism and a complete picture of neural function can only be determined by studying both its inputs and outputs.

I am reminded of the acronym GIGO from the computer industry. This stands for gold inputs = gold outputs. However, it could also imply garbage inputs = garbage outputs.

The nature of memory

In order to secrete coherent thoughts, we need to have access to a database, or memory bank, in brain terms. Neural connections have been compared to both wax, in that they can remain the same for long time periods, and plastic, in that they can be shaped and moulded quickly. In the same way that a strengthened synapse gets bigger, so perhaps can a revisited memory coalesce and become stronger, feeding into different synaptic neural networks. In the case of traumatic memories, these are stored piecemeal and dysfunctionally. Here, the normal hierarchical structure of memory storage and retrieval has broken down. Lower excitatory sensory inputs have overwhelmed the normal upper inhibitory mechanisms. It seems likely that memories are stored as patterns generated from interconnecting neurons. Connectionist neuroscientists have proposed that "If two neurons are repeatedly activated simultaneously then the connections between them are strengthened in both directions" (Seung, 2012, p. 81).

They also proposed that "If two neurons are repeatedly activated sequentially, the connection from the first to the second is strengthened" (Seung, 2012, p. 82).

These rules have become known as Hebbian rules of synaptic plasticity, from Hebb's 1949 book, *The Organization of Behaviour*. The connectome is where nature meets nurture and experience plays a key role in the development of memory. The links between memories and connectomes is a key task for the future as technologies advance to become equal to the task. In summary, Seung (2012, pp. 76–82) stresses that we can change who we are for the better by means of the four Rs:

1. Reweighting.
2. Reconnection.
3. Rewiring.
4. Regeneration.

I would add a fifth R: reprocessing. This can be achieved with BART psychotherapy, as described in the text.

In the same way that the water in a stream and the earth underneath are involved in a constant two-way exchange of information, so the neural network in our brains works the same way. I have explained how our moods can fluctuate from the frozen state of numbness to the hyper-aroused state of the rapids. When our neural activity is becalmed, we operate within an effective window of tolerance. As the waveform patterns of neural activity are produced, our connectomes drive our present experiences, leaving an impression behind that becomes accessible memories of the past. If the waveform of neural activity enters the frozen state, we can become dissociated with hypo-arousal. If, on the other hand, the pattern of neural activity enters the rapids, then the dissociation will be because of hyperarousal. Through attuned use of BART psychotherapy, we can guide our patients and clients towards safety of the calmer Narrow Water Castle.

The origin of philosophy

According to Bertrand Russell (1945), philosophy as a discipline emerged with the work of Thales in the sixth century BC (McGilchrist, 2009, p. 266). The famous words, "Gnothi Seauton": "know thyself", were inscribed over the entrance to the Temple of the Oracle at the Greek city of Delphi. This was said to be the site where the flight paths of the male and female golden eagles intersected. Thus, X marked the spot where these two birds landed. A camp was set up and civilisation began. The gods, such as Zeus, were all-powerful and had dominion over land and sea and all creatures on earth. This can be seen as another creation myth to help explain in aural tradition some of life's mystery.

As Greek culture developed, the LH, as represented by the god Apollo, gradually took precedence over the RH, as represented by the god Dionysos (McGilchrist, 2009, p. 199). Gradually, over the centuries, the dominance of the LH worldview prevailed. The influence of the Greek and Roman cultures, which sought to integrate the hemispheric perspectives, waned.

BART psychotherapy is designed to reattune the LH (emissary) to its master, the RH. This can help to rebalance the global approach and unconscious attention from the RH with the re-presentation and analysis from the LH. I also see this as a realignment of eastern and western medical viewpoints, which can be collaborative and not mutually exclusive, as explained in the following illustrations. The myth behind the Oracle at Delphi was that two golden eagles were sent out in opposite directions from the same point. They were to drop a stone at the point where their paths crossed. These stones landed at the Delphic Oracle, symbolising the meeting of east and west. I would also suggest that the intuition of the right hemisphere and the rationality of the left hemisphere intersect at this famous landmark. The Oracle can be likened to the corpus callosum.

An amazing analogy occurred in July 1969 with the Apollo 11 moon landing. Neil Armstrong the commander of the spacecraft, announced as the lunar module commenced its descent, "Mission Control in Houston. The *Eagle* has wings". Later, he was to famously declare "Houston! Tranquillity Base here, the *Eagle* has landed." This was the site on the moon chosen for landing. Eagle was the name of the lunar module that separated from the spacecraft, taking Neil Armstrong and his crew both to the moon and back to the mother craft. An eagle was also the astronaut's symbol and was worn as an emblem on their space suits. In Native American culture, the eagle is revered as representing their essential spirit: it is one of the three components of the scorpion astrological sign. The eagle is believed to be closest to the spirit as it can climb higher and see further than any other bird. This again shows the confluence of scientific achievement and mystical symbolism. In the same way that the astronauts blasted off from earth on a Saturn V rocket, perhaps the stones dropped by Zeus's eagles were rock-ettes, or small rocks.

I believe a new philosophy is possible through the application of BART psychotherapy. Patients can be helped to achieve new insights and awareness towards the Delphic goal of Gnothi Seauton. They will have greater knowledge of the feelings deep inside themselves. They will be supported to allow an intense dialogue to be initiated with these feelings at a cellular, visceral, and linguistic level.

The Renaissance saw a resurgence in the RH perspective on the world. This meant opening up the eyes to the world of experience. The body and soul were considered inseparable. Primacy was afforded to implicit understanding, intuition, myth, and metaphor. This was not to last, and soon individual ambition and competition thrived alongside the influence of the LH. The Era of Enlightenment and the Age of Reason dawned on civilisation. Thus, over time, we have seen the foundations laid for the concepts behind the evolution of thought across cultures and time.

1. From the Greek, we get *nous*, or wisdom, which is allied to the RH worldview.
2. From the Latin, we derive *intellectus*, which is allied to the primacy of the analytic LH
3. From the English language comes *sensus communis*, or common sense. This, I believe, integrates both hemispheres and links their perspectives to the meaning derived from sensation and feeling. It may also be related to the primacy of the word "commons". In the rural village of Newtownhamilton, where I grew up, the site of the agricultural market where pigs and cattle were bought and sold was known as the Commons. It was where all farmers would meet to conduct trade and exchange local news and information. Today, the most important part of the legislature is the Commons. If we take the neural network analogy, the trunk neuron would be the Houses of Parliament at Westminster leading to millions of branches of smaller common areas across the country. Taking the analogy further, it could be said that lines of communication from one to the other have become severed and that MPs are disconnected from the grass roots. The parallel to nature is striking and may suggest a root and branch review to restore interconnectivity from the epicentre of political power to

the peripheral regions. This would be similar to the connections already outlined between our central and peripheral nervous systems.

Nous grasps first principles by induction. Thus, the primacy of the RH is that it is the basis for the LH's rationality. The body and soul are integrated, and reason is subservient to unconscious awareness, metaphor, and imagination. Descartes's world was one where the mind and body were separate and primacy was given to the role of the LH. The integration of the world of art and science involves the embodied ambiguity of the RH with its implicit investigation. Creations of the RH come to us via the senses and are a forerunner of the English common sense approach. I conceive this book as an integration of the art and science of both psychotherapy and peak performance.

Implications in the field of psychiatry

Patients with the diagnoses of anorexia nervosa, multiple personality disorder, and deliberate self-harm share the symptom of dissociation. The patient feels cut off from her feelings. The self is fragmented and emotions lack depth. The patient's capacity to empathise is reduced. There is an underactive RH and overactive LH. In autism spectrum disorders, the LH is especially relied upon, with consequent hypo function of the RH. One of the goals of BART psychotherapy is to reverse the imbalance in these disorders via continuous bilateral cerebellar activation followed by affective reprocessing and conscious directed thoughts.

In autism, there are deficits in social intelligence and difficulties in understanding implicit meaning. Patients with autism have difficulty interpreting tone of voice, prosody, humour, irony, and deceit. The functions of empathy and imagination are more dependent on the RH than the LH. The over-analytical LH of the child with autism may interpret parts of the person rather than the holistic whole. There could be an obsession with mechanical parts, such as the spinning drum of a washing machine, which occurred in a three-year-old child with autism referred to me. Children with autism often refer to themselves as "he" or "she" as they become alienated from self and develop a distorted self-perception. As the eyes convey a pure form of theory of mind, children with autism find meaningful eye contact difficult. One of the pathognomic features of autism is poor eye contact. This scores highly in the autism diagnostic observation scale, or ADOS. The function of face recognition is dependent on global cerebral function and is, therefore, impaired in autism.

My hypothesis is that BART psychotherapy assists with the rebalancing of hemispheric functioning with improved oxygenation and blood flow to the compromised areas of the hypo-perfused RH. In autism, there appears to a compensatory hyper-functioning of the LH. From a sensorimotor perspective, immobility would be expected on the left side of the body, consequent to RH hypo-function. Careful attention to, and scaffolding of, fine body movements would be the goal of stage 4 BART psychotherapy to rewire right cerebral hemisphere brain axons ready for transmission.

It seems essential for our full consciousness and imagination that the RH is put in a position whereby the LH cannot overrun it. The RH "believes" but does not know; the LH "knows" but is unable to believe. The master "trusts" his emissary, yet this very trust may be misplaced. With cooperation between both hemispheres, they become invincible whereas, if there is domination by the LH over the RH, then both hemispheres suffer. Chaos ensues when the RH (or left hand) does not know what the LH (or right hand) is doing.

Our brains reflect, both in structure and function, the substance of the universe around us. We come to understand our world through the metaphorical use of language. I believe this is helped by bilateral activations of the cerebral hemispheres being enabled to reprocess thoughts, as in BART psychotherapy.

Theories on the origin of the universe

Ideas about origins of the universe are related to the development of conscious awareness in man. There are new ideas emerging from the Perimeter Institute in Toronto about these origins. Its director, Professor Neil Turok (Leonard, 2010), hypothesises that as one big bang ends another bounces into existence as a way to explain conservation of space–time and the laws of physics. Lerner, in his book, *The Big Bang Never Happened* (1991), provides a counter-argument to the preeminent theory on the origins of the universe. The corollary for psychotherapy is that the Jungian concept of collective unconsciousness is timeless. By increasing the vibratory frequency of our own individual consciousness, we may be able to tap into this universal awareness, or cosmic mind. I believe that doing this during sessions of BART psychotherapy has the potential to further resolve traumatic memories.

Analysis of dreams

It is during dreams that we suspend the physical three-dimensional world of daily life on planet earth. In dreamtime, it is believed that we have access to eleven dimensions of space–time. This is analogous to the eleven multi-verse dimensions predicted by superstring theory and quantum mechanics. Many cultures speak of the predictive nature of dreams, from the stories in the Bible to the Aborigines in Australia.

In western science, Frederick August von Kekule was having difficulty conceptualising the structure of the benzene ring—the organic chemical compound made up of a ring of carbon atoms. He had a dream of whirling snakes. He reported the dream in a speech made in 1890 at a dinner commemorating his discovery many years after it took place:

> I turned my chair to the fire [after having worked on the problem for some time] and dozed. Again, the atoms were gambolling before my eyes. This time the smaller groups kept modestly to the background. My mental eye, rendered more acute by repeated vision of this kind, could not distinguish larger structures, of manifold conformation; long rows, sometimes more closely fitted together; all twining and twisting in snakelike motion. However, look! What was that? One of the snakes had seized hold of its own tail, and the form whirled mockingly before my eyes. As if by a flash of lighting, I awoke . . . Let us learn to dream, gentlemen and then perhaps we shall find the truth . . . but let us beware of publishing our dreams before they have been put to the proof by the waking understanding. (Roberts, 1989, p. 80)

Figure 41 depicts von Kekule's snake grasping its own tail.

In his book, *The Act of Creation*, Koestler (1964) called this the second most important dream in history after that of Joseph predicting seven years of plenty followed by seven years of famine. In this

Figure 41. Image of the ouroboros in von Kekule's dream.

story, none of the Pharaoh's magi could interpret his dream. Then Joseph was called for and then Pharaoh said to Joseph,

> Behold, in my dream I stood on the bank of the river. Suddenly seven cows came up out of the river, fine looking and fat; and they fed in the meadow. Then behold, seven other cows came up after them, poor and very ugly and gaunt, such ugliness, as I have never seen in all the land of Egypt. In addition, the gaunt and ugly cows ate up the first seven, the fat cows. When they had eaten them up, no one would have known that they had eaten them, for they were just as ugly as at the beginning. Therefore, I awoke. In addition, I saw in my dream, and suddenly seven heads came up on one stalk, full and good. Then behold seven heads, withered; thin, and blighted by the east wind, sprang up after them. In addition, the thin heads devoured the seven good heads. So I told this to the magicians, but there was no one who could explain it to me. (Genesis, 41)

Joseph was able to explain that the seven fat cows represented years when the harvest was plentiful and everyone had enough to eat. The seven lean cows represented seven years of hardship and famine when disease and pestilence would befall the world. The crucial part of the dream was the sting in the tail in that the thin heads devoured the fattened heads.

Joseph, through his interpretation of the dream, could predict the future. Most countries would feast during the good years but not put any provisions aside for the lean years, when millions would starve to death. Therefore, he suggested to Pharaoh that a good percentage of the harvest should be set aside and preserved so that his people could be fed enough to survive the seven years of famine.

The Pharaoh was so pleased with Joseph that he put him in charge of all of Egypt. In due course, the seven years of plenty arrived and there was much merriment, laughter, and wastage. When the lean years arrived, people in every land fought one another for food. Only in Egypt did everyone have enough to eat and God saw that Joseph had listened to him.

An experienced manager of an NHS trust stated that during the years 2001–2007, money was poured into the NHS. Then, when the financial collapse happened in 2008, he predicted that there would be seven years of hardship for the cash-strapped NHS. No money would have been put aside during the good years to help with the economic crisis and many trusts would struggle to survive. Many more would perform so poorly that they would be subjected to a rescue plan equivalent to emergency resuscitation. The parallels with the biblical dream of Joseph are apparent.

Summary

Conscious thought is believed to represent only five per cent of human brain activity. Research is ongoing into ways we can usefully access the brain activity of the remaining ninety-five per cent non- or unconscious activity. Most of the techniques so far have examined military applications. The role of the connectome and how the brain's wiring makes us who we are is discussed. This includes a recent definition of the field of connectomics and how this features in our understanding of memory. BART psychotherapy will prove useful in treating the effects of dysfunctional memory storage via the fifth R, which is reprocessing. Various ideas of the neuroanatomical origin of consciousness are proposed, such as the periaqueductal grey matter in the midbrain. The philosophical origins are also mentioned. New insights, such as those once achieved by the Ancient Greeks at the Delphic Oracle are proposed. As we moved from the Age of Enlightenment to the Age of Reason in society, so did our world perspective shift from the right to the left hemisphere. This has had major implications in the field of psychiatry, with many more patients experiencing mental ill health because of being cut off from their feelings. The role of BART psychotherapy in redressing this balance is proposed. Comparisons with the American moon landings are made. This leads on to scientific and mythological ideas on origins of the universe, which are proposed to be compatible. There is a final section on dream analysis with an account of the scientific breakthrough made by von Kekule in his discovery of benzene's structure and Joseph's interpretation of the Pharaoh's dream, which saved the people of Egypt from starvation.

CHAPTER EIGHT

Guidelines for practitioners on conducting a BART psychotherapy session

Procedure

First, specially adapted headphones or glasses with a bilateral sensor are placeed where glasses rest on the ears. The aim is to facilitate bilateral stimulation over the bony protuberances known as the mastoid processes. The frequency is adjusted to the highest level tolerated by the patient. This can range from 0 Hertz to 60 Hertz. It is said that 40 Hertz is the optimum frequency for thalamocortical coherence. This point also achieves maximum cerebellar stimulation, enhancing the reprocessing of thoughts during BART psychotherapy.

Then, after taking a detailed trauma history, the client is asked to describe the issue or traumatic event that they wish to work on and to continue the narrative from the point of the significant event up to the present moment. They are helped to maintain contact with the narrative by allowing them to reflect on their experiences. I pay attention to their body language during this process, through constant feedback and interaction with the patient or client.

When I have asked the patient to retell their story, this will be divided into more and less manageable parts, each with a subjective unit of distress score (SUDS). I then ask them to hold either a "magic remote" (for children) or video/DVD remote (for adults) in their left hand while they are replaying the narrative in their mind. This will tap into the visuospatial and imaginative capacities of their right cerebral hemisphere. I then ask them to allow the worst part of the memory to emerge, which is usually when they felt most upset. They are asked to describe their gut reaction or instinct associated with the specific traumatic experience. If the patient is finding it difficult to tap into their gut reaction, I will give them a "menu" to help them describe their initial instinctive reaction to their trauma (Table 11).

Often, the patient will come up with the worst aspects of the traumatic memory spontaneously; if not, it is helpful to have this "menu" to hand. The precise options offered will depend on the nature of their traumatic story and the unprocessed sensory fragments within it. The client then places his hands, which are holding the tactile zappers, over the area of the body that experiences the above feelings most intensely.

Table 11. Menu of options to give to the patient or client if they are having difficulty in tuning into their bodily reactions during the BART reprocessing session. Created by Sorcha O'Malley.

Menu of possible patient reactions
Gut reaction, instinct or feeling
Sensation
Taste
Gut feeling
Sensation
Picture
Image
Sound
Expression or word
Odour, smell or aroma
Butterflies or heaviness in stomach
Tension or pain like tightness in chest
Choking or anxious feeling in throat
Speechless
Heart racing
Chest thumping

As BART psychotherapy proceeds, the sensations, feelings, emotions, and movements associated with the trauma are brought to the surface from the relevant abdominal viscera. By making contact with these experiences, at a more superficial level, they become less intense, lighter, and change in location in line with the chakra energy points, as formerly discussed.

The patient is observed for any change in temperature, sensations, feelings, or emotions being processed at a higher-energy level. The goal is to register these experiences at a heartfelt level consistent with the energy level of the fourth, or heart, chakra. These are often registered as painful sensations in the chest area, associated with loss and traumatic grief. As BART psychotherapy continues, a block to the flow of information processing is often found at the level of the throat chakra, or thyroid gland. The information must first be transferred to the master hemisphere and then its emissary, as described earlier. The patient or client either crossing her hands to the lateral aspects of her neck and tapping gently, or placing the zappers there, can achieve this. An awareness of body language by the patient is encouraged during reprocessing. The flow of information is facilitated by getting the patient to tap his feet alternately and to track internal bodily sensations in a figure of eight, from head to toe.

If a cul-de-sac in information reprocessing is reached, the patient is encouraged to mindfully connect with the "stuck" feeling and its bodily location. The patient is then asked to float back to the first, or the worst, time they experienced that traumatic feeling or sensation. The patient then recounts the narrative, as if in stage 2. Invariably, an unconscious memory, or physical sensation, comes to consciousness. The patient is then able to verbalise these experiences and make sense of them. The patient is asked to allow the most upsetting aspect of the traumatic memory to emerge into conscious awareness. This moment is captured using a freeze-frame technique, which helps to titrate the associated stress within their window of affect tolerance, emotional regulation, and safety (see Figure 23).

The patient's original "target" memory is revisited until the SUDS scale is reduced to the lowest possible level. The initial gut reaction will now have been registered at a heartfelt level. This is a sign that the brain is now ready for reprocessing of the information on an intuitive level. My belief is that the extent of learning, reflection, and intuition possible from BART psychotherapy is dependent on the person's age and stage of neurological development. Reprocessing may be blocked by earlier traumas stored at a bodily level. That might be in the enteric nervous plexus, where they become isolated in the abdominal viscera, or at the root chakra level if the narrative is one of sexual assault or abuse. Information about the trauma may also be blocked at the level of the cardiac ganglia (or nervous system), especially when associated with childhood traumatic grief. Improving gut-brain, heart-brain, and head-brain connections are an essential component of BART psychotherapy. The holistic intelligence of the mind and body can be enhanced through the therapeutic process of vibrating at a higher resonant frequency. This is made possible with the BOKA machine, using the zappers bilaterally, within BART psychotherapy. When the patient is asked to re-view the image following reprocessing, they often report that it has faded. One patient said, "It's as if it has been covered by clouds and it is no longer associated with any distress."

I may incorporate techniques from sensorimotor psychotherapy. If the traumatic memory involved an assault, it is often helpful to ask the patient to stretch out his hands as if pushing the attacker away and creating a safe boundary around him. A change in posture, for example, getting the patient to stand up from a sitting position allows him to have greater confidence in imaginally confronting his assailant.

The continuous low frequency bilateral cerebellar stimulation is unique to BART psychotherapy. This lasts for the 90–120-minute therapeutic session. This maintains the patient within the calmer WATERS and avoids the dissociation associated with the RAPIDS or FROZEN states. I attempt continuous psychoeducation during the BART psychotherapy session as the patient becomes more receptive to language. I ensure attention is paid to any residual affective dysregulation. Over the ninety minutes, there is gradual transfer upwards of information from the lower to the higher chakra energy centres. Patients report sensations moving from the right to left cerebral hemisphere. I believe this is evidence for integration of information as the master hemisphere connects with its emissary. In my clinical experience, at this stage the patient is likely to commence yawning and report feeling tired. This is a reassuring sign that the brain pathways involving REM sleep have been activated. Stickgold (2002) reported that this is secondary to the production of pontine–geniculate–occipital (PGO) waves from brainstem stimulation.

The two forms of bilateral stimulation used in BART psychotherapy directly activate the brainstem centrally. This has the effect of neurological activation of the cranial nerves three, four, and six. These oculomotor, trochlear, and abducens nerves move the eyes in all possible directions. In my work as a consultant child and adolescent psychiatrist, I find that children whose optic tracts are immature are unable to track movements across the midline. Thus, other forms of bilateral stimulation are preferable. In BART psychotherapy, I combine bilateral cerebellar stimulation at the level of the mastoid process with bilateral tactile stimulation using zappers. In my clinical experience, young children with attachment disorders often report lack of sensation or feeling in their feet. My hypothesis is that lack of neurobiological regulation from poor maternal infant bonding has damaged neurological processes in the periphery, such as proprioception. I have found that placing the zappers in the child's socks and asking him to stand up while experiencing bilateral stimulation can reactivate impaired neurological connections. The child reports an improved self image and goes on to draw a more complete representation of self. This can then help the child to repair damaged attachment relationships. During reprocessing, the therapist notices how their distance from the patient, tone of voice, and posture interact and influence the patient's progress in the session. Further awareness of these factors will be achieved by gaining experience in sensorimotor psychotherapy (Ogden, Pain, & Minton, 2000).

My EMDR supervisees often report feelings of exhaustion after intense EMDR sessions. I believe this is due to negative emotions, feelings, and sensations released from the patient. Supervision must address the need for therapist repair and restoration before the next therapeutic session.

Images used with the patient or client who is undergoing BART psychotherapy and peak performance

Certain images are useful to help the patient or client understand the process of therapy and help to map out the individual BART stages of reprocessing. They also serve as an introduction to the chakra energy fields, which will be unfamiliar to most patients or clients educated purely in allopathic medicine. However, patients or clients from eastern cultures will have more extensive knowledge of the application of the increased levels of vibrational energy accessed as they get in touch with higher chakra levels.

Figure 21 (p. 33) shows total integration of all stages of BART psychotherapy. Figure 22 (p. 33) is a lateral view of the chakras and their relationships to the essential bodily organs: the gastrointestinal tract, liver, stomach, heart, and lungs.

Taken together, these diagrams represent the different stages of BART psychotherapy. The patient or client enables their gut instinct (heartfelt sensation, thyroid sensation (lump in the throat)) to be reprocessed and recognition in the brain can take place as a final step in their reprocessing of thoughts. These are crucial stages in BART psychotherapy. Once the body sensations are digested and reprocessed via bilateral affective stimulation, the scene is set for the cerebellum to link up with the orbitofrontal cortex so that learning and meaning can emerge from any significant and traumatic life experiences.

The two diagrams mentioned above illustrate how BART psychotherapy relates to the patient's endocrine, immune, vascular, nervous systems, and chakra energy systems. I believe these show a genuine interrelationship, physically and functionally, between the theories of western and eastern medicine. The initial focus of reprocessing is to identify a bodily location for a physical sensation or gut reaction associated with the traumatic memory. The process then expands to a wider area; the enteric plexus feeds into heartfelt emotions of traumatic grief, loss, and sadness. The throat chakra is often blocked with unexpressed feelings; once overcome, there is interplay of reprocessing between the bilateral cerebellae, which directly connect to the prefrontal cortex, and the sixth chakra, or third eye of the pineal gland. There is also a parallel interplay of reprocessing between the cerebral hemispheres. Thus, the initial ascending reprocessing lessens the trauma intensity, facilitating descending patterns of stimulation, which complete the patient's reprocessing pathway. Alternate foot tapping and observation of other movements of the body's periphery manipulate the figure of eight pathway illustrated in the diagrams above. This allows identification of any blocks to information processing consequent to the patient's traumatic experience.

The human endocrine glands correspond to the body chakras illustrated, as described below.

Crown (anterior, posterior, and intermediate pituitary gland secrete ten hormones regulating homeostasis)

1. Growth hormone.
2. Thyroid stimulating hormone.
3. Adrenocorticotrophic hormone.
4. Beta endorphin.
5. Prolactin.
6. Luteinising hormone.
7. Follicle stimulating hormone.
8. Antidiuretic hormone or vasopressin.
9. Oxytocin, which regulates mother–infant bonding.
10. Melanocyte stimulating hormone.

Forehead chakra

This is located one inch above the third eye chakra and extends outward from the centre of the forehead between left and right frontal lobes. It appears to have been ignored by meta physical science. However, the hypothalamus is a major endocrine organ. The word hypothalamus is derived from the Greek for "under room". The hypothalamus has many functions, as listed below.

1. Medial preoptic nucleus releases gonadotropin releasing hormone GnRH.
2. Supraoptic nucleus releases vasopressin or ADH.
3. Paraventricular nucleus releases thyrotropin-releasing hormone, corticotropin-releasing hormone, and oxytocin. The latter is a fundamental part of mother–infant bonding.
4. Anterior hypothalamic nucleus governs thermoregulation, sweating, and inhibits hyrotropin. Thus, the HPA axis is part of a feedback loop similar to the rising and ebbing of the chakra energies themselves.
5. The suprachiasmatic nucleus regulates circadian rhythms.
6. The lateral nucleus governs thirst and hunger.
7. Dorsomedial nucleus regulates heart rate, blood pressure, and stimulation of the gastrointestinal tract.
8. Ventromedial nucleus governs appetite and neuroendocrine cell secretion in lungs and adrenals. Stress can stimulate hypothalamus to release these carcinogens.

9. Arcuate nucleus releases dopamine, growth hormone-releasing hormone, and regulates feeding. Stress can, therefore, decrease growth hormone and result in stunted growth.
10. Mamillary nuclei are part of mamillary bodies and are believed to be important for recollective and spatial memory. They are part of the Papez circuit, which forms a limbus shape around the brainstem.
11. Posterior hypothalamic nucleus is involved in regulation of the autonomic nervous system (Cavdar, Onat, Aker et al., 2001), with inputs from brainstem and subcortical structures. This study showed this nucleus connected to the lateral and medial septal nuclei of the forebrain. It also revealed widespread connections to the amygdaloid body, which helps to regulate emotional stimuli. Other studies have shown that the insular cortex receives a visceral input and connects with the autonomic nuclei of the forebrain (Cechetto & Saper, 1987). The midbrain periaqueductal grey directly connects to this nucleus. The PAG regulates defensive and anti-nociceptive behaviour, along with regulation of the cardiovascular system. This nucleus may regulate sympathetic outflow via the raphe nucleus synapses with the adrenal glands. Finally, links to the cerebellum have also been shown.

Taken as a whole, the hypothalamus has input from the nucleus tractus solitarius governing visceral input and is a centre for integrated thinking (Mantyh, 1982). It appears that the connections are reciprocal, that is, go both ways.

The third eye. The pineal gland secretes melatonin, which regulates sleep–wake cycle and represents intuition and activation of the Mer-Ka-Ba.

Throat thyroid and parathyroid balances cerebral rationality with emotional expression of the heart; represents spiritual and physical communication.

Heart chest (heart and lungs) and *thymus* represent harmony and love.

Solar plexus (stomach and pancreas) represents creativity and personal energy.

Sacral and umbilicus. Ovaries/testes dealing with sexuality and emotional balance.

Root and base of spine. Adrenals related to fight or flight and physical survival and represents grounding and security.

It is interesting that each chakra is anatomically associated with different endocrine glands. When a patient or client experiences toxic stress, the HPA axis is stimulated. Initially, this causes secretion of adrenaline from both adrenal glands. In severe depression, left untreated, the symptoms will often last nine months. CT scans taken of the adrenal glands show that they increase markedly in size during the course of the illness. (Professor Ted Dinan, personal communication.) Chronic toxic stress further stimulates the adrenal glands. This time, they secrete corticosteroids and mineral corticoids such as aldosterone. The corticosteroids act on receptors in the central nervous system. This down-regulates the ability of the neuron to function. The chemical neurotransmitters are not released and the lock and key mechanism I referred to earlier does not occur.

Each endocrine gland secretes a different hormone. Each hormone has a unique molecular structure, which vibrates with a specific resonant energy. This is akin to the idea of chakras in eastern medicine. Finally, the pituitary gland is associated with ten hormones of different vibrational energy. The crown chakra is said to have 1,000 petals in most eastern traditions, but only thirty-three in Tibetan culture. Of importance is the recognition that the anatomical location of the crown is associated with the development of pure consciousness. In Judaeo-Christianity, Jesus Christ was mocked and adorned with a crown of thorns. This could be taken to imply that he was able to activate his crown chakra and access higher planetary and cosmic planes of consciousness.

Leonardo da Vinci famously depicted this in his portrayal of Vitruvian man (Figure 42). The body chakras related to this image are shown in Figure 43.

The root of psychiatry is from the Greek words *psyche* and *iatros*. These mean soul healing, and I have devised BART psychotherapy in the spirit of the Ancient Greek physicians who did not subscribe to the mind–body dualism of Descartes.

Case example 3

A heavy goods vehicle driver was referred to me in 2011. He had been involved in a fatal road traffic accident in 2008. Since then, he had attended more than ninety individual sessions of CBT. He spoke of

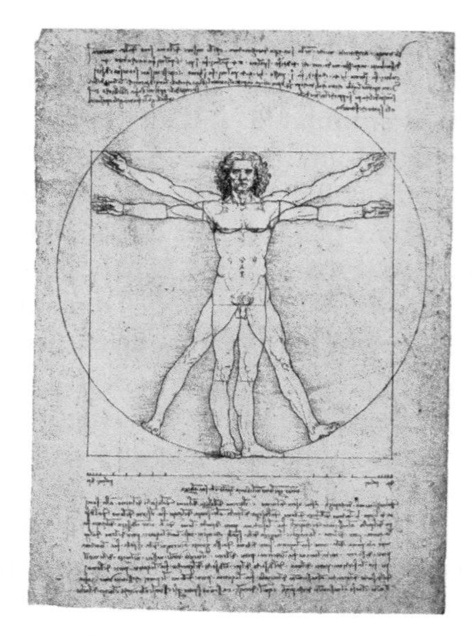

Figure 42. Vitruvian man, by Leonardo da Vinci.

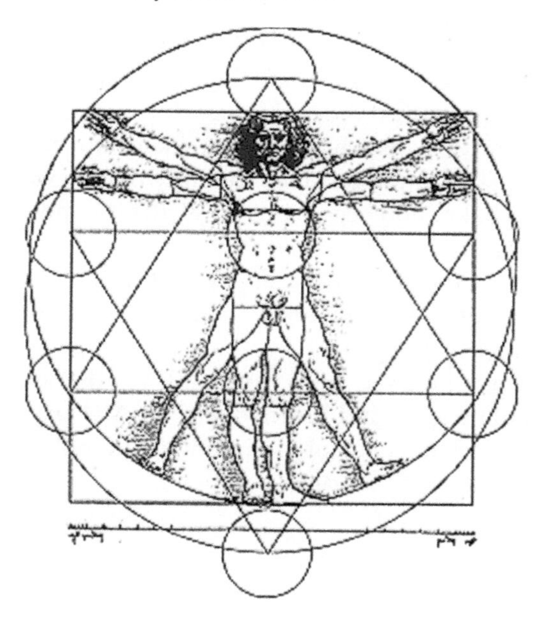

Figure 43. The body chakras in Vitruvian man are shown surrounded by an electromagnetic energy field known as the Merkaba. This can be conceptualised as the Mer-Ka-Ba, which is seen in many cultures as a transport vehicle for the soul. Reprinted with permission from Bob Frissell at www.bobfrisell.com.

how he dreaded these sessions, as he was asked to repeat the history, which became increasingly difficult because of the accompanying dysregulated affect. He was in a state of speechless terror and experienced continuous fear and hopelessness. This had led to severe depression with suicidal intent. During BART psychotherapy, I used bilateral cerebellar stimulation to regulate his affect. I asked him to imagine the chair as the driving seat in the heavy goods vehicle. I asked him to hold the zappers in each hand as if holding on to the steering wheel. I used the freeze-frame technique to slow the reprocessing into manageable bytes. His peripheral nervous system became reactivated as if he was reliving the event *in vivo*. His grip tightened on the tactile zappers and at the point of impact his right leg shot forward. My patient had his eyes closed and was unaware of this motor impulse. When I drew his attention to the instinctive movement, he realised this was when he applied maximum pressure to the brakes. Metaphorically, it was as if his life had been put on hold since the accident, as he, at a somatomotor level, was still applying the brakes. During the BART psychotherapy session, he was encouraged to mindfully let go of these brakes in order to get his life get back on the road. This stoic Yorkshireman was able to relive the experience and grieve appropriately, realising that the driver who swerved into his path was the guilty party and that his driving was not at fault. The physical injuries he suffered from the accident and the associated traumatic images of the driver he had killed were readily dealt with in several further sessions. His latest feedback was that he had recovered his previous zest for life and was well on the road to recovery.

Trouble shooting with BART psychotherapy and peak performance

The patient may show "stuckness" in trauma processing via a movement impulse, as in the above example, a physical sensation, a gut feeling, reaction, or instinct, a core belief, or intense affect or destructive thought process. Individual therapies that focus on one or two of these might miss the vital factor causing the blockage to information reprocessing. In the later stages of BART psychotherapy, wider chains of association to the original trauma are made with the patient. This allows any residual pockets of trauma to be located so that they can be actively reprocessed towards resolution and recovery. The patients usually respond by saying they feel lighter and as if a weight has been lifted from their shoulders.

I encourage the patient to notice further reprocessing that may occur after the session. This often comes in the form of a new insight or dream moving on from the original traumatic experience. I encourage patients to write this down and/or email me so that we can discuss its meaning for them at the start of the next session. The patient can then be in a position to avail himself of peak psychotherapy in moving towards positive psychiatric and psychological change. This is an area often neglected by therapists who are restricted to trauma resolution. Once traumatic stress has been processed, patients are able to ascend Maslow's hierarchy towards an integration of mind, body, and spirit. Specific goals can be worked on to achieve their chosen areas of peak performance.

Summary

This chapter outlines the practical steps a practitioner needs to take in order to conduct a BART psychotherapy and, ideally, peak performance session. A menu of possible patient responses is provided, as this approach will be new to both practitioner and patient or client. The whole process is made possible by the BOKA machine, which can be explained as the patient's body having the necessary knowledge (in terms of the menu already described). However, this knowledge is not in an accessible form and must be activated by gradually increasing its resonant frequency (i.e. "body of knowledge activator"). To help both therapists and patients or clients, illustrations are included. These show how the endocrine glands correspond to the chakras, and the surrounding energy fields. There is a detailed description of the ten hormones secreted by the pituitary gland and comparison is made to the beliefs of the thousand-petalled lotus of the crown chakra. It could be said that when the ten hormones are released, they cascade across the HPA axis and their effect is magnified ten times, giving direct equivalency to the thousand petals of the lotus flower associated with the crown chakra. However, those people of Tibetan faith ascribe to the view that the crown chakra has thirty-three petals. This can be seen to equate to the number of years Jesus Christ is said to have lived on earth. In the Christian faith, Christ is said to have ascended to heaven on the third day. This equates to a vibrational energy of 0.3 recurring. By ascending, he would have increased his vibrational energy to 1,000. The chapter concludes with a case example illustrating the process and how to troubleshoot with patients or clients.

CHAPTER NINE

Taking a trauma and developmental history

Assessment template

I have developed an assessment template, which is partly based on the attachment interview of the child by Dr Charles Zeanah (Oppenheim & Goldsmith, 2007) and the *Health of the Nation Outcome Scales* for children, adolescents, and adults (HoNOS, HoNOSCA, Gowers, Bailey-Rogers, Shore, et al., 2000). In addition, I have added a chronology of stressful life experiences and traumas. This starts at conception and moves through pregnancy and all stages of the patient's life. It is critically important to identify an informant who can relate significant trauma up to age five. I have termed this schedule HoNOSCA-revised. Thus, preverbal traumas can be brought into conscious awareness during BART psychotherapy (Chapter Thirteen). A key point is to identify patients who were born premature, that is, at less than thirty-two weeks gestation. A paper in *Archives of General Psychiatry* in 2012 describes how they have a much higher incidence of severe mental health problems in adulthood in comparison to those born at term. The lead author, Nosarti (2012), said that the increased risk of severe psychiatric disorder shown in the results was likely to be the result of "subtle alterations of brain development". This study indicates that of the one in thirteen children born prematurely in the UK, between one and six per cent will go on to develop severe psychiatric disorders. Nosarti recommends that all preterm children should be monitored at the age of five. To fulfil that role, clinicians can use this developmental questionnaire. Early identification of this cohort may lead to prevention of this level of co morbidity.

In taking a trauma history, I recommend assessment of the twelve cranial nerves for possible involvement in the relevant significant life events. Any unresolved trauma at a neurological level requires an appropriate intervention to integrate the sensory fragments of the experience into a coherent whole prior to reprocessing.

The cranial nerves originate from the base of the brainstem. The nerves branch out bilaterally in terms of motor and sensory fibres to the rest of the body. These connections are to the senses of smell in the nose, vision in the eye, movements of the eye, muscles and facial sensation, facial muscles, balance and hearing, the motor and sensory functions of the vagus, motor and sensation of the tongue and pharynx, muscles involved in the startle reflex, and muscles of the tongue. The olfactory nerve synapses with the nerves in the cribriform plate in the nasal epithelium. It is the only cranial nerve not to access the cerebral cortex. In traumatic stress involving smoke, fire, or other acrid smells, these can stay with the patient and be very resistant to resolution. Bilateral olfactory desensitisation can be achieved with BART psychotherapy. Using knowledge of the cranial nerve pathway and function informs the therapist's taking of the patient or client's trauma history. BART psychotherapy can then be reliably targeted to focus on reprocessing the functions of the affected cranial nerves. The relevant questions in relation to the twelve cranial nerves are as follows.

I Olfactory: The patient or client should be asked if there are any odours, smells, or aromas relevant to the traumatic episode. This could be the aftershave of a male sexual assailant, or exposure to smoke and fumes from a vehicle accident or house fire. Patients traumatised following a hospital procedure often report the smell of antisepsis, anaesthetics, or the hospital environment itself as traumatic. Patients who have witnessed a decaying body find it difficult to eradicate the smell from their nostrils. I have used bilateral olfactory stimulation to help eliminate these noxious odours. This can be done by imagining a favourite childhood smell, for example, wild flowers, or using tissue suffused with a favourite natural perfume placed over the nose and inhaled through each nostril alternately. I have proposed a device which would allow the appropriate soothing aroma to be delivered to each nostril via a mask separated into two chambers, each connected to a nasal spray.

II Optic nerve: The optic tract travels to the occipital cortex of the opposite side and processes images from the visual fields of the left and right eye. Any particular distressing image can be processed to resolution during the stages of BART psychotherapy.

III Oculomotor nerve, IV trochlear nerve, and VI abducens nerve: these motor nerves act on the eyes to move them in all possible directions. In my clinical experience, peripheral tactile bilateral stimulation and bilateral cerebellar stimulation activates the brainstem where these nerves have their anatomical origin. BART psychotherapy allows attention to be paid to the subsequent direction of the patient's eye movements. My hypothesis is that looking upwards is an effort by the patient to extract meaning equivalent to engaging with their prefrontal cortex. Looking with both eyes to the right (or therapist's left) is usually a sign that the patient is accessing a past memory. Looking with both eyes to the patient's left (or therapist's right) tends to occur when working on a future template. Each patient may have a different meaning for his or her eye movements depending on which cerebral hemisphere is dominant. The beauty of BART psychotherapy is the constant therapist–patient dialogue, which allows each hypothesis to be confirmed or refuted. This is different to neurolinguistic programming (NLP), which has a fixed attribution to the various eye movements. However, when Dr Richard Bandler and Dr John Grinder introduced NLP in the 1970s in California, they emphasised reading eye patterns for useful information. These are further described by Molden and Hutchinson (2007, pp. 89–94).

Visual thinking mode: Looking up and to the left implies recall of a visual memory. Looking up and to the right implies constructing an image. Looking up and to both the right and left alternately indicates that both recall and construction of images are occurring. The conversation of visual communicators includes phrases such as: Can you see what I mean? It's clear and bright. I'll paint you a picture. Let's zoom in on this point. Patients often speak quickly in a high-pitched voice and use shallow chest breathing.

Auditory thinking mode: A lateral left movement of the eyes implies the patient is remembering sounds associated with the trauma. A lateral right movement implies reconstructing a sound or conversation. An auditory communicator uses phrases such as: I hear what you say. That rings a bell. It sounds OK to me. It's music to my ears.

Internal dialogue thinking mode: When the eyes point down and to the left they suggest that the patient or client is conversing with them. The patient may put their hand next to their face or chin in classic "thinker pose". Paying attention to these micro movements is emphasised in sensorimotor psychotherapy and gives vital information to guide the reprocessing of traumata.

Kinaesthetic or feeling mode: According to NLP, eyes pointing down and to the right imply that the patient is immersed in a feeling experience. They will tend to use phrases such as: That feels right. I can go with that. Let's keep in touch. I hope to be on an even keel from now on. I am getting the hang of this therapy now.

In practice, most patients use a combination of states in learning and social interaction. Several questionnaires are available to assess if there is a dominant style. I use a quick and easy method. The patient is asked to close their eyes and imagine sitting down to taste their favourite dessert. I usually suggest an ice-cream of their own choosing in terms of colour, flavour, and toppings. With their eyes still closed, they move the index finger of either hand to the point in space where they imagined the ice-cream. The commonest point is in the middle of the forehead. This represents the third eye, pineal gland, or sixth chakra and implies that the person is predominantly a visual learner and communicator. If the patient locates the area of the auditory cortex on either side, this implies a preference for auditory learning and communication. Patients who are predominantly kinaesthetic have difficulty pinpointing a location in space and, if pressed, tend to locate either parietal cortex bilaterally.

Three types of eye movement are recognised.

1. Convergence is used for depth perception and ensures that the image of the object lands on the correct spot in each retina.
2. Saccades are short and rapid eye movements, which are unconsciously controlled at a frequency of 4 Hertz. A larger area can be scanned with the high resolution or fovea of the eye.
3. The eyes make smooth pursuit movements both when tracking an object's movement and when fixed on a single point.

Fixate on a hand 30 cm away, as in EMDR. When the hand moves rapidly from side to side at a greater frequency than 1 Hertz the fingers appear blurred. Now ask the person to hold index and middle finger 30 cm away. Then move your head as fast as possible up and down and from side to side. The person's fingers and hand remain clear. The head-brain can move the eyes in relation to a fixed hand image following a hand movement. When the pursuit system fails, a blurred image results. This tends to explain why the practice of EMDR using simulated eye movements generates a blurred image during its protocol driven procedure.

V Trigeminal nerve: This nerve is sensory to the mandible, maxilla, and nasal sinuses. It is motor to the muscles of mastication. With the patient, it is important to enquire about any direct damage here during trauma to the face.

VII Facial nerve: This nerve is motor to the muscles of the face, sub maxillary, sublingual, and lacrimal glands (tears). It also provides sensation to the anterior two thirds of the tongue and soft palate. I often find that patients reprocessing head trauma will display unconscious movements of the tongue and jaw as they move towards resolution and recovery with BART psychotherapy.

VIII Vestibulocochlear nerve: This nerve provides the senses of balance and hearing. Most traumatic experiences are initiated by an orientating response to sound. This then triggers a startle response to look towards the sound source. Hence, we hear the sound of the ambulance's alarm before we turn around to see its blue light flashing. The traumatic sound information is stored in the auditory cortex in milliseconds. In taking a trauma history, we must be aware of the disabling impact of sudden unexpected noise before we can initiate reprocessing of the whole event.

Case example 4

A twelve-year-old boy described how he was lying asleep on the couch with his parents and sister asleep upstairs around midnight. Suddenly, four gunmen burst in, threatening to shoot. Although the gunmen were disturbed and left suddenly, the sounds of the break-in and the sight of the men in balaclavas haunted him. Using BART psychotherapy, we were able to freeze-frame the initial moment as his auditory cortex registered the attack. The butt of the gun was used to shatter the wooden doorframe and it was the sound of broken wood and glass that activated his startle reflex. By means of a combination of the seven-element exercise (*vide infra*) and desensitisation to the sounds picked up by the VIIIth nerve, he was able to make a full recovery.

* * *

IX Glossopharyngeal nerve: This nerve provides sensation to the posterior one third of the tongue, tonsils, pharynx, and middle ear. It is motor to the stylopharyngeus and pharyngeal musculature.

Case example 5

A thirty-year-old female patient was on holiday in Spain and enjoying an evening meal. She suddenly stood up and drank a glass of water. A lump of meat lodged in her trachea. She started to choke and was having a "café coronary". No one came to her aid until an off-duty fireman realised what was happening. He rushed to her side and performed vigorous abdominal thrusts, causing her to expel the piece of meat stuck in her throat. Several years later, a colleague who worked as a consultant psychiatrist in psychotherapy referred her to me. We ran a weekly clinic in parental and infant mental health. Her obsession with liquidising all her food was affecting her ability to adequately care for her infant. As she progressed through the stages of BART psychotherapy, we were able to adequately reprocess the holiday incident. However, she was left with the fearful sensation of a lump in her throat. By getting her to imagine the fireman reapplying the abdominal thrusts, this sensation dissolved and she was able to recommence solid food and care for her infant. Any trauma to the throat, tongue, and neck will affect the glossopharyngeal cranial nerve.

* * *

X Vagus nerve: The term vagus comes from the Latin word for "wanderer" because of its undulating course throughout the body. It is motor to the pharynx, heart, lungs, bronchi, and GIT. It provides sensation to heart, lungs, bronchi, trachea, larynx, pharynx, GIT, and external ear via the auricular branch. It is now known that gentle massage of the earlobe has a direct calming effect on the heart via these fibres. This might have a role in counteracting a patient's hyperarousal associated with the RAPIDS state.

XI Accessory nerve: This is motor to the sternomastoid and trapezius muscles. It is activated at times of trauma, causing the startle reflex. Cranial accessory fibres of the nerve supply intrinsic muscles of the larynx, pharynx, and palate.

XII Hypoglossal nerve: This supplies the intrinsic and extrinsic muscles of the tongue. These are responsible for automatic/reflex tongue movements and are often implicated in patients' traumatic experiences. The course of the twelve cranial nerves is described in *Gray's Anatomy* (Williams, Bannister, Berry, et al., 1995).

Effects of severe depression on cellular aging

This process is thought to occur at the cellular level of telomeres. Telomeres are specialised nucleic acid proteins that cap the ends of DNA, protecting it from damage during replication. The final part of the telomere fails to be replicated during each cell division in what has become known as the "end-replication problem". This results in progressively shorter telomeres. When telomeres reach a critically short length, cells can die prematurely (Verhoeven, Revesz, Epel, et al., 2013).

Stress and trauma are believed to contribute to telomere shortening. However, telomerase is a ribonucleoprotein enzyme that elongates telomeres by adding nucleotides to the end of chromosomes. This leaves the possibility of longer telomere length and more accurate DNA replication during cell division. I inform my patients that stress reduction and relaxation is associated with increased levels of the enzyme telomerase. This can result in an anti-aging effect and is mentioned in the following script issued to patients to get them in the right frame of mind for BART psychotherapy.

The seven-element relaxation exercise (earth, air, water, heat/warmth, ether, light, and love)

For patients who present with affective dysregulation, I have modified Laub and Shapiro's four-element exercise (2008). The description to the patient is as follows.

As you are sitting comfortably in the chair, I want you to mindfully place both feet on the floor. Imagine your feet penetrating through the floor to the earth below. You may want to imagine yourself on a warm, sandy beach with your feet in contact with the sand or standing in a garden next to a tree. Imagine the roots of the tree giving support to you as you lean against the tree trunk. The second element is the fresh sea or forest air all around you as you let your mind rest on your breathing. As you breathe in and out, notice how more oxygen reaches your brain and your heart rate slows. This will improve your concentration as BART psychotherapy proceeds. The third element is water. Seventy per cent of the composition of our body is water and, as you drink from the glass, imagine swallowing water mixed with saliva. This contains the enzyme amylase, which will relax your stomach and gastrointestinal tract. Any knots or butterflies in your tummy are eased as the tension relaxes. The fourth element is heat or warmth which percolates throughout your body as regional blood flow increases during the session. We will pay attention to any areas of blood flow, which are associated with hot or cold sensations of the RAPIDS and FROZEN states we have discussed. At all times, we will seek to return to the calm WATERS. The fifth element is the ether, or atmosphere of calm, generated by you as your trauma is reprocessed during BART psychotherapy. I will now draw your attention to your favourite colour of light. This will be imagined to come from the cosmos of universal light energy. It will be drawn down through the gateway, or stellar, chakra to your soul and then into your body through the third eye, or pineal gland chakra. As it gains increasing focus and strength, I shall encourage you to visualise a colourful light energy as it divides into two streams. One stream connects with the thirty-three petals of the crown chakra and moves upwards. Another stream connects from the brow to the throat chakra, aiding spiritual and physical communication. From here, your favourite colour of light energy moves to the chest, heart, lungs, and thymus, increasing your awareness of harmony and love. From here, the light energy reaches the solar chakras, giving creativity and concentration. The sacral chakra connects to your innate sexuality before moving to infuse the root chakra, ensuring that you are secure and grounded to commence therapy. As you imagine the light entering your body, it combines to create energy, as predicted by Einstein's famous equation $E = mc^2$. The relaxation spreads to the double helix of your cellular DNA. The levels of the enzyme telomerase are increased. This allows the DNA to replicate exactly and you experience an anti-aging effect. Finally, I invite you to create a mental image

> of those people whose presence creates a loving atmosphere. You are aware of this room as a safe or peaceful place. You can think of figures real or imagined, person or animal, someone from a book or film. When you get a strong sense of the nurturing quality of the figure, tap your feet alternately, tapping in this resource. I ask you to visualise this loving and nurturing energy surrounding, strengthening, and enabling you to deal with whatever trials and tribulations are currently being faced.

This last resource can be added to with nurturing and protector figures and wise inner advisers, as described by Parnell, (2013).

The patient will then pause before continuing to resonate at the level of the earth star chakra. This exercise will return the universal energy to its stellar origins. One of the fundamental laws of physics is that energy can be transformed, but neither created out of nothing nor destroyed without trace. Einstein stated in his famous equation: Energy equals mass multiplied by the velocity of light squared, where E is energy, m is mass, and c is the velocity of light.

I encourage patients to be mindful of this state, usually at the end of our 90–120-minute sessions so that they can imagine that they leave the room enclosed in an insulating bubble of this atmosphere. We rehearse how they can use this to de-escalate any rising tension in the atmosphere when they leave the office to return to home or work.

Each time the patient has reprocessed an aspect of the trauma, they scan the event mentally, aided by the real or "magic" remote. The goal is to isolate or freeze-frame any remaining disturbing images from the replayed traumatic event. To augment processing, I give the patient bilateral tactile units, or, with young children, castanets can be useful. As the patient's somatic map of the territory changes, any negatively charged words used by the patient to describe their experiences are reframed positively. To allow reprocessing to continue at an effective pace, attention is paid to the patient's body language, eye contact, tone of voice, and unconscious movements for any signs of autonomic hyper- or hypoarousal. The pace of reprocessing is either slowed down or speeded up, to ensure the patient remains within their window of affective tolerance and emotional regulation. Typically, the patient will notice that the sensations associated with the trauma move from the solar plexus to the chest to the throat, in line with the chakra energy system. Any blocks to reprocessing are identified and resolved using BART psychotherapy before, ultimately, a transfer of information occurs at the interhemispheric level to the prefrontal cortex at the level of the third eye, or sixth chakra (pineal gland). Once the trauma narrative appears reprocessed with minimal affective disturbance, the patient assesses imaginally for any remaining disturbance in the past (trace back), present (go above), and future (move forward). Where areas of disturbance are identified, patients are asked to cross their arms, with or without holding tactile zappers, to facilitate sequential bilateral transmission of information along neurological channels. Patients who have been grabbed by the throat by an assailant often experience distressing sensations around their throat and neck. I encourage the patient to gently massage these areas with their fingers until relief is felt. Patients who have suffered injury to an arm, chest, shoulder, leg, or other body part will experience a shift in painful sensations in these areas. In my experience, asking the patient to gently place the tactile zappers over the area until the distress is relieved can relieve the emotional component of the residual pain.

As the stuck traumatic information is reprocessed, the tension within the patient's neuromuscular system is released. As the physical symptoms diminish, the cerebral hemispheres reinterpret the flow of information. Meaning is made of their experience as linked neural networks are activated. Patients are shown illustrations to facilitate their understanding of the transformation they have experienced. Patients often report at this stage tingling sensations, especially in the periphery. My interpretation of this is that thinking space in the cerebrum has been created, allowing new synaptic connections to be made. The patient is in a calm state and able both to learn from the experience and gain insight into their behaviour. I like to address resilience by asking the patient to imagine coping with the incident if similar circumstances were to occur in the future. Stage Four suggests that Brain Axons are Rewired for Transmission, and the patient is set up to be resilient.

The final thirty minutes of a 120-minute session of BART psychotherapy allows the patient time for reflection on the reprocessing achieved during the session. By then, the patient will have experienced ninety minutes of continuous bilateral cerebellar stimulation, as well as intermittent peripheral tactile stimulation accompanied by self-tapping if necessary. This may have precipitated them into a rapid eye movement (REM) state and they often report feeling tired and might commence yawning. This promotes an optimum level of integration of information between the cerebral hemispheres before reaching the analytic, executive functionality of the prefrontal cortex. Then the patient is asked to review the reprocessed traumatic incidents completed during the session to become aware of any new

- thoughts;
- beliefs;
- feelings;
- sensations;
- impulses;
- meanings, that is, things they have learnt about themselves and how they have survived their traumatic experiences.

Any new positive thoughts, beliefs, feelings, sensations, and lessons learnt are reinforced using a future template (Figure 44).

In my clinical experience, I have found that the patient goes through the stages of arousal followed by deepening and then relaxation before having time to think and reflect on the session.

The end of the session allows for reflection on what lessons have been learnt and for sense to be made of their experience. The patient

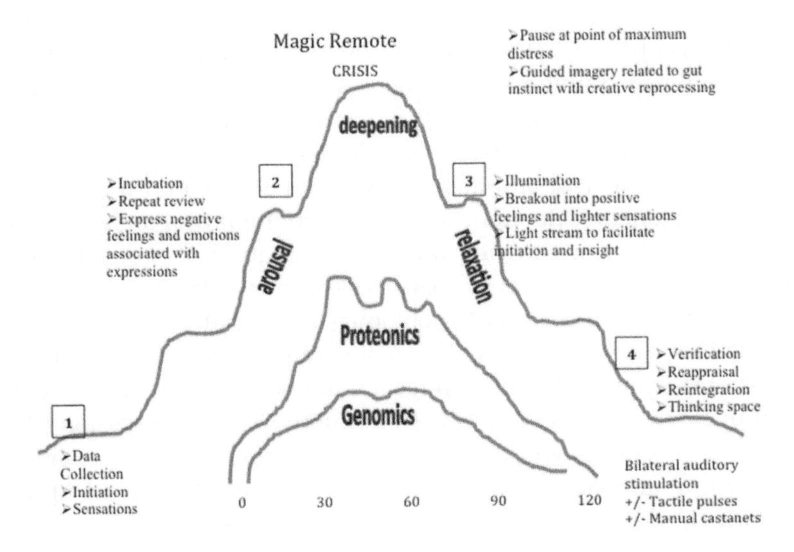

Figure 44. Model of BART psychotherapy session compared to neuroscience model of Rossi (2004). Drawing created by Sorcha O'Malley and adapted from original by Ernest Rossi.

or client's thinking space is freed in the prefrontal cortex and my hypothesis is that new neuronal pathways are laid down *in vivo* towards the end of the two-hour session. Reprocessing continues after the session in the subsequent days, giving the opportunity for further synaptic potential. I ask the patients to notice any continued reprocessing and, in particular, to note any significant dreams related to the session. Most patients send this information by email so that I can have my formulation hypothesis ready for the next session.

Summary

In taking a developmental and trauma history of the patient or client, I discuss how particular attention should be paid to assessing sensory and/or motor involvement of the twelve cranial nerves. All of the cranial nerves except the olfactory synapse with the brainstem. As explained earlier, this will trigger a brainstem, instinctive, or reptilian response. Many therapists have discussed with me their difficulties in helping their patients or clients get rid of odours, smells, or aromas associated with the traumatic or abusive experience. No amount of traditional or trauma-focused CBT or EMDR is able to relieve this olfactory sensation. I have proposed bilateral olfactory stimulation using BART psychotherapy to relieve the patient's distress. A key component of successful therapy is having the patient in a calm, relaxed state. The use of the seven-element relaxation exercise is described, and this can be interwoven into the session. Rossi (2004) has proposed a neuroscientific model of psychotherapy. I apply this to BART psychotherapy, showing the initial elevating of arousal, then deepening the therapeutic experience, followed by relaxation. The real time changes of genomics and proteomics are hypothesised to occur in parallel, as illustrated. This has major implications for the effectiveness of therapy and would suggest that one two-hour session per patient or client is much more effective than two one-hour sessions. In my clinical experience working in the NHS, I have never come across two-hour appointment sessions apart from the ones I have set up in the traumatic stress clinic. It is my conviction, based on my own experience and reviewing the neuroscience literature, that there should be a paradigm shift to sessions of this duration for patients with complex and severe traumatic stress instead of the more traditional approach of the fifty-minute hour first promoted by Freud at the end of the nineteenth century (Freud, 1905d). I propose this appointment schedule is more appropriate for the provision of twenty-first-century health services. It has been my experience that six hours of this trauma-focused therapy spread over three two-hour sessions can dramatically reduce the patient or client's impact of events scale scores and their associated subjective unit of distress score (SUDS).

CHAPTER TEN

Influence of some research in trauma therapy by neurobiologists and how this has affected my development of the integrative approach of BART psychotherapy and peak performance

There are a number of scientists whose work has had a profound effect on my approach to therapeutic work with patients and clients.

1. *Biology of Belief* (2011), by Dr Bruce Lipton

Bruce Lipton is a cellular developmental biologist who has proposed that multicellular organisms use the same proteins for multiple functions. The caenorhabditis worm has 1,000 cells, compared to fifty trillion cells in humans. However, it has 24,000 genes compared to 25,500 in the human genome. Thus, genes are only part of the story of perception. Thus, he is suggesting a new biology to describe perception and has co-written a book entitled *Spontaneous Evolution* (Lipton & Bhaerman, 2011). Dr Lipton's latest work, *The Honeymoon Effect* (2013a) develops this idea one step further and is an attempt to understand the molecular basis of consciousness. The book introduces the term honeymoon, which refers to the state of married bliss of newly-weds who often go on a romantic holiday. However, the term was used in 1546 as "hony moone". There are reports that the father of the groom provided mead for a month to the newly-weds. The state was said to wane like the moon in that time. Indeed, today, the twenty-eight day lunar cycle is close to one month. An extract reveals the honeymoon effect in his (Dr Lipton's) own life:

> After decades of failure, that's what I finally manifested! Because so many people have asked how we did it, Margaret and I will explain in the Epilogue how we have managed to create our happily-ever-after Honeymoon Effect for seventeen years and counting. We want to share our story because love is the most potent growth factor for human beings and love is contagious! As you will find when you create The Honeymoon Effect in your own life, you will attract similarly loving people to you—and the more the merrier. Let us . . . revel in our love for each other so this planet can finally evolve into a better place where all organisms can live their own Heaven on Earth. My hope is that this book will launch you on a journey, as that instant in the Caribbean launched me, to create The Honeymoon Effect each and every day of your life. (Lipton, 2013a, p. xviii)

Lipton (2011), in his book, *Biology of Belief*, discusses the interaction of endocrine, immune, and nervous systems with the culture medium of the body and mind (Figure 45), or gut-brain, heart-brain, and head-

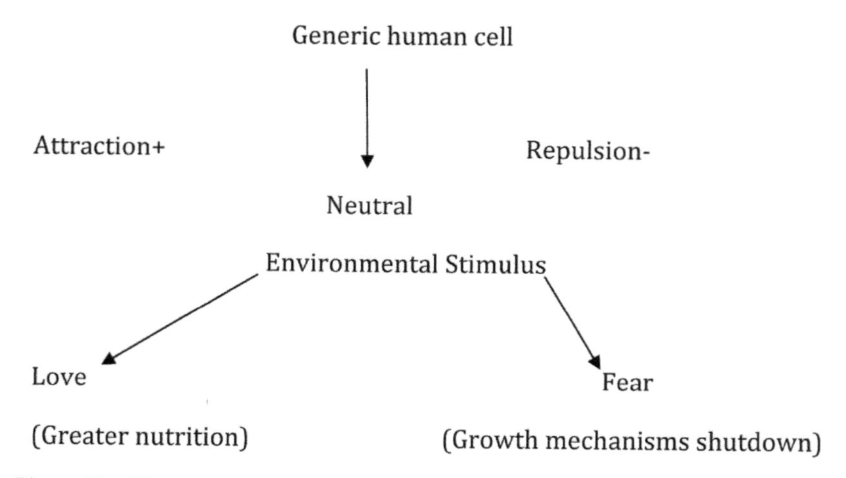

Figure 45. The concept of the biology of perception from environmental stimulus to growth of cell. This was conceived by Dr Bruce Lipton. This series of interactions leads to growth of viscera centrally and muscles of arms and legs in the periphery in the human subject.

brain, as I have discussed earlier. Exposure to toxic stress causes these body substrates to release stress hormones into the bloodstream. Those such as adrenaline prime our muscles so we can escape from impending danger.

The human cell contains mitochondrial and nuclear DNA inside and is surrounded by the cell membrane.

Lipton performed experiments to locate the cell's brain. He concluded that it was not DNA, as, when the DNA was extracted, the cell survived. Eventually, the protein receptors in the cell membrane acted as the cellular brain. Our sensory receptors are composed of protein and receive information via neuropeptides before transmitting a signal to the nucleus for encoding. This signal creates DNA to enable it to adapt to the environment. Dr Lipton concluded that "Our perception of the environment directly controls the activity of our genes" (Lipton, 2013b, p. 177).

Thus, our beliefs directly affect the molecular structure of water in our body. This has relevance to the head-brain, which is ninety per cent water. This water is affected by emotions and changes in vibrational energy. It comes in many forms: the ocean bathing our cells, blood, lymph, cerebrospinal fluid, capillaries, and visceral organs. Stuck unexpressed emotions can consolidate as belief systems. This directly influences our bodily fluids, resulting in chronic disease and illness. Recognising and reprocessing these stuck emotional states can be achieved with BART psychotherapy.

In the 9/11 attacks in New York, many survivors continued running for miles, well away from the danger zone, until their immune system gave way and they collapsed from exhaustion. According to Dr Lipton, during the first six years of life, we "download" behaviour programmes from our parents, siblings, and from other experiences and social interactions. As well as the Darwinian "survival of the fittest" theory of natural selection, it is now believed that we also evolve via cooperation within communities and collaboration for the greater good of society, not just in terms of success of the individual. It is also known that the epigenome is more powerful than the gene, in that it determines which genes are switched on or off. This can be expressed as shown in Figure 46.

Thus, the signals in the environment drive epigenetic activity and switches on healthy or unhealthy gene activity. Each person, based on the scientific evidence, can ask himself or herself the following: what

Environmental signal - Frequency of love or fear

Wave interaction with DNA codons

Regulatory protein changes shape

Protein sleeve comes off deoxynucleic acid DNA

Messenger RNA molecule copied

New proteins go into production from component amino acids

Figure 46. Pathway from the emotions of love or fear to DNA, RNA, and new protein formation from essential amino acids. Diagram by Sorcha O'Malley.

are the environmental signals I perceive? Destructive emotions, such as fear, generate a waveform pattern that only interacts intermittently with the base pair codons of DNA. This will lead to a limited range of instinctive or reactive responses. The associated stress has the possibility of coding for harmful proteins in the body's cellular nuclei. If, however, we perceive a loving atmosphere or environment, a completely different waveform is expressed. This emotion has an increased frequency and, therefore, interacts with all codons in the DNA double helix. This gives us the potential to activate all sixty-four codons possible within the known DNA double helix structure. This means that by being better attuned to the emotional energy of the ambient environment, we can avoid fear and access a more loving emotional experience. When the human genome project was completed in 2000, scientists were surprised that only around 30,000 genes were decoded, accounting for ten per cent of cellular DNA. The remaining ninety per cent of DNA did not appear to code meaningfully for proteins and was perceived to be genetically redundant, or "junk", DNA. Given the knowledge we now have of epigenetics in switching genes on or off, one hypothesis is that this remaining ninety per cent of DNA has yet to be activated epigenetically. The question to pose is: what genetic energetic frequency of emotional energy will interact sufficiently to trigger an mRNA response in the remaining forty-four codons?

The Human Brain Project

This was launched in August 2013 with a seventy-eight-page vision statement: www.humanbrainproject.eu. The goal is to map out the million billion synaptic connections of the brain over the next decade. This will be a multi-disciplinary effort led by Professor Markam from EFPL in Lausanne, Switzerland. The work will be divided into three strands:

1. Future neuroscience.
2. Future medicine.
3. Future computing.

Six strategic objectives have been set:

1. Design, develop, deploy, and operate computers for researchers in the above fields.
2. Stimulate research into the brain's structure and function including the causes and diagnosis of brain disease
3. Generate and collect strategic neuroscience data, which can inform objective 1.
4. Implementation and analysis of any innovation and results for its social and philosophical implications, involving citizens and researchers in a far-reaching conversation about future directions of research.
5. Training of scientists of Europe across disciplines to enable convergence of information and computer technology and neuroscience, creating enhanced capability for academia and industry across the European continent.
6. Providing a coherent approach to leadership and project management so that regional, national, and European research programmes are effectively aligned.

This ambitious project is analogous to building a human brain with input from the periphery (European countries) to the centre (Project Headquarters at Lausanne in Switzerland). Crucial to its success will be a two-way flow of information, as happens between neurons in the human brain. At the nerve centre will be someone with sufficient synaptic capacity to hold the big picture in mind and focus on the end goal of the key six strategic objectives for the full flagship (SOFF). This is a good analogy, as when the ship sets sail, we can all climb aboard and journey across the ocean waves to our new destination.

In mythological terms, this is reminiscent of the voyage to a new land taken by Noah, his chosen people, and animals in the Ark of the Covenant.

The power resources for this project are enormous. Whereas the human brain uses about 30 Watts, the output of many power stations will be needed to generate sufficient computer capacity to build realistic models of the brain's phenomenal computing power and its thought output.

How can humanity reactivate their double-stranded DNA to take maximum advantage of what scientists have referred to as the ninety per cent junk DNA?

From the research I have done, a sea change in the earth's planetary orbit is required for sunlight of a higher frequency to reach humanity from the star system. It has been suggested that the most likely time for this to happen is after the winter solstice of 21 December 2012. This date has long been flagged as the moment when our solar system aligns with the galactic centre. This epoch comes around once every 26,000 years. Humanity has no record of historical events from that time. Indeed, the oldest scientifically dated monument is that of Gobekli Tepe ("belly hill" in Turkish), near Istanbul. These megalithic stones predate Stonehenge by over 6,000 years. It is believed to be the site of the world's oldest temple, a cathedral on a hill. It is situated thirty minutes from Urfa, an ancient city in south-eastern Turkey. Layers of stone carvings have been built up, leaving the hilltop covered in sand as it stands today. It is now believed that building this temple led to the development of complex civilisations. Klaus Schmidt is the German archaeologist who has been excavating this site for the past ten years. Ninety-five per cent of the site has yet to be revealed. We await his theories on the purpose of these mysterious structures from this ancient Turkish civilisation.

Despite the fact that only five per cent of this site has been excavated, the detailed stone carvings found make this the most important archaeological site currently being excavated anywhere on earth. The structure of the stones uncovered so far dates from 12,000 BC. The site was used for "religious purposes". However, no stone tools have been recovered on the site. The creators of this monument went to great lengths to bury it in sand and debris. This fortuitous act preserved it from destruction. The collective wisdom of the researchers is that this civilisation intended to leave a message for their descendants. In the above view, I am struck by the similarity to the triple spiral symbols central to the Newgrange monument in County Meath, Republic of Ireland. It is believed Stone Age man communicated using the Ogham language. This was based on knowledge of the frequencies of underground structures, such as the location of reservoirs of water, which could be divined by dousing. In addition, the "OM" mantra from India has similarities to this triple spiral. The spiral is the basic expression of three-dimensional energy progressions and can be measured with a pendulum.

The K52 entrance stone to the Newgrange Megalithic site in the Boyne Valley, County Meath, Republic of Ireland is adorned with carvings of spirals and, in particular, the triple spiral. The significance of these are not fully understood.

The "OM" sound may be used to open up the third eye chakra, or pineal gland. This has been used in India since longer ago than 3,500 BC. The frequency of this sound might represent the copying of double-stranded DNA by messenger ribonucleic acid (mRNA) to make a new strand of DNA.

One striking characteristic is the variation and significance given to the triple spiral symbol across different cultures. From listening to Michael Poynder give a presentation based on his book *Pi in the Sky* (1992), I think this might relate to a previous capability humanity had in terms of the double helix of DNA. This might be represented by the various symbols for the caduceus throughout history. The engravings at Newgrange, on both stones K1 and K52 and in the inner chamber itself, most beautifully illustrate this. If, indeed, humankind had a genetic structure composed of fully activated double-stranded DNA, this would allow for the vastly increased range of codon possibilities and could explain how we were once able to utilise what is now called junk DNA.

This term was first introduced by Ohno (1972). Now, genetic science describes this section of DNA as "introns". It is seen as part of our common ancestry with other species of life on planet earth.

Wan and colleagues (2014) reported that a second layer of information was embedded in all RNA transcripts in the form of an RNA secondary structure. This RNA structure was found to influence almost every step in the process of gene expression. The extent of this influence is unknown at present. There are both coding and non-coding RNAs in the human genome. In conclusion, the broad contribution of RNA structure and its variants to the regulation of our human genes was reported. This scientific finding shows that we are more than a double-stranded DNA helix, as first thought when Crick and Watson discovered DNA in 1952. We have the potential, through epigenetics, to activate these additional RNA structures.

According to the myth of Atlantis, prior to its fall humanity had reached a state of "God-like evolution". Man risked self-destruction, and to prevent this a catastrophic fall, perhaps of water, occurred. Many creation myths from different cultures around the world attest to a catastrophic deluge enveloping the earth. Few survived what has been described as a worldwide *tsunami*. Even today, several descriptions exist of dreams where people are swept away by waves higher than a mountain. This would explain a vessel floating on a spherical surface of the ocean, as in Noah's Ark. As described in the Old Testament, it was only when the rains subsided and the raven came back with a leaf from an exposed branch that landfall could occur on Mount Arafat. This is one of the highest peaks in Turkey.

Assuming ninety per cent of the world's population was wiped out, man then might have regressed to a more primitive species and hypothetically lost his advanced form of genetic DNA. The earliest known resurrection of civilisation myth in the post diluvian era was in Sumeria and Mesopotamia. The monument covered up in Gobekli Tepe could relate to the structure of the DNA as it replicates from the double strand of DNA to a third strand, via messenger ribonucleic acid (mRNA). This statement is speculative on my part and not backed up by scientific evidence. Instead, I am responding to my intuition, or gut instinct. This is a good example of how the left and right hemispheres evaluate evidence. When undergoing BART psychotherapy, clients and patients have the best of both worlds: an integrated holistic perspective.

The symbol for "OM", recorded in India around 3,500 BC, is said to represent the universal void of creation. In addition, it is possible that the purpose of the chants of OM before, during, and after meditation was to increase the energy of the chakras, perhaps to assist with DNA replication and protein synthesis. This would fit in with the model I have proposed for BART psychotherapy. Perhaps the way to scientifically evaluate the impact of BART psychotherapy is to measure its impact on telomere shortening. My hypothesis would be that exposure to the gamma frequency of bilateral cerebellar stimulation would increase the enzyme telomerase, thereby diminishing the deleterious effect of telomere shortening on DNA replication.

Biology of perception and natural selection

According to Lipton's book, *Biology of Belief* (2013), our new perception controls our genes and selects what genes are expressed. By looking at the historical achievements in monuments such as Newgrange and Gobekli Tepe, we can surmise that these peoples had access to more of the genetic DNA potential than humankind does today.

Cairns, Overbaugh, and Miller (1988) discussed the origin of mutants in their article on "adaptive" mutations (i.e., mutations that are not random). They found that some forms of bacterial mutation occurred spontaneously before there was any outward sign of the utility of the mutation. The conclusion was that bacteria have some choice over the mutation they produce. The human corollary is that an individual human genome may profit by experience. Thus, it is possible that genetic instability (leading to a greater risk of mutation) can be switched on by living in a stressful environment, but switched off when that stress has been treated successfully.

This could be a cellular representation of the last universal common ancestor (LUCA). All seven billion inhabitants of earth can trace their ancestry back to LUCA, which first appeared on earth 3.8 billion years ago, according to Professor Brian Cox (2013). We now exist as leaves derived from different branches of the tree of life. Mitochondria and nuclei have combined in the above cellular representation to form the diversity of life known today. This can help to place in perspective any conflicts or difficulties with others, as, ultimately, they can be seen as part of the main, that is, ourselves.

2. Contribution of Raichle and Snyder (2007) to the field of research into the neurobiology of trauma

Raichle defined the default mode network (DMN) in 2001 as an area within the brain which is active when the brain is at rest. It consists of the following areas:

- post cingulate cortex (PCC);
- ante cingulate cortex (ACC);
- medial prefrontal cortex (mPFC);
- parietal lobe;
- temporal lobe (middle temporal gyrus).

Over different ages, the default mode network architecture matures from a "local" organisation to a "distributed" organisation. There is a dynamic development between the two-task control networks, the default network, and cerebellar networks. Initially, there is segregation of local, anatomically clustered regions. In children, regions are largely organised by their anatomical location, but, with age, anatomically clustered regions segregate. The cluster of frontal regions best demonstrates this segregation. In children, the more distributed adult functional networks are, in many ways, disconnected. In time, the functional networks integrate. The isolated regions of the default mode network in childhood that coalesce into a highly correlated network best illustrate this integration. Organisation of the DMN shifts from the "local" arrangement in children to the "distributed" organisation commonly observed in adults.

The DMN functions less well under high working memory load. An intact DMN is necessary for:

1. Theory of mind (TOM). This is the capacity to attribute mental states, desires, beliefs and attributes of another person.
2. Autobiographical (episodic and semantic) memory.
3. The ability to look forward and plan for the future.

In the patients with PTSD, they often re-experience the traumatic events by reliving their worst sensory fragments. Their working memory becomes overloaded and these fragments are stored in a disorganised way. They are often completely unable to think about the future. They are preoccupied by reliving their traumas in the present and have a fragmented sense of self. This affects how they think about themselves.

They tend to expect the worst, have symptoms of dissociation, and feelings of shame and self-loathing. The research points to a disturbance in the DMN as a biological substrate for PTSD. BART psychotherapy can help traumatised patients with the above symptoms. It is known that, in PTSD, the DMN shows little connectivity between the post cingulate cortex and the medial prefrontal cortex. My hypothesis would be that after five two-hour sessions of BART psychotherapy, the patient with PTSD would start to display the connectivity at rest consistent with a healthy DMN. Thus, the PCC would be able to recognise objects and salient past events, the medial PFC would enact self-referential awareness, the lateral parietal lobes would embody the self, and the temporal lobes would sub-serve all aspects of memory. Under fMRI, these four brain areas would be fully interconnected post treatment if this hypothesis is correct.

In a child aged seven to nine, the DMN is similar to that of a patient under chronic stress. Thus, developmentally, the adult traumatised patient only has the capacity to respond at rest with the DMN of a 7–9-year-old. My goal in this book and the explanations underlying the neurobiology of BART psychotherapy is to prove that the DMN can be restored and brought back online, so that it can start functioning like the DMN of a healthy adult.

3. Northern and southern neural pathways of Professor James Austin

Austin (1999) has described an upper, or northern, pathway, which is egocentric and involves the upper occipital cortex. It is specialised for action and pays attention to what is above the visual horizon. This includes your lucky stars, blue skies, clouds, and mountains. The immediate environment might include a sabre-toothed tiger; this pathway processes visual image colour processing and hearing. The lower, or southern, pathway is allocentric. It processes the proprioceptive and parietal environment of what is within arm's reach. For women, their fusiform gyrus processes the facial features of a newborn baby while their hands provide afferent feedback to take care of their infant. For men, they are able to hold a tool such as a hammer in their hand and accurately hit a nail on its head using this pathway. Hence the saying: "You just hit the nail on the head", which means to represent something exactly.

Both pathways combine egocentric and allocentric awareness. The three hotspots of the DMN are activated at rest, generating a sense of psychic self-identity and helping us safely navigate through our environment. The hotspots are active when we are involved in self-related activity and cool down when an external acute task is attempted. It is now known that these areas of high and low activity, as seen on functional MRI, change every twenty seconds. This is the intrinsic cycle of human brain activity. When there is a wish to go into a meditative state, a triggering stimulus, such as a gong, shifts the allosteric pathway upwards in awareness and lowers the attention paid by the egocentric one. Hence, referential reprocessing of the other is increased while that of the self is decreased. These techniques can be incorporated into BART psychotherapy sessions.

Symptomatically, the patients would experience enhanced emotional awareness, improved sense of self, greater affective regulation, and, finally, better social functioning. Research into, and dissemination of, the techniques of BART psychotherapy for both trauma and peak performance will, I hope, allow this question to be answered definitively over the next decade. Crucially, patients and clients must be enabled to grieve the unresolved traumatic grief and losses. They must also be helped to reconnect their social friendship, work, and educationally related networks. As both patients and clients often present with a distorted sense of their own self-worth, it is vital, via BART psychotherapy, that they become aware of their inner affective state. They then experience, through affective reprocessing, how both to widen their window of affect tolerance and develop a capacity for emotional regulation. Once out of the disabling dissociative states of hyper-arousal (RAPIDS) and hypo-arousal (FROZEN), see Figure 23, they are no longer hijacked by emotions and will benefit from the later stages of BART psychotherapy. The patient is able to experience the present truthfully. The self-reflection during the last thirty minutes of a session allows them to plan for the future and derive meaning from the experience.

What can the patient or client learn from their collective experiences?

Many patients see themselves as broken or damaged goods before referral to the therapist. However, the following tale will help to change that perspective.

> Two Africans lived in a village with no running water. Each day, they carried a ceramic pot down to the river, filled it up, and brought it back to the village. However, each person always seemed to have less water to give to the villagers at the end of their journey. This was difficult to understand, as the pots were the same. Time passed and different members of the village went to collect the water with new metal pots, which did not leak. They retraced the steps of their predecessors. To their surprise, they found that along the path back to the village, rows upon rows of beautiful flowers had sprung up where the old ceramic pots had cracked and leaked.

Thus, our patients and clients who might have seen themselves as broken and damaged can realise that an unbroken wholeness exists within them, which can coexist with the brokenness. They can both be messed up and very all right at the same time. By inviting our patients and clients to hold on to these thoughts, we can metaphorically water their souls and wait for their own flowers to bloom.

My BART psychotherapy has a key role to play in managing the patient and client's response to that stressful environment. The aim could be to prevent the development of traumatic stress for such at risk individuals.

A recent Danish study by Bernsten and colleagues (2012) followed a cohort of 746 soldiers before, during, and after deployment to Afghanistan. They found that the greatest risk for developing PTSD was linked to childhood adversity experiences (i.e., stressful living environment) rather than the specific war experiences. Indeed, a less well-educated group with the most childhood adversity had reduced levels of PTSD in the theatre of war. They reported that the camaraderie of their fellow soldiers was something they had never experienced before. On returning to their troubled civilian lives, their PTSD levels increased. This finding had never been reported in the literature before. It confirms my thesis of how being in a loving, supportive environment of the army on active service can be sufficient to counteract the fear of attack by enemy combatants.

According to proverb, the Muslim mystic, Rumi, said, in the twelfth century, "It is only through our wounds that light can enter to start the process of healing".

I would suggest to our patients and clients that by allowing pure vibrational light energy to enter our physical and emotional wounds and scars, the path to healing could begin. This is the first step of their road map to the ultimate destination of recovery and peak performance.

Summary

In this chapter, I have looked at a new biology of perception and belief first espoused by Dr Bruce Lipton, a developmental cellular biologist. His latest book, *The Honeymoon Effect*, proposes that changing our beliefs and perceptions can prolong the state of wedded bliss that follows on from marriage. A flow diagram of the behaviour of the human cell shows the frequency of attraction as love and that of repulsion as fear. Dr Lipton proposes that environmental stimuli affect cell growth and that it is our perception of this environmental stimulus that switches gene activity on and off. There is a brief mention of the human genome project and the mammoth task of the human brain project, which is proposed for the next decade. Scientists have identified junk DNA in the human chromosome. A description of monolithic sites at Gobekli Tepe and Newgrange is given. These sites are aligned with the orbit of the sun. In Newgrange, for 8,000 years or more, the sunlight pierces the inner sanctum and is reflected upward by a polished stone shaped like a parabolic mirror. Approximately thirty-three modern-day humans can fit into this space and experience this natural illumination. This might have religious significance for Stone Age man. I hypothesise that it might also reactivate this "junk DNA", starting with accessing the increased vibratory frequency predicted to reach earth after the winter solstice marking the end of the Mayan Calendar in December 2012. All of the above mechanisms would explain how different genetic characteristics are expressed, both helpful and harmful. This allows for a recalibration of the nature–nurture paradigm of evolution. A different perspective can inform the Darwinian theory of natural selection, survival of the fittest, and genetic determinism. This takes account of modern scientific enquiry and looks back in time at what was achieved by some of our earlier greatest civilisations. We can move to a state of attraction to positive environmental stimuli, such as living within a loving and supportive family, so that we can more rapidly activate our "lost DNA introns". The research related to the default mode network of the brain, proposed by Raichle and Snyder (2007), is presented. This has been subdivided into a northern–southern pathway, by Professor James Austin (1999), which engages the person in different functions based on eye gaze (up or down), and the other somatosensory functions being used. The concept of an intrinsic rate to the brain's activity, which alternates between these pathways, was also suggested. This knowledge is fundamental to effective reprocessing, as the DMN is rendered ineffective by unprocessed significant life events. Finally, a 2012 study of Danish troops in Afghanistan is mentioned, emphasising the role friendship networks play in overcoming adversity and, using a parable, I explain how patients and clients can learn from their collective experiences. The chapter ends with a quotation from the mystic poet, Rumi.

CHAPTER ELEVEN

Living in a hypothetical world dominated by the left hemisphere's perspective, and summary of the five stages of BART psychotherapy

Introduction to our current worldview, which is dominated by the perspective of the left hemisphere

In the western world, where the perspective of the left hemisphere dominates, the first aspect of life to suffer is its central coherence. The "bits" of something assumes greater importance than the whole picture. Gathering information "bit by bit" is a poor substitute for knowledge gained from experience. This allows the big picture to be seen. Expertise (Latin, "one who is experienced") is based on LH theory, or abstraction. Quantity would take preference over quality: the principle of "what" over "how". People are reduced to the impersonal, that is, to mechanical perspective and number crunching: pure data without context. Societal cohesion is put at risk with lack of trust and paranoia predominating among the populous. This worldview has cascaded from the political and financial elite since time immemorial. Indeed, this cabal has been called the illuminati and has links to the freemasons and other religious groups.

Previously, society demanded of its doctors, teachers, and priests a vocational and altruistic role. When we have only the left hemisphere perspective, these attributes may be viewed with suspicion. In many organisations today, this view predominates. Doctor–patient relationships, which are based on mutual respect, have been damaged by management in the organisation to enable the hierarchical system to retain power and control. Certainty and security are sought out obsessively by management. This power structure cannot tolerate uncertainty or insecurity. Anything that challenges the status quo is too risky. This idea of being in control is promulgated by the left hemisphere perspective. Doctors, however, are taught to tolerate and embrace uncertainty and this requires a whole-brain approach.

There is a scientific comparison with Heisenberg's uncertainty principle, which is a concept from quantum mechanics and was proposed in 1927. This image of concentric circles illustrates how we can never be certain of the exact location of any particle in space.

A common sense view involves both hemispheres, is based on intuition, as mentioned in my introduction (p. xvi), and depends on interhemispheric collaboration. In a world dominated by LH thinking, this common sense view breaks down. Behaviour associated with aggression and anger escalates as these emotions find expression in the LH. Insight is channelled via the RH and it, too, diminishes. There is a lack of autonomy and a tendency to act as if by rote, that is, without conscious awareness. The human mind becomes technocratic with a distinct lack of its sense of uniqueness, awe, or wonder.

According to McGilchrist (2009), increases in our material well-being do not correlate with happiness. Happiness levels in Britain were reported to be fifty-two per cent in 1957 and only thirty-six per cent today. Happiness depends on "the breadth and depth of one's social connections". In so-called primitive societies, most interactions occurred face to face. Over the course of first world development, globalisation and urbanisation with fragmentation of communities has increased the levels of unhappiness if correlated with the rising prevalence of mental illness. It has also been established that social integration counteracts the harmful effects of smoking, obesity, hypertension, and a sedentary lifestyle.

The Conservative Party's Manifesto (2010, pp. 36–40) announced, as a policy objective, the Big Society. This may be a flawed concept in that in order for the Big Society to exist there must be feeder networks from the smaller social networks dotted all around the political landscape. If these are not joined up, then the goal of the big society is unlikely to happen. Currently, the Conservative Party (founded in

1834) has a membership of 134,000 and falling, whereas the Countryside Alliance (established only in 1997) has a membership of 100,000. The former currently has 303 MPs and uses top-down methods of recruitment, whereas the latter has grown exponentially, initially by amalgamating like-minded bodies and appealing directly to the grassroots. As I have already explained, this bottom-up approach is how our neural networks survive and thrive. The lesson for political parties is clear—adopt this approach or wither on the vine. The use of large-scale mass media campaigns by political parties seems not to have encouraged increased membership among an increasingly disaffected public. The single-issue organisations and political parties, such as UKIP, seem to be able to mobilise and harness grassroots opinion.

The expression "I heard it on the grapevine" refers to the spreadng of ideas through rumour or gossip, perhaps by people working in vineyards. This form of communication by word of mouth is a successful example of bottom-up reprocessing as used initially in BART psychotherapy. This is later combined with top-down cognitive reprocessing for the most effective outcome.

Summary of five stages of BART psychotherapy peak performance

Stage one: B*ilateral* A*ffective* R*eprocessing of* T*houghts*

The bilateral and reprocessing phases remain constant throughout the five stages. Ideally, each stage can be completed in either one two-hour session or two one-hour sessions. In the first stage, the key goal is affective reprocessing. This can be illustrated by:

> *A*ctivation of the
> *F*elt bodily sensations (primordial bodily feelings, gut reactions or instinctive response to the traumatic event).
> *F*ight, flight, freeze, fright, feigned death or fall reactions are reactivated safely within the window of affect tolerance.
> *E*ngagement of emotions associated with the core or genetic (proto) self.
> *C*erebellar and cerebral activation of consciousness, leading to
> *T*ransformation and
> *I*ntegration of somatic maps of the patient's

*V*isceral (i.e., bodily organs')
*E*xperience of the traumatic memory being processed.

Thus, by the end of stage one, the autonomic nervous system of the patient has been activated from the periphery through the brainstem and cerebellar pathways. This allows the original traumatic event to be felt less intensely.

The patient will often place the zappers over their abdominal region when initially processing the traumatic event. This is usually accompanied by a feeling of sickness or nausea. They are encouraged to stay in touch with this feeling until it subsides and reprocessing moves to a higher vibratory level.

In stage one, the goal is to establish bilateral cerebellar stimulation and start the reprocessing of thoughts from the gut via the heart to the brain.

Stage two: B*ody's* A*ccelerated* R*ecognition of* T*houghts*

During the second stage of BART psychotherapy, the patient's level of autonomic arousal in the aftermath of trauma has been further reprocessed. This occurs while preventing the patient from lapsing into the dissociative states of either hypo- or hyper-arousal.

The therapist maintains a focus on the patient's feelings, emotions, and sensations in relation to their traumatic experiences. The patient's narrative is contained and transformed via their imagination. The events are reviewed repeatedly using the Magic Remote© until they are experienced factually with minimal distress and having a low SUDS score (0–2). Patients are relieved that their memories are no longer associated with the previously unbearable, emotionally charged traumatic events.

The re-cognition or recognition of thoughts is a tautology, which emphasises the impact BART psychotherapy has in the resolution of trauma. The scene is set for BART psychotherapy to be used to identify specific unhelpful thoughts. It is at this stage that the most successful aspects of trauma-focused CBT can be employed, as the patient is better able to extract meaning from their traumatic experience.

At stage two, the goal is to establish the therapeutic relationship and, by mutual attunement between therapist and patient or client, they can start to re-think (recognition of) their previous thoughts.

Stage three: Brain's Autonomic *nervous system is* Resilient *and* Together

The patient's different brain systems (gut, heart, and head) and autonomic nervous system (immune, endocrine, and linked to the chakra system) are given resources to enhance resilience during the third stage of BART psychotherapy. Any fragmented personality parts of the dissociative identity disorder (DID) are pulled together. The DID patient may have the following parts: helper, lonely, parental, sexualised, school attendee, enraged, infantile, and promiscuous. The patient will be held in a safe mental state in order to come to terms with these different parts of their personality. Techniques such as ego-state therapy can be incorporated into BART psychotherapy at this stage of the patient's treatment. Attention is paid to any triggers leading to an increased affective discharge by the patient. Sensory cues, such as smell, sound, movements, touch, sight, taste, and posture, are identified and reprocessed. The technique of imagining an internal "padded" room helps to dissipate any negative affect experienced by the patient. The parts of the personality of the DID patient are brought together when they can hold the individual parts in conscious awareness. The patient is asked to check on the nature and function of each emotional personality (EP 1, 2, 3, etc.). It might be that their apparently normal personality (ANP) has become fragmented and requires integration. Colours are used to express different emotions associated with the different emotional personalities. Bilateral stimulation is applied during reprocessing of each EP until a new, more integrated aspect of the patient's personality emerges. Healthy emotional states associated with these EPs can be blended by getting the patient to imagine a "comfort" room, or, for adolescents, a "chill-out" room. Continual attention is paid to the patient's gestures during reprocessing and these are fed back to the patient with suggested hypotheses in relation to their potential meaning. The advantage of doing this during BART psychotherapy is that these hypotheses can be tested for reliability and validity with the patient in real time.

By stage three, the patient or client has used his head-brain to integrate all the sensory and motor information from his visceral and enteric nervous systems. This helps to shield him from stress while any disintegrated personality parts are drawn resiliently together. This stage encourages the therapist to work with the client or patient to link or associate any dysfunctional emotional personalities. The parasympathetic and sympathetic nervous systems are optimally activated during this stage.

Stage four: Brains' Axons are Rewired for Transmission

As Hebb stated in 1949, neurons or cells that fire together, wire together. When a positive stimulus fires the cell neuron, it will go on to develop healthy synapses. A negative or abusive experience will tend to wire neuronal cells towards a development of an aggressive response. During adolescence, there is a spurt of brain development similar to the first few years of life. Axons lengthen, but some neuronal growth is stopped, especially from the ages of ten to fourteen. This can correlate with the "moodiness" of the teenager, when they are particularly unable to express themselves. This could be related to their underlying emotions. This is also a period when myelin from glial cells increases their transmission 100 times, especially in the prefrontal cortex. The process of myelination in the prefrontal cortex continues throughout adolescence. Synaptic pruning enables neural networks to become efficient, especially when categorising sounds. Growth of the corpus callosum continues until approximately the ages of twenty-five (women) or thirty (men). Earlier in the evolution of our Homo sapiens species, this was the expected lifespan. Thus, it was essential that pair bonding and procreation occurred early if the genes were to be passed on to the next generation.

Testosterone production slows synaptic pruning, making adolescent boys more awkward than adolescent girls. However, white matter continues to be myelinated in a linear manner throughout life. This is the normal state of brain development, provided the patient has not suffered major adverse experiences in childhood. If so, then the BART psychotherapist will be tuned in to the need to focus on this stage of the therapeutic process. By stage three, the patient or client will have experienced bilateral activation for approximately six hours. Following on from this, the goal of stage four is to have optimised the potential of the patient for axonal rewiring. This will enable transmission across newly created neural networks.

Patients or clients will have remained within their specific window of tolerance. Using the BOKA machine, the frequency of this bilateral activation will have been optimised to ensure transmission of their narrated experiences. Using the BOKA machine, the headphones and zappers can be set to resonate at different frequencies. I would suggest starting the headphones at a low frequency of less than 10 Hertz. This will converge with the Schumann frequency mentioned earlier. I would suggest starting the zappers at a higher frequency of 15–20 Hertz. This equals the beta waves emitted by the awake brain when our eyes are open. This frequency should be maintained while the zappers are reprocessing traumas located in the body.

As the patient or client continues reprocessing, they activate the solar chakra, then the heart chakra, to the throat chakra. I would increase the frequency of stimulation until they are able to tolerate the maximum frequency of Hertz associated with thalamocortical concordance. The sensory thalamus will forward its information, first to the cerebellum bilaterally, and then on to the cerebral cortex. This allows the patient to both digest and reflect on the meaning of each traumatic experience. The last thirty minutes of the session allows for the bilateral stimulation of the zappers to be switched off and for the patient to recover from what has been experienced. I liken the session to having a brain workout.

Stages three and four of BART psychotherapy are interchangeable, depending on the developmental age of the patient or client. This therapeutic engagement results in achieving neuronal potential where it has been arrested through traumatic experiences, or where the goal is to stretch the synapses to allow the client to reach peak performance.

Brain development during adolescence

Bilateral innervation starts from the peripheral nervous system (upper and lower limbs) and goes to the central nervous system (pons medulla and midbrain). At least ninety per cent of fibres of the lateral corticospinal tract cross the midline at the level of the brainstem. This provides a theoretical underpinning to the continuous bilateral cerebellar stimulation and the foot tapping as part of the figure of eight exercise, which is explained to the patient or client. The figure of eight represents the flow of information that I want the patient to achieve so that they overcome traumatic blocks to processing and, for the client seeking peak performance, to experience the flow, or being in the zone.

During BART psychotherapy, I get the patient into a state of information flow. When they are in the zone, the information travels up from the initial gut reaction to the heartfelt sensations associated with grief and loss before registering in the quintessential elements of the brain. Crucially, for resolution of the traumatic stress, I get the patient foot tapping. This aids the circulation of sensations throughout the body from top to toe and *vice versa*. There is a parallel in ancient history for this form of processing as illustrated by the ouroboros symbol, which shows the snake or serpent completing the circle by biting its tail. Clockwise represents the flow of information across the body from left to right and *vice versa*. This is also the image in Kekule's dream that led him to discover the chemical structure of the benzene ring.

Often, the ouroboros symbol involves the image of two serpents each biting its tail. I use this metaphor to conjure up a figure of eight image positioned either vertically or horizontally in space. Patients or clients are encouraged to track the movement of sensations and feeling from their root, or sacral, chakra up to the crown and third eye chakras.

At this point, the reprocessing can often become stuck and I suggest to patients and clients that they tap each foot in turn to kick-start the reprocessing. Sometimes I notice that this can happen spontaneously.

Dan Siegel reported in a lecture of his that I attended how one elderly patient was unable to speak about the traumatic grief he had experienced. Thus, his Broca's area was in need of stimulation. Once his right foot started to tap, due to the crossing of the corticospinal tract in the brainstem (pyramidal decussation), his Broca's area was activated and he started to speak.

There is a Gnostic gem from Roman-era Egypt (1st century AD), with an ouroboros surrounding a scarab and *voces magicae*, characters representing magic words. This shows that the ouroboros symbol is ancient and can resonate effectively with the patient or client undergoing BART psychotherapy. (Figure 47).

Stage five: Better Active, Recovered, and Triumphant

By stage five of BART psychotherapy, the patient is on the way towards resilience and stability. As they receive high frequency

Figure 47. Ancient depiction of the ouroboros symbol.

gamma waves (40–60 Hertz) at the level of the cerebellum, they resonate with increasing intensity throughout the brain and brainstem. The anterior cingulate cortex no longer has to act as a brake mediating between the sympathetic HPA axis and the bidirectional vagal complex. Instead, the patient develops a mellow, whole system integrated response. The patient's autobiographical self merges with their core self, as first described by Damasio (2010). This allows the patient to feel what is happening now. The patient can experience the depths of this ancient neuronal circuitry. They are able to activate their parietal lobes in order to integrate all past somatomotor experiences. The calm feeling tone generated within the final stage of BART psychotherapy enables the patient to experience the sense of dual awareness, where gut reactions related to a traumatic experience can be tolerated without generating an instinctive reaction.

By retraining the patient's response to threat, I explain how their amygdalae are now better inhibited by their frontal lobes. This allows for the impact of insight. This creative process by the patient activates new synaptic connections, allowing traumatic events to be seen or visualised differently. As the neurons are stimulated bilaterally at a gamma frequency of 40 Hertz, experiences are felt at both a brain and heart level. Hippocampal storage of new memories can change the previous traumatic memories permanently.

The following stages of development, showing the path of continued progress from insight, wisdom, Samadhi, and non-dual awareness to elevated levels of consciousness are possible to achieve with both our patients and clients:

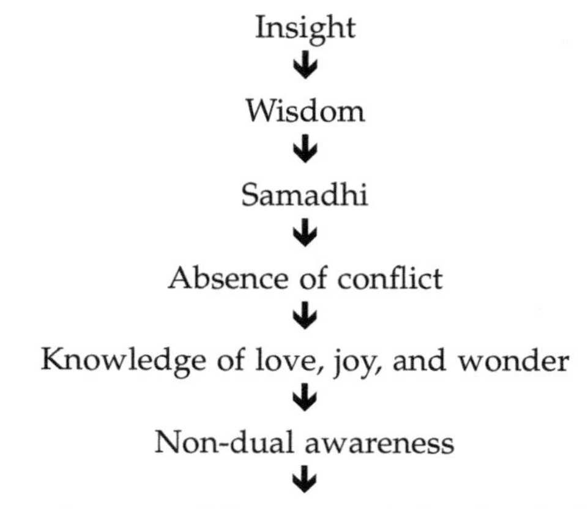

The goal of this final stage of BART psychotherapy is for the patients, in conjunction with therapist, to recognise when they are better able to be active, fully recovered, and able to be triumphant.

Case example 6

A teenage boy had suffered a violent attack by a dog in which his arm was almost severed by the vice-like grip of an animal bred to be aggressive. He had held his arm over his face in an attempt to protect it. His mother grabbed a brick and repeatedly hit the dog over the head in an effort to get it to release its grip on her son's arm. In a recent demonstration on the BBC 2 television programme, *The Wonder of Dogs*, viewers were shown how terriers were employed as rat catchers in the linen mills across England. The instructor offered the edge of a Frisbee to the small terrier. The dog started to shake its head vigorously from side to side without relinquishing the Frisbee. If this had been a rat, the dog would have shaken the rat to death. In the same way, the cross-breed dog who attacked the boy held on to the boy's arm. He described to me how he heard the bones in his forearm snap and shatter into multiple pieces. This animal was considered dangerous under the Dangerous Dogs Act as it was a cross-breed between a Rhodesian Ridgeback and a Pit Bull terrier. Its owner made no effort to control his dog's aggression and, because of the attack, the boy underwent years of reconstructive surgery on shattered radius and ulna bones. The mother was terrified to leave the house due to her own traumatic stress symptoms. Both mother and son responded to several sessions of BART psychotherapy. After two sessions, the boy's symptoms of PTSD had regressed and he was no longer terrified by the sound of dogs barking. His impact of events scale had reduced from seventy to normal.

Moving on from BART psychotherapy

The next step from insight is to develop wisdom. This occurs when the mind is in a quiet and reflective state. The patient is able to achieve affective regulation of thought at a body and soul level. In this state of Samadhi, conflict is absent and knowledge of love, joy, and wonder abound.

Einstein (1946) said, "The significant problems we face cannot be solved at the same level of awareness that created them" (Calaprice, 2011).

This is an apt metaphor for BART psychotherapy. The initial trauma is experienced at a gut level and this is gradually transcended at a higher level of consciousness. Non-dual awareness leads to a unity of consciousness at an individual level. The truth of what is awakens in the patient's mind. Change occurs as needed as resistance is overcome. The potential for alchemical transformation exists when the patient achieves unity of consciousness. Behaviour based on previous trauma is addressed during this stage of BART psychotherapy and peak performance and various types of future templates are used.

This last stage of BART psychotherapy aims to fully integrate the functions of the LH and RH. These are somewhat artificially divided in Table 12, as in reality both hemispheres are inextricably linked in structure and function. These functions will be further clarified by the six SOFF stated in the vision statement of the Human Brain Project as it undertakes its work over the next ten years.

Summary of final stage of BART psychotherapy

The final stage of BART psychotherapy brings the capabilities of both hemispheres together to resolve the patient's traumatic events. As

Table 12. Functions of the right and left hemispheres.

Right hemisphere master	Left hemisphere emissary
Noradrenergic neuronal transmission in ventrolateral thalamic nuclei	Dopaminergic neuronal transmission in corpus striatum
Overall, how we come to understand the world	Increased ratio of grey to white matter
Spatial working memory	Verbal working memory
Global	Local
Perceives curves and circles (natural phenomena)	Perceives in straight lines (unnatural mechanistic phenomena)
Coordinator or unique	Categorical
Engagement	Alienation
Processes negative emotions	Processes positive emotions
Incarnation	Abstraction
Monitoring of environment	Production in environment
General	Particular
Episodic retrieval	Episodic encoding
Right prefrontal cortex active	Left prefrontal cortex active
Whole aspect and metaphor	Part aspect and literal
Verification and checking	Semantic processing
Sees things in the round	Cognitive sequential processing style
Processing of faces with a global perspective	Assimilation of information bit by bit into the whole picture
Appreciation of context and function	Linear processing and analysis
Processing of music, body movement, rhythm, and dance	Unidirectional, goal bound, processing
Left hand	*Right hand*
Sinister, awkward, weaker	Dextrous, on God's side, stronger
Associated with mental ill-health	

Table 12 illustrates, each hemisphere is partially insulated from the other from a functional standpoint. Normally, performance is improved by decreasing interhemispheric interference. The stimulation of activity in one hemisphere tends to suppress activity in the other. However, co-operation occurs when there is reprocessing across hemispheres. This is especially important when task complexity increases. Spatial and verbal working memory is then fully engaged.

The corpus callosum has more than two hundred million white matter neurons. These are only partly myelinated and it takes 100–300 milliseconds (ms) for synapses across hemispheres to interconnect. This compares with other brain regions as follows:

	Neuronal recruitment (ms)
Brainstem	40
Cerebellum	120
Limbic system	240
Frontal cortex	500

This is the time it takes the initial stimulus to reach a point of conscious awareness where we are capable of thought. The advantage of BART psychotherapy and peak performance is that continuous bilateral stimulation during the therapeutic session can enable the patient to access more efficient interhemispheric communication. It is widely recognised that during our waking moments ninety-five per cent of our behaviour and thought patterns emanate from the unconscious. Only five per cent of our behavioural patterns are under conscious control (Leonard, 2012). BART psychotherapy aims to help the patient or client recover from their emotional "stuck points" related to their traumas. They can then live in harmony with the environment rather than constantly react to it as if the trauma was still present.

The RH experiences the body through its spiritual and emotional resonance and aesthetic appreciation of the environment. Medicine is at its most effective when addressing these issues. Patients undergoing BART psychotherapy and peak performance have the opportunity to restore these aspects of their life. The emphasis on the senses of smell, touch, taste, vision, hearing, balance, and proprioception enables patients to reconnect cerebrally with the specific somatosensory aspects of their traumatic events. The bilateral cerebellar stimulation that is integral and unique to BART psychotherapy helps to connect thoughts, emotions, and embodied experiences of both hemispheres with the brainstem, motor, and sensory tracts supplying the limbs, skin surface, and deeper feelings and sensations registered at a visceral level. During reprocessing of the patient's trauma, she is asked to activate the associated gut reaction or instinct. Typically, this is felt in the region of the solar plexus before transferring to the chest and heart area. These heartfelt sensations and feelings usually relate to unresolved grief and loss, and enough time is taken to resolve any distress located here. During BART psychotherapy, I have addressed concepts associated with eastern medicine by focusing on energy levels within the body.

Typically, the seven chakras are located at points of maximal activity of the immune, nervous, and endocrine systems. Each chakra resonates at a specific frequency. This increases as we ascend towards the higher levels of consciousness. Frequently, the patient will have become overwhelmed by their trauma at an energetic level. Depending on the frequency of this emotion, it is likely to manifest as a blockage at any of the first five chakras. The flexibility of the process of BART psychotherapy and peak performance encourages the therapist to locate this blockage though a process of patient observation and feedback to determine the location of affective dysregulation. This affect is then activated using bilateral stimulation (preferably with tactile units) until the reprocessing has been transformed. The blocked information can then travel along pre-existing neural pathways. Invariably, patients report a lump in their throat. This indicates a block to information processing at the level of the thyroid gland, or throat chakra. Patients are relieved when this distressing sensation dissipates.

The information superhighway comes to the intersection, or sensory gateway, of the thalamus. The thalamus takes stock of the information and, if resonating at the correct frequency, allows this information to pass through to the cortex. If the patient is in a dysregulated state of arousal (RAPIDS or FROZEN), then the thalamic gateway is closed and the patient is only capable of reflex instinctive responses. The BOKA machine uniquely has the capacity to apply the optimum thalamic frequency of 40 Hertz bilaterally. This, theoretically, allows the activation of thalamocortical pathways and cerebellar frontal pathways. These are facilitated by the patient's corpus callosum. This integrates the information with that of the Master (RH) and his Emissary (LH). The patient is in an ideal place to make meaning and learn from her reprocessed experiences. By the fifth or final stage of BART psychotherapy, the patient is:

feeling *B*etter,
physically *A*ctive,
on the road to *R*ecovery.
able to have a sense of *T*riumph.

Philosophical aspects of BART psychotherapy

My BART psychotherapy adheres to the principle of dialectic growth espoused by Heraclitus, quoted by McGilchrist (2009, pp. 30–31), "Increscunt animi, virescit volnere virtus. The spirit grows and strength is restored by wounding".

In many ways, this links to the idea that the wounded healer is the best therapist. It also echoes the quote from Rumi mentioned earlier.

The worldview as seen from the perspective of the right hemisphere

The cultures from the east tend to see the world from the perspective of the RH. "Shizen" is the Japanese word for nature and means "of itself". Everything in nature has "kami", or spirit (McGilchrist, 2009, p. 453). All aspects of the biosphere are connected and can communicate with each other. Like Heraclitus's river, it is constantly changing but always itself (McGilchrist, 2009, pp. 30–31). In the modern western world, the predominant perspective is that of the LH. Currently, the global perspective of the RH from the east is starting to predominate, with the rise of Brazil, India, China, East Asia and Japan. In the west, we must not usurp the role of the RH, so that once again it can become our master and the LH its emissary. BART psychotherapy and peak performance seeks to draw together the mystery of life from the complementary perspectives of east and west. Awareness of non-duality, oneness, and integration of the information from the gut, heart, and head sets us on a path that is free from suffering.

In my experience, BART psychotherapy can help to reduce the patient's pain, conflicts, or crises to enable a deeper connection to be made to the awareness of unity. The patient and client's body and mind are brought into balance and stability. BART psychotherapy can help the patient achieve the combination of non-dual awareness and freedom from suffering.

In theomorphic steps down, several stages are involved.

1. Prakritti, universal creative energy, steps down into our personal vision.
2. Ether steps down, bringing mental impulses into the physical body.
3. Air involves the attachments and aversions at the heart of our movement.
4. Fire, our personal power directs energy into the world.
5. Water, we give birth to our self-expression.
6. Earth involves completion of the process and release of stored energy.

The ouroboros is represented by two snakes coiled around a central staff. This is the universal symbol known as the caduceus. It comes from the Ancient Greeks, whose physician, Aesclepius, used this to cure disease. It has always been associated with healing. The universal creative energy (Prakritti) steps down theomorphically into the personal vision of the patient or client. Through the ether, mental images step down into the physical body. Through breathing (air), the heart displays our loves and hates (attachments and aversions). Through generating warmth via the fire element, our personal power directs energy out into the world around us. Through the seventy per cent of our body that is water, we give birth to our self-expression. Finally, by connecting to the earth with our feet, we complete the cycle and release any trapped energy. This illustration uses some of the same components of my seven-element relaxation exercise. The order is reversed and this can be facilitated with the patient or client at the end of therapy.

By now, ideally, the chakras will be fully energised. It is clear that the heart chakra gives off the most radiant energy. The electromagnetic, auric, and nervous system fields can reach all other chakra energy points to ensure maximal communication at all micro and macro levels for our patients and clients.

In BART psychotherapy, a key goal is to integrate the western ideas epitomised by the psychologist Maslow (1943) with eastern ideas of energies radiating from key chakra energy points. For me, this resonates historically with the philosophy of the Greek *iatric* at the Delphic Oracle. Indeed, this is the origin of psychiatry (*iatros* and *psyche*). It comes from the Greek meaning, "healing of the soul". My goal is to reacquaint psychiatrists with the origins of their chosen discipline in the work of Heraclitus and Aesclepius, who first used the caduceus for healing. The original rod of Aesclepius had one serpent coiled around a staff. This originated from the following myth.

Aesclepius was the God of medicine and he noticed a serpent was badly injured. Another serpent came along and administered healing herbs, saving the wounded serpent. I like the symbol of the eagle's wings as part of the caduceus on the cover of this book. The coiled serpents can represent the energy of the *kundalini*, which, when activated, opens up the third eye chakra associated with the pineal gland and wisdom. The significance of the pineal gland is represented by the pinecone sculpture outside the Vatican (Figure 26, p. 47).

This highlights how the chakras coincide with key endocrine structures in the body and suggests that the eastern mystics had a sophisticated knowledge of how the immune, nervous, and endocrine systems interacted. They perceived health in terms of the different coloured light frequency emanating from the chakra energy systems.

In western thought, science tended to explore the cells microscopically, as illustrated by what follows.

Hypothalamic–pituitary–adrenocortical (HPA) axis. The hypothalamus secretes corticotrophic releasing hormone, which induces the pituitary to secrete the adrenocorticotropic hormone, which induces the adrenal cortex to secrete cortisol, which feeds back and regulates activity in the hypothalamus and pituitary. Cortisol also circulates systemically. I have shown earlier how activation of the endocrine glands along the HPA axis mimics closely the energy points associated with the chakras. This shows how western and eastern ideas are becoming harmonised.

Brain–immune system interactions. The brain regulates the immune system through the autonomic and neuroendocrine systems. The sympathetic innervation of the adrenal medulla secretes epinephrine, and there is both sympathetic and parasympathetic innervation of lymph nodes from synaptic connections in the hypothalamus. Glucocorticoids from the adrenal gland act on innate and adaptive immune cells. Neural connections exist between the hypothalamus, brainstem nuclei, and autonomic ganglia. Neuroendocrine influences that alter immune function and that emanate from the hypothalamus consist of the hypothalamic pituitary axis, prolactin, and growth hormone, which, together with epinephrine, influence innate and adaptive immune cells that secrete cytokines. In addition to autonomic feedback, several different types of cytokines and interleukins feed back to multiple sites in the head-brain. From here, adrenocorticotrophic hormone is released to act on the adrenal medulla. Prolactin and growth hormone are released into peripheral blood.

The interaction of immune, endocrine, and nervous systems is a key discovery of western medicine. I have also shown how these interactions are compatible with the eastern traditions and beliefs in terms of chakra energy systems. BART psychotherapy capitalises on this architecture to get the best result for both patient and client and is the only therapeutic approach to combine the best in western and eastern medicine.

The activation of the body's immune system has been equated to the triumph of the human spirit in that it protects us from antigens and has our highest good at heart. These principles are consistent with BART psychotherapy.

Summary

Life in a world according to the perspective of the left hemisphere starts this chapter, with the implications outlined. This does not happen due to the existence of the corpus callosum, which shares information between hemispheres. The five stages of Bilateral Affective Reprocessing of Thoughts are explained. Each stage is explained in images and then words. This appeals to the strengths of the right and left hemispheres, respectively. The aim is for therapist, patient, and client to have a coherent overall view of the process, which will enhance their therapeutic gain. A key reason for the success of BART psychotherapy and peak performance is that, to the best of my knowledge, it is fully informed by affective neuroscience and neuroanatomy, especially given the fact that ninety per cent of neural information is homolateral up to the brainstem before it becomes ipsilateral and crosses to the opposite cortical hemisphere. This flow of information is enhanced using figure of eight and ouroboros symbols. The functions of the hemispheres are tabulated to provide a focus to boost areas of perceived weakness and augment areas of strength. Philosophical aspects are mentioned with discussion of the ancient symbol of healing the caduceus. By now, the chakras are shown as fully energised and linked to optimised endocrine functioning. The newest research into the links with the HPA axis and the brain–immune axis are briefly discussed.

CHAPTER TWELVE

Using BART for peak performance in sport, business, academia, and any pursuit where anticipatory anxiety impairs results

How to become an expert in your chosen discipline

According to Ericsson and Lehmann (1996) at Florida State University in Tallahassee, it normally takes 10,000 hours of practice to become an expert in any discipline. The skill-hungry years, from the perspective of neurological development, are from age eight to twelve. Thus, starting at age eight in your chosen discipline, one would require three hours of practice daily for fifty weeks per year until age eighteen. In Russia, China, and other Eastern Bloc countries, children as young as four are often exposed to this level of practice. Theoretically, they would then be at "peak performance" level at age fourteen. However, their adolescent growth spurt and neurological improvements via synaptic pruning are yet to emerge. The long-term consequences for such an athlete could be long-term physical injury and psychological impairment.

Flow is being able to concentrate effortlessly in performing all types of skills appropriate to your chosen discipline, be it chess, football, hockey, or any other sport. Time slows as you concentrate on the activity in hand. Enjoyment in the pursuit is the key to success. There are four essential components to being in a state of flow:

1. Lack of awareness of time. In this state, participants lose all sense of time due to their intense, focused absorption in their chosen task. It is as if watching the clock would become a distraction and impair performance. In my experience, during a session of BART psychotherapy, both the patient and I become jointly focused on achieving our reprocessing goals for the session. Sometimes, the 90–120 minutes are over in an instant. Conscious time appears to slow down as we enter the realm of reactivation and reprocessing of unconscious memories, feelings, emotions, and sensations. These principles would apply equally to an athlete seeking to improve their personal best, or to a team whose form had inexplicably dipped below its best.
2. Autotelicity. This is the conviction that your chosen activity is rewarding for its own sake. Following an intense session of BART psychotherapy, patients will confirm that they feel less burdened with worry. They also report feeling better mentally, emotionally, physically, and even spiritually. I am able to see evidence for these changes in the patient's posture, demeanour, and the different "vibe" emanating from them compared to the start of the session. I would expect a similar uplifting response to occur with anyone seeking to optimise their performance in school, university, the workplace, or in the world of sporting achievement.
3. The "sweet spot". This is the point at which flow "flows", for example, the ability to hit the tennis ball on the part of the racquet where its response is true to the player's intent. Also, when the footballer strikes through the ball so that the imagined trajectory becomes a reality. In my clinical experience of using BART psychotherapy, the narrative reciprocity that develops helps to alleviate the patient's distress. I remain alert and fully focused on the therapeutic process. In contrast, many of my patients report attending countless therapy sessions (e.g., of unmodified CBT) where they end up more frustrated due to the lack of progress in therapy. This might relate to the therapist not being tuned in to the patient. Thus, they are unable to "hit the sweet spot" with the patient and, consequently, there is no "flow" to the session. BART psychotherapy offers a completely new potential in working with athletes across time and distance.
4. Automaticity. This is when the healing within the BART session appears as if it is happening by itself. I believe this happens when

> the patient is able to resonate at a higher vibrational frequency, overcoming past traumas. They can tap into the heightened awareness of the therapist. Both patient and therapist then have the potential to tune into "Source", "All There Is", or "Unitary Consciousness". This invariably leads towards resolution of the patient's traumas and soul healing, or *psyche iatros* (the forerunner of psychiatry).

All of the above requirements can be achieved with the athlete, student, writer, worker, or sportsperson who wants to improve performance, minimise performance anxiety, enhance creativity, bring dreams to reality, recover fitness after illness, or implement in competitive matches the skills learnt in training.

The set-up to achieve flow is enhanced by my seven-element relaxation exercise. Breathing and heart rate slows down as the client reaches a state of relaxed concentration. Conscious thought takes a back seat as the client focuses on his body. The muscles that are attended to will depend on the client's requirements and the demands of the task. For example, improving hand–eye coordination and visualisation would be a key skill for sports such as golf, hockey, football, all racquet sports, archery, and most track and field events. BART for peak performance uses the same template as BART psychotherapy. The target will be a past performance that triggered anxiety or frustration. It could relate to being dropped from the team or being substituted when the client believed he was performing well. The highly trained client will have no difficulty tapping into her triune-brains, or neural network responses, that is, gut reaction, heartfelt response, and headwork. These will be accompanied by somatic sensations and movement impulses, as described previously. In this relaxed state, the client has an increased production of alpha waves and an initial suppression of activity in the prefrontal cortex as, initially, blood flow follows the flow of attention to the neural networks of the body, especially the enteric and cardiac plexi. It has been my experience, at the end of a BART psychotherapy session, that the patients experience a new feeling of a tingling sensation in this most recently evolved part of the brain. My hypothesis is that, as experiences are resolved at lower energy or chakra levels, then interhemispheric resolution occurs. The pineal gland marks the point of the sixth chakra. This is also where the right and left prefrontal cortices meet. The tingling sensation might reflect new synaptic activity as the patient generates ideas consistent with recovery. The same response would be expected with clients seeking to improve performance.

Wulf and colleagues (2002), kinesiologists at the University of Nevada in Las Vegas, also believe that the best learning occurs when you turn off conscious thought. The external focus of the body allows the client's flow of information to become automatic. Both client and therapist focus on a positive, goal-directed outcome for the session. If both are able to resonate at similar frequencies in terms of their attunement, an augmented and swifter response is possible.

Factors relevant to developing optimal, or peak, performance

In an article discussing the performance of twelve Olympic gold medallists, Fletcher and Sarker (2012) develop a grounded theory of psychological resilience in Olympic champions. Resilience was defined as "a dynamic process encompassing positive adaptation within the context of significant adversity" (Luthar, Chicchetti, & Becker, 2000, p. 544). As such, many factors impede the athletes' performance. These include:

1. Stressors, which were of three types:
   (a) loss of form;
   (b) organisational, for example, related to sports politics;
   (c) personal, for example, related to family circumstances and relationships.

   Exposure to stressors was found to be a prerequisite for future outstanding performance. Many of those interviewed said that without exposure to these stressors, they would not have become Olympic champion.
2. Challenge appraisal.

   The best athletes in the world look on stressors as an opportunity for growth, personal development, and mastery of their technical discipline. They push themselves to train harder than the opposition in the expectation that this will give them the competitive edge.
3. Meta cognition, a term coined by Flavell (1979). It is described as an individual's knowledge of, and control over, their emotions. It is divided into three stages:

(a) metacognitive knowledge;
(b) metacognitive skills;
(c) metacognitive experience.
Five psychological factors were found to exert influence on challenge appraisal and metacognition:
(i) a positive personality;
(ii) motivation;
(iii) confidence;
(iv) focus;
(v) perceived social support.

In this study, peak performance was described as fulfilling their athletic potential, rather than becoming Olympic champion. They have the higher mental faculties to reflect on their own initial reaction to stressors and learn from this experience. The emotional reaction, for example, disappointment in competition, is then used to spur achievement in the next competitive event. This harnessing of affect or emotion, rather than succumbing, is critical to the evaluative stages of BART psychotherapy and peak performance elaborated on throughout this book. I would propose tapping into the three major components of metacognition (knowledge, skills, and experience), using BART psychotherapy and peak performance as a cornerstone in developing psychological resilience in athletes.

Being in the zone: use of BART psychotherapy for peak performance

When you are in the zone, you are barely aware of the world around you. Time seems to slow down as you focus on the task. Being in the zone can help to bring each person in touch with his or her element. Robinson (2009) has discussed this concept in detail in his book, *The Element*.

BART psychotherapy and peak performance can help the client prepare to stay "in the zone". Imaginal re-experiencing of their chosen task while experiencing auditory and tactile bilateral stimulation can lead to future peak performance. Mind and body merge as one with gut instinct, heart feelings, and headwork effortlessly synchronised. The last thirty minutes of the session are a chance for reflection and reason to emerge. The neural networks associated with new learning are laid down. These can be put into practice at the next training session. Then recalibration and feedback from training can occur at the next BART peak performance appointment. A key element of BART psychotherapy and peak performance is achieved by allowing the somatic sensations to synapse with the central nervous system (CNS). This is then reconnected with the peripheral nervous system (PNS), initially by rhythmically tapping first one foot and then the other. This allows a figure of eight wave impulse to be generated from head to foot. Latest research suggests that when this wave resonates throughout the body, a climate of joy, wonder, and love occurs, as the client's own DNA is stimulated maximally and the potential for replication of new codon combinations by messenger RNA exists. The opposite happens when the client is describing or experiencing a climate of fear and cell growth shuts down.

The client feels that they are in the zone when a sense of authenticity and freedom emerges in the session. Their neural networks or synapses are freed to connect in novel patterns optimal for peak performance in their chosen discipline. Each client, when they have resolved past failures or difficulties with BART psychotherapy and peak performance, has the potential to achieve a higher plane of achievement. This might involve accessing an energy field normally out of reach. They can be assisted to be in harmonic convergence with this meta state. Usain Bolt provides an example of tapping into higher energy fields as he uses his signature thunderbolt pose to assert his conviction that he is the fastest man on the planet and "a bolt from the blue" (Figure 48).

During the night, the individual goes through stages of non-REM and REM sleep with associated brainwave activity. In the awake state, the client produces beta and alpha waves. Non-REM (stage 1) or light sleep produces irregular, shallow waves. Stage 2 has bursts of rhythmic brain activity characterised by sleep spindles and K complexes. Stage 3 produces regular deep brainwave activity and stage 4 has delta waves. REM activity comes next and is present for increasing periods during the night in ninety-minute cycles. Each individual BART psychotherapy and peak performance session is designed to mimic the ninety-minute sleep–wake cycle of circadian and ultradian rhythms to get the maximum benefit from reprocessing therapy. It is essential that athletes travelling to competitions across time zones

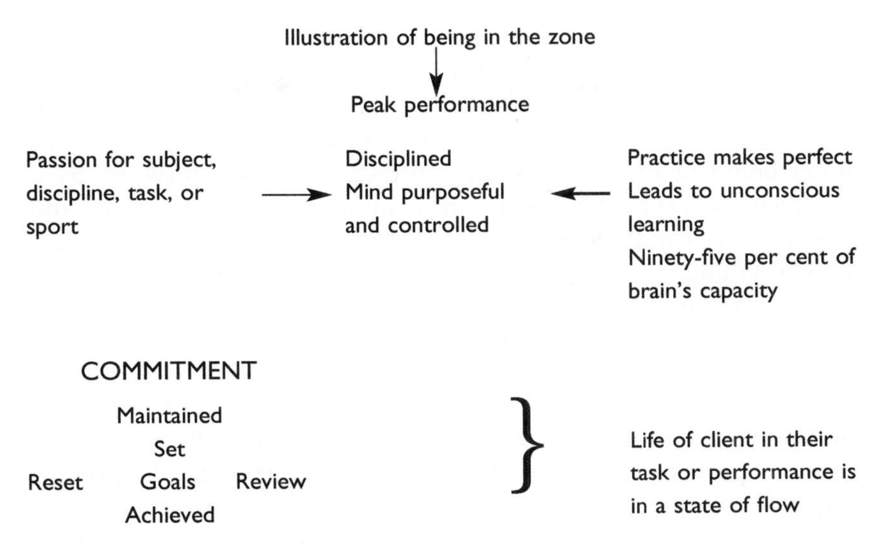

Figure 48. Illustration of being in the zone.

optimise their sleep–wake cycle without resorting to hypnotics. This can be achieved using education on the above cycle and BART psychotherapeutic peak performance. Recently, a poor performance by the England football team was attributed to the widespread use of hypnotics as the players wanted to sleep after travelling across several time zones by plane.

When the patient or client is unable to produce a normal sleep cycle with regular periods of REM, this is an early warning sign of unprocessed traumatic stress and often is a precursor to mental ill health or burnout.

Applying BART psychotherapy and peak performance for athletics, sports, business, stage performers, artists, and anyone keen to achieve their goals

According to Waters (2013), in his spiritual dynamics newsletter, life can get easier. He suggests that instead of working hard to complete a project, it all just flows together in one easy-moving path towards perfect completion. This is the promise of the eastern philosophy of Wu Wei. This promotes the idea of doing without doing, or action without effort. Patients or clients can experience a state of flow that enables them to move through the task with ease, grace, and efficiency. The message of Wu Wei is to develop deeper states of inner awareness. In a state of flow, the action is guided from within and the inner being of the client is fully attuned with the universe. Synchronicity and coincidences become commonplace. People, ideas, and materials appear at the right time and place. There is a time and place for everything to come together for effortless achievement. The realm of being becomes manifest in the world of action.

Western scientific thinking has been applied to the principle of Wu Wei by an American-Hungarian professor, Dr Mihaly Csikszentmihalyi. According to him (1990), goals for clients should be set just outside their current performance range, but realistically matched to future expected performance based on strength conditioning, coaching, assessment of training, and learning from past performances.

Any negative feelings, sensations, emotions, or associations with previous injuries are reprocessed with BART psychotherapy. The flow of information is activated from being stored in the body to the cerebral hemispheres. The client is able to activate the appropriate neural pathways, achieving enjoyment and success. Using guided visualisation, the chosen imaginal exercise stimulates mirror neurones and muscles as if they were performing live and the procedure becomes intrinsically rewarding. When the client or their team are performing well, the state of joyful feedback allows players to access the higher energy levels which helps sustain peak performance. The five stages of BART psychotherapy and peak performance are modified, focusing on the future template. An assessment is always made of recent and previous significant life events. Negatively charged ones are reprocessed to resolution, while positively charged ones are incorporated into the seven-element relaxation exercise.

Examples of a successful sporting team

I believe one of the reasons for the continued success of the New Zealand Rugby Team is their unity in embracing and performing the Haka (New Zealand Folksong, 2011). The chants and associated actions of the Haka are outlined in Table 13. The "Ka Mate" Haka generally opens with a set of five preparatory instructions shouted by

Table 13. The Haka. Words and translation reprinted from www.eu.wikipedia.org/wiki/haka.

	"Ka Mate"	
Leader:	*Ringa pakia!*	Slap the hands against the thighs!
	Uma tiraha!	Puff out the chest.
	Turi whatia!	Bend the knees!
	Hope whai ake!	Let the hip follow!
	Waewae takahia kia kino!	Stomp the feet as hard as you can!
Leader:	*Ka mate, ka mate*	I die, I die,
Team:	*Ka ora, Ka ora*	I live, I live
Leader:	*Ka mate, ka mate*	I die, I die,
Team:	*Ka ora Ka ora*	I live, I live,
All:	*Tēnei te tangata pūhuruhuru*	This is the hairy man
	Nāna i tiki mai whakawhiti te rā	. . . who caused the sun to shine again for me
	A Upane! Ka Upane!	Up the ladder, Up the ladder
	Upane Kaupane	Up to the top
	Whiti te rā,	The sun shines!
	Hū!	Rise!

the leader, before the whole team joins in. It has been criticised because its sole purpose is to intimidate the opposition. As an exercise in bilateral stimulation, it causes the blood powerfully to perfuse the blood vessels. The associated language, such as "stomp the feet as hard as you can" mimics the gentler figure of eight stimulation of BART psychotherapy and peak performance. I would propose that my multi-user machine could replace the Haka in the dressing room for teams preparing to go out to the field of play.

This shows schematically the postures and movements of the players during the Haka. From observing the *in vivo* performance, you notice the ferocity and energy, drive, and passion shown by native Maori and white New Zealander alike. They are prepared to lay down their lives for their teammates. However, the goal of rising up to the top, where the sun shines, is articulated.

Anyone watching the All Blacks will notice the ferocity of the Haka, which is designed to strike terror into the hearts of their opponents. The lyrics suggest activation of the chakras from stamping their feet, slapping their thighs, and inflating their chests to climbing up to the top of the ladder where the sun shines as they rise and emerge victorious. This evolved as a thank you from a Maori chief. He hid in a food storage hole and when he eventually climbed out, a friendly chief met him. This Maori tradition has been adopted by New Zealand and used with success for more than 100 years. This was spectacularly demonstrated during 2013. The All Blacks won all fourteen games they played during that year. They were the first rugby team to achieve this during the professional era.

European Champions League football 2012–2013

Another example of peak performance is the triumph of football artisans Chelsea against the artists of European football in the Champions League semi-final of 2012. Barcelona were 2–0 up before half-time and coasting when Chelsea scored just before half-time. Chelsea gained self-belief and pressure started to mount on Barcelona. When their talisman Lionel Messi twice hit the woodwork, it appeared as if fate had decreed they would lose. Barcelona continued to exhibit their elegant style of play, but this was not sufficient to breach the determined Chelsea defence, which grew in confidence in the second half. In the end, Chelsea progressed against all the odds to the Champions League final by beating Barcelona 3–2. Barcelona were caught off guard and were no longer in their "element", or in control of events on the pitch. Perhaps if the team had imagined a scenario where Chelsea could win using BOKA and BART psychotherapy and peak performance, they could have changed tactics. Instead, they stuck to their tactics of slick passing with movement off the ball and lost.

Further examples from the world of Champions League football include the battle between Real Madrid and Manchester United. The latter have won three Champions League trophies while Real Madrid are chasing *la Decima,* their tenth victory. They were managed by two of the most successful managers of their generation in José Mourinho, then aged fifty, and Alex Ferguson, then seventy-one. The score from the first leg was 1–1, with all to play for in the second leg. With both teams evenly matched on the pitch, the key was in the psychological preparation of the players and the mind games of the managers via the enthralled media and public. In the end, Real won 2–1, with their star Christiano Ronaldo scoring in the sixty-ninth minute. He described the match as "an emotional night" for him. The key difference might have been his drive, desire to win, and ability to keep his emotions in check. He was able to keep his cool and prevent the red mist from descending to impair his razor-sharp performance.

The individual and team peak performance, from the neurological and mind–body standpoint outlined in BART psychotherapy and peak performance, could possibly give that team the cutting edge necessary to progress to the next round. It is interesting that Alex Ferguson has announced his retirement and his replacement is fifty-year-old David Moyes, the Everton manager. Whether he has the capacity to repeat Alex's success will be closely watched. He has been given a six-year contract, in recognition by the board that success is unlikely to be immediate.

Meanwhile, José Mourinho returned to manage Chelsea in September 2013. In a recent Champions League match against Romanian champions Steaua Bucharest, Chelsea demolished them 4–0 away from home. Commentators reported how Mourinho had infused his intense desire and passion to win to each player. From the prodigal return of Juan Mata to the tireless running of Ramires, to the enterprise of the German Schurrle, there were heroic performances across the team. Mourinho embraced Schurrle for his assistance in facilitating the third Chelsea goal. This shows how Mourinho has adopted the peak performance principles espoused in this book. He said:

> I put the players under a lot of pressure for this game and they coped well. They used that as a motivation. I don't want to play in the Europa league, but I also thought that was a way they can grow up faster, faced with that pressure. (Fifield, 2013)

With his own affective expression and movement stimulation, which is often bilateral, involving both arms, he engages in reprocessing his own thoughts. These feelings are then effectively communicated to his players. The similarities to BART psychotherapy and peak performance are evident.

This was recently highlighted in a Premier League match where Mourinho protested vigorously that the opposing team were time wasting. He was banished to the stands and had to celebrate Chelsea's victory alongside the spectators.

His passion for Chelsea was evident by his bilateral gesticulations, which no doubt helped him to process his obvious anger. He was charged with misconduct by the Football Association and decided to refrain from commenting on the incident until he heard from the referee why he "was prevented from doing his work". This episode had no adverse impact on the team and on Tuesday 22 October 2013, Murinho's team beat Schalke 3–0 away from home, with Fernando Torres scoring twice on his one hundredth appearance for the club.

Getting accurate feedback from your past performance to improve future ones

Figure 49 shows how to gain accurate feedback from your performance so that the prediction of performance in the future will become more accurate.

Another example from the world of football is Louis Suarez, who plays for Liverpool. In the past, he has been given a ten-match ban for biting an opponent. Although he said he was sorry, he was known to have bitten an opponent before. He also received a seven-match ban for racially abusing Patrice Evra. This suggests that his default mode

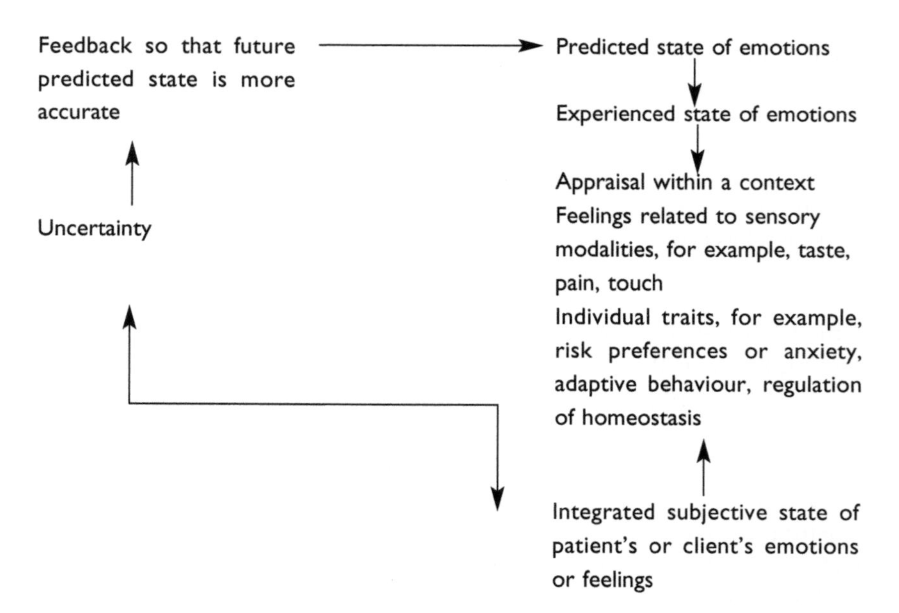

Figure 49. Plan to get optimal feedback from your performance.

network (DMN) is stuck at a pre-juvenile level. When his body and mind perceive threat, he communicates either like a baby or toddler, who often bites due to frustration, or calling someone names, as would happen in a playground where there is bullying. Suarez's obvious talent on the pitch is sabotaged by these outbursts. I would suggest three sessions of BART psychotherapy and peak performance would heal his traumatised DMN and allow him to manage any anger outbursts when they occur. To quote Dr Steve Peters, he would learn to box in the frustrations and talk to the angry, primitive part of his mind that is looking for instant gratification.

The five stages of BART psychotherapy for peak performance

The process of moving towards peak performance following on from BART psychotherapy can be broken down into five PARTS.

Part one: P*ractice* A*ctivity* R*eview* T*ransition*

The key goal of part one is to make the transition from the reprocessed thoughts developed from the five stages of BART psychotherapy. Depending on the client's state, it may be possible to omit some or all of these stages. However, I would advise cataloguing any significant life events, as they may hijack performance at a later stage.

As stated by Robinson (2009) and Sayed (2011), it will take 10,000 hours of practice to get one's neurons firing in a repeated pattern which can be replicated at will to achieve the pinnacle in the client's chosen sport performance or activity. The person is beginning the journey from conscious learning, involving the prefrontal cortex, to eventual unconscious learning, involving the deeper structures of the brain such as the cerebellum and cingulate cortex. The corpus callosum is essential for interhemispheric learning, and the bilateral stimulation described in BART psychotherapy has a role to play in facilitating this process. The client is encouraged to review the achievements from the hours of practice in their chosen activity.

The role of deliberate practice in acquisition of expert performance was originally studied by Ericsson, Krampe, and Tesch-Röma (1993, p. 363). They said,

> The theoretical framework presented in this article explains expert performance as the end result of an individual's prolonged efforts to improve performance while negotiating motivational and external constraints. In most domains of expertise, individuals begin in their childhood a regimen of effortful activities (deliberate practice) designed to optimize improvement. Individual differences even among elite performers are closely related to the assessed amounts of deliberate practice. Many characteristics once believed to reflect innate talent are actually the result of intense practice extended for a minimum of 10 years.

Practising for twenty hours per week for fifty weeks per year over a ten-year period equates to 10,000 hours. This is the figure quoted in Gladwell (2008) and Colvin (2008, pp. 39–42) and is known as the 10,000 hour rule.

Following the years of practice, the client has created a neural network, or pathway, which allows them to make the transition to improve performance in the actual event, competition, examination, presentation, or other chosen task.

Part two: Planning for Action and Revved-up for the Trials

The key goal of part two is to become absorbed in the chosen task or activity. This allows the client to adapt so that they lose track of time when fully engaged in the performance. The action plan, or planning for action, is also crucial, as this demands complete concentration. This state of absorption is a prerequisite to reaching a state of "flow". This is defined as that feeling of effortless concentration common to those giving outstanding performances in different areas of skills and techniques. Working with the client by accumulating data from research on the relevant performances of others, that is, competitors in the chosen field or expertise, allows for gearing or revving up for the trials. This is a very important stage where difficulties can be worked on, adjustments made, and any doubts or niggles ironed out. This sets the framework for the next parts of the process. Bilateral cerebellar stimulation during BART peak performance facilitates interhemispheric learning and optimisation of the functions of right and left hemispheres.

Part three: P*hysic-al* A*utotelicity nerve* R*eflexes and* T*oned muscles*

The key goal of part three is to harness the previous psychological advantages with the physic-al emphasis. The word physic comes from the Greek, meaning the nature of healing, and, when combined with the suffix -al, incorporates the strength of the body as well as the mind. This part emphasises speed of thought and action, stamina, and drive to complete the project, a systems approach to integrate gut-, heart-, and head-brains with immunological and endocrine organs. Again, the zappers can be used to provide bilateral stimulation to the key groups of muscles being used by the client. The hockey player will want to hone their hand–eye nerve reflexes. They will also strengthen and increase the flexibility of their leg muscles. We will also work imaginally on set plays and tactics: for example, those associated with the short corner. Staying focused with frequent substitutions during the game is also a key component in preparing for matches. Video analysis can provide useful feedback on past performance.

Autotelicity is defined as the client having the sense that the activity they are involved in is rewarding for its own sake. Through physical exercise, they will have developed the ability to perform with the flexibility of a baby moving all its limbs, but with the added control derived from the desire to achieve.

The final part of this stage involves the neurological reward from knowing your nerves respond reflexively and, consequently, the muscles needed are toned and effective. The final *T* can also represent the need for the client to be aware of tablets and toxins. These take the form of essential vitamins needed for muscle development, and are listed in Table 14.

The recommended daily allowances (RDAs), if exceeded, can be toxic, so knowledge of nutrition is essential for all performers. The world anti-doping agency (WADA) is in a constant battle to stay ahead of those seeking to artificially boost their performance. The athlete's biochemical passport has been introduced to prevent blood doping. Knowledge of the physiological systems outlined in this book will equip all clients to stay abreast of WADA requirements and testing policies.

Part four: P*innacle of* A*utomaticity by* R*ehearsing* T*echniques*

The key goal of part four is to embed the learning already achieved. The client can see the peak of Mount Everest ahead and is preparing

Table 14. List of thirteen essential vitamins with recommended daily allowances, effects of overdose, and original food source.

Vitamin	Chemical name	Recommended daily allowance (RDA)	Overdose symptoms	Food source
A	Retinol Beta carotene	900 μg	Hypervitaminosis A	Orange Yellow fruits
B1	Thiamine	1.2 mg	Drowsiness	Pork Brown rice
B2	Riboflavin	1.3 mg		Dairy products
B3	Niaicin	16 mg	Liver damage	Meat, eggs
B5	Pantothenic acid	5 mg	Diarrhoea	Meat, avocados
B6	Pyridoxine	1.5 mg	Nerve damage	Meat, vegetables
B7	Biotin	30 μg		Egg yolk
B9	Folic acid	400 μg		Bread
B12	Cobalamine	2.4 μg	Rash	Meat
C	Ascorbic acid	90 mg	Diarrhoea	Fruits, vegetables
D	Cholecalciferol	10 μg		Fish, eggs
E	Tocopherols	15 mg	Heart failure	Spinach Liver
K	Quinones	120 μg	Clotting if patient is on Warfarin	

to climb the summit. Essentially, they are marshalling their resources at base camp and getting ready for the challenge to perform on the next day or even within hours.

Automaticity means that the client can reproduce the necessary performance automatically, that is, without thinking. This has been achieved by switching the location of the brain neurons that have been fired and wired together. Learning any new skill requires the processing power of the prefrontal cortex, which acts like an orchestra bringing in the other neuronal networks of the brain according to need. Once these pathways have lit up, the respective associative cortices can forge a direct neural connection, obviating the need for orchestrated input from the prefrontal cortex. Now the activity is harmonious and plays to its own tune and rhythm. The prefrontal cortex takes a back seat. The neurons involved in the ninety-five per cent of unconscious processing take over. This unconscious learning, when reactivated, allows the client to be "in the zone". It has come about by repeatedly rehearsing technique so that nerves and overwhelming emotion are contained. This allows an opportunity to re-explain the RAPIDS, narrow water and FROZEN model of hyper- and hypo-arousal mentioned earlier.

Part five: Performance Actually Reaches Target

The key goal of part five is success in that the client's performance actually reaches the desired target. In order to perform, the client must harness his or her own mind and body architecture. This includes 213 bones, 500 muscles, and seven miles of nerves. By dint of their personal vision, positivity, philosophy, and passion, they can now stand on the podium. They can realise their full potential. BART peak performance via integration of top-down and bottom-up processing with the information transferred between left and right cerebral hemispheres can assist in this process.

Ideally, the performance of the client actually hits the target. During the performance, brain scans have shown that there is decreased activity in the prefrontal cortex. The client remains focused and quiet mentally. Any over-thinking at this stage is likely to interfere with the automaticity of the flow process and impair performance.

Use of BART peak performance in the world of golf

Rory McIlroy was the number one golfer in the world in 2012. He relinquished this accolade when he pulled out of the second round of the Honda Classic when seven over par. He later admitted that he was not in a great place mentally and that he had walked off the course impulsively. Prior attention to the detailed workings of the mind discussed here might have altered that fateful decision. By October 2013, he had slipped to sixth in the world and was without a victory in 2013 until his fortunes changed. This shows how even the most talented of athletes can succumb to external pressures and media expectations. Jack Nicklaus, in his textbooks on how to play golf, described how he would imagine the trajectory of the golf ball prior to addressing the ball. He attributes much of his success to this disarmingly simple technique. By using his imagination, his mirror neurons were firing and, therefore, his unconsciously learnt nerve reflexes associated with each golf swing could be activated on demand. He had found a perfect way to counteract what golfers call the "yips". This is the loss of fine motor skills associated with any sport and is termed focal dystonia. It has ruined many golfers' careers. Recently, there have been reports in the literature of it being cured by emotional freedom technique (EFT). Given that this approach is designed to activate the body's meridians, I believe that BART psychotherapy and peak performance can also effect a cure.

Normally, there is a surge of alpha waves produced just before the golf shot, the arrow release, or when about to deliver a speech or presentation. This allows the client to focus attention on the target. Other sensory inputs can be suppressed, such as the throbbing pain of a toothache. It is as if time stands still at that precise moment. Indeed, one of Rory McIlroy's explanations for his dip in form was a toothache.

When about to start the race, match, or presentation, the athlete or client enters a state of relaxed concentration accompanied by physiological changes. These include reduced respiratory rate, pulse rate, and blood pressure. This may be considered to represent the previously undescribed seventh, or hyper-focused, "F" state of the autonomic nervous system. This is "flow", where the client hits the sweet spot and everything flows towards the ultimate target. It is my hypothesis that this can be achieved by working through the five stages of peak performance illustrated above.

It would also be helpful to identify any unresolved traumatic stress in the golfer's life. In Rory McIlroy's case, he was forced to deny on his Twitter account rumours that he was about to separate from his girlfriend, tennis star Caroline Wozniaki, and was involved in legal action over a dispute with his management team. In recent press conferences, he has refused to talk about his private life.

> Rory McIlroy has said "countless hours spent with lawyers this year" have been a "distraction" as he heads into this week's World Tour

Championship in Dubai still seeking his first win of 2013. (BBC Sport Online, 2013)

He said that his head was full of stuff that he should not have to deal with when out on the golf course. It is likely that this thinking forced Rory to engage his orbitofrontal cortex. This would have the effect of inhibiting the state of flow described above. Without access to this unconscious learning, his ability to hit the golf ball on the sweet spot would be affected. Such issues can be treated using the techniques described in BART psychotherapy (Chapters Eight and Ten). A key component of treatment would be access to bilateral stimulation at a frequency of 40–60 Hertz to help clear all the extraneous "stuff" from his head so that he does not have to think about it on the golf course and can focus on each shot during the round. McIlroy concluded by saying: "But it would be nice next year when things hopefully are a bit calmer, if I can look forward to just playing golf" (BBC Sport Online, 2013).

This implies that his current state of hyper-arousal, indicated by the RAPIDS in Figure 23a, will benefit from the calmer waters of the window of affect tolerance and emotional regulation.

By openly stating that the pressures sportsmen and woman were facing in order to succeed, he acknowledged the risk of stress-induced illness affecting their performance. I saw this as cathartic statement acting like a valve releasing the extraneous stuff in his head. As a result, he was able to focus on golf, winning the Australian Open in November, clinching victory with a birdie on the final hole. This was to give him his first victory of 2013. A victory in his first event of the year in Abu Dhabi was prevented by a two-stroke penalty for inadvertently putting his foot over a white line when taking a shot after a relief shot.

McIlroy has regained the number one spot in golf by winning the Open in Hoylake, Liverpool and the WGC Bridgestone event in Ohio in July and August 2014, respectively. This confirms his ability to produce peak performances under pressure. He then displayed his mental maturity by winning his fourth Major, the PGA Championship, or Wanamaker Trophy, 7–10 August. McIlroy said that he "gutted it" down the back nine. This is a good example of his ability to control his gut feelings and instinct, which is the key aim of BART psychotherapy.

Clients and patients can be encouraged to set their own specific goals and objectives. Examples include:

- scoring the winning goal in the match;
- winning the race;
- achieving their personal best performance;
- completing the 5,000 km race for charity;
- completing a university dissertation (with honours);
- success in running a business;
- graduation with first- or second-class honours;
- getting a promotion at work;
- publishing a book, either in print or electronically;
- giving birth successfully and bonding with the newborn baby.
- becoming an airline pilot;
- enjoying family life and the company of their children;
- winning an Olympic gold medal in their chosen sport;
- winning the world championships in their chosen discipline;
- making a successful patent application, which leads to an important invention;
- success in giving a presentation, either in school, university, or work.

Think about what your chosen ambitions would be, and write them down. As the saying goes, the world is your oyster, or, as I like to say, your brains (gut, heart, and head) can become the centre of your universe.

Roy Keane, retired captain of Manchester United Football Club, recently stated that when Darryl Southgate tried to chop him in half, he over-reacted and was sent off. It is in cases like this, when the so-called red mist descends, that volatile players such as Wayne Rooney and, in the past, Eric Cantona would have benefited from being able to instantly control their anger to prevent it turning into aggressive behaviour.

All three players have learnt from their experiences. Roy Keane was appointed as assistant manager to Martin O'Neill for the Republic of Ireland in November 2013. Wayne Rooney is arguably playing the best football of his career under new manager David Moyes. Eric Cantona has forged a career as an actor following his retirement from football.

Zappers

The name I have coined for the tactile units attached to the BOKA machine and used for BART peak performance is the "ZAPPERS". This stands for the

> *Z*one (i.e., being in the zone for optimal performance)
> *A*ctivating
> *P*eak
> *P*erformance,
> *E*xcellent
> *R*esults and
> *S*uccess.

It also implies applying determination and extra vibrational energy to achieve the desired outcome. This can be achieved by applying the principles outlined in the five stages of BART peak performance.

Use of BART peak performance in the world of musical rehearsal: peak performance session for Denis

Background to the BART peak performance session

Saxophonist Denis was preparing for his final year performance, playing jazz. Denis had rehearsed the pieces he would be playing many times. This session is designed to identify any aspects of the performance that might be associated with anxiety, which could impair performance. We used the techniques outlined in this chapter to enhance his performance. The outcome was that Denis sailed through the performance without difficulty and passed with flying colours.

Exploration for any relevant trauma history

Prior to this peak performance session, Denis reprocessed an incident at a bus stop where a drug addict threatened him with a knife and demanded he hand over his mobile phone. Denis processed this memory very well and managed to get his SUDS rating down from eight to zero.

During the complete duration of the reprocessing session Denis received bilateral cerebellar stimulation using headphones placed over each mastoid process, just behind the ear. Then, during reprocessing of the knife incident, the zappers were moved around the body, tracking the areas of maximal dysregulation.

When adhering to the BART peak performance protocol, Denis held the zappers next to his throat until the sensation of using his laryngeal muscles to optimise the blowing of the notes on the saxophone was achieved. This is how the session went.

Art: Just imagine that you are playing or starting and what you are telling me is that you have done the chord changes and chord practices so much that you do not want to have to think about those.

Denis: Yeah.

Art: Imagine that the part of your body that is reacting to . . . and it might be that you . . . so just hold your hands in whichever way they are going to be comfortable. There might even be a way of holding your hands here. [Here, Denis changed his posture.] You are going to be standing?

Denis: I will be standing but . . . yeah . . .

Art: So, just imagine that . . .

Denis: Yeah, I just want some . . . Because if I feel loose playing, I will just, I would feel like I'm like this. Just relaxed.

Art: So, if you just . . . you are feeling like that. Do you get a cue from the band? Do they say: one, two, three, four . . .?

Denis: I will be directing it all, yeah.

Art: Are you using . . . in front of you?

Denis: No, not at all. It's memorised.

Art: Memorised. And do they have music . . .?

Denis: Depends if they've done their job. They are allowed to have music so they don't have to memorise it, but I'd rather if they did, because it looks better.

Art: And in terms of the look of the group, do you need to dress in a certain way?

Denis: Not at jazz . . . well . . . I think we might need to have to have suits on or something but I'll check that. My drummer, I've never seen him in anything like that in my life.

Art: So, just let the music that you will be playing be heard in your head; notice how you are producing the sounds, just test out in your body and in your mind, so look for anything between now and then that needs to be fine-tuned.

Denis: Yeah, intonation probably.

Art: So, think about the intonation and just hear it or sense it or feel it, just get into a position that is comfortable and the body position necessary to work on the intonation.

Denis: That is all here. It is in my face.

Art: So just put it on your face.

Denis: That will be on my cheeks.

Art: Yeah, on your cheeks. Yeah. So, the saxophone is on your cheeks. And what I want you to do now is just get relaxed while you are doing this and this is going to be all memory that your cheeks are going to remember and put the best intonation into practice. So, I want you to feel the intonation and the rhythm and I want you to know if you can balance this intuitively with both parts of your brain. This is where you want to look at what you are doing here. It is the two sides of the experience you will have. I think music is very interesting because it is sort of taps into the functions of both right and left parts of the brain. So, as you think about that, let whatever intonation come to mind. Bring all elements of that music together. A part of it will be non-verbal. A part of it will be a sort of intuition. So, this is all on the right side [of the brain] still.

As I am saying these words, I want you to become aware of what your right hand is feeling. Are you sort of noticing how the emotions of the music and the sensations of your facial expressions are changing? Be aware both of your own and other people's reactions and the images that go with that. Images that maybe will come up as you play your music . . .

We know all about your survival responses [related to the knife incident] but we doubt that they are involved here. What we are particularly linking into are your emotions and your sensory motor reactions and how you visualise the performance.

The left side [of the brain] is very much more analytical, but it takes full part in what the right side produces. It accesses information from the right cerebral hemisphere and breaks those images into linear pieces for analysis. It looks for the perceptions and the rationale behind things. So, I imagine, for you it is always going to be one step ahead of what the right brain is producing, the left brain is always going to be thinking about the next note or musical phrase; there is that constant interaction.

And you know that the left brain is something that brings the divergent holistic right brain back down to the reality of the left-brain narrative. But, for the normal language functions of the left brain, you can substitute music as well. So, a link exists between the sensory information that you are feeling and that the rhythm is bringing to your experience with the language, which is the music that is linked to intonation.

I want you again to get the idea as you are sort of seeing your brain in front of you and know the sort of impact you will have by drawing on all of the years of experience just for this forty minutes of jazz performance. All of that intuitive information is brought to bear without effort because it is through the lack of effort that the unconscious learning can be effectively utilised. This is 95% of the brain's capacity for unconscious processing, while only 5% relates to conscious learning.

Denis: Yeah.

Art: Be aware of the continuous bilateral cerebellar stimulation as it helps the information to be shared between cerebral hemispheres.

Denis: Yeah, I think . . . I think my subconscious would . . . Because I don't see it . . . I wouldn't see it as left and right . . . but I'm kind of getting it now because when I'm improvising, I'll be thinking, when I'm thinking of the changes or when I'm not listening. When I am thinking rather than listening and then you'll be thinking, thinking, thinking . . . and then you'll realise yourself: I'm not listening.

Art: Just what you did right then was very interesting. When you touched your left ear with your left hand—just do this again. [This is an example of a somatic experiment.] What does it tell you when you do that? As you are thinking, is it coming together? As that is the left side, when you are saying that you are linking into that side of your brain in a way.

Denis: Yeah, that is probably subconscious. Yeah.

Art: Yeah, exactly! So it's just, again, part of it. So that's really useful information and the two sides of the brain are related. They are separated by a physical structure also. I mean it is not . . . the way I see it, it's just that as emotions are felt by the heart, this can stop language being generated by the left side of the brain. [When the window of affect tolerance and emotional regulation are exceeded.]

Denis: Yeah, because I will start thinking: "right, I need to listen", then I will start listening, and then I will be subconscious. I am probably . . . it might sound the same to someone else but . . . in some way it is different for me.

Art: What I want you to tell me, if you can, is what that felt like when you are sort of holding the intuition [in mind] and just noticing it, just following the intonation. Then you will fine-tune that intonation and we want it to be tuned to the right level. You want it to be there for just that forty minutes, so it is always a work in progress.

Denis: Yeah.

Art: But as of now, where is it going to and where does it need to go?

Denis: I just need to be able to do the performance without thinking. I just need my sax to start here and here. [Denis demonstrates his ideal position for the saxophone.]

Art: Hold it there . . . just hold one buzzer [zapper] there . . . and link it to where the next one needs to go in the other hand.

Denis: Yeah. It needs to be here. [Denis holds the zappers in the ideal position in each hand.]

Art: So, what I want you to do is imagine that the sax is now linking your body and linking your throat and the blower with the stomach, which is the sort of gut reaction or gut feeling, and just get a sense of how you can imagine the connections, the vocal connections, the music connections, the musical connections, the instrument connections, link those parts of your body. Some people visualise it like a waterfall or river connecting up all the synaptic nerve connections.

Just see what makes sense with you and also that it helps to make those elements of the music come together as you desire it for your sax performance.

Denis: I like to think about it as a didgeridoo, because when you blow it is not just [sound for blowing]. You have to make a sound in your throat. You have to visualise the sound in your throat. So, if you want to hit a high E, you have to [Denis makes high-pitched sound with his throat], like your throat goes like that when you sing a high E, so your throat has to be closed or you will not be singing it. But, if you are doing a low one, it's like I need to widen my windpipe.

Art: So, if you just imagine that you are widening your windpipe and just allow the air, the muscles, and the cricoid cartilage in the throat to produce the right sounds. It's very much like what is coming to mind as you imagine playing your instruments.

So, imagine that your windpipe is equally under that level of control and that you are able to create that didgeridoo sound.

Denis: Yeah . . .

Art: How does that feel? [Sensation locations reported by Denis have zappers applied bilaterally and are moved in accordance with the reported changes in sensation.]

Denis: It makes me want to pick up my sax, to be fair.

Art: I've just noticed that it gives you the pleasure of playing the sax as I can see a smile on your face. Notice where that pleasure is and the feeling, as I want you to get in touch with that feeling.

So just follow that through and see that the music is being formed the way you want it to be.

Denis: I can see my drummer smashing away. [Denis laughs.]

Art: And is the drummer in front or behind?

Denis: No, he will be behind me, but he is the best drummer I have played with.

Art: So, just hold that in mind. So, it's a bit like there is a team behind you.

Denis: Yeah, it was just like I'm bouncing off him . . . because I do when I'm playing. I feed off him like mad.

Art: So, feed off him. So, imagine you are feeding off him and his music is actually coming into your ears, as he is behind you, so it's coming directly to your ears.

Denis: Yeah . . .

Art: And notice the continuing bilateral cerebellar stimulation as a background rhythm as I turn up the frequency to maximum so that you can integrate this experience.

Denis: Because I'm at the front, it's like, I'm only playing the sax but it's like, now, it's like I'm base guitar, drums, piano . . . it's all coming into the same direction and I'll probably be loudest of all.

Art: Just stay in that moment and bring the other members of the band in as much as they are in, but you are basically the leader of the orchestra and chief executor here, basically the one that brings all the elements together and puts them into play, so you can imagine the orchestra components . . . bringing . . . players through jazz. Feel yourself getting into the rhythm of the stage performance. That said, imagine that you are halfway through the performance.

And know that you can do this and it's just the matter of how you can conserve your reserves of energy for the rest of the performance.

If you need to, see the audience supporting you.

This is a good opportunity to look out for anything that could potentially crop up, for example, an alarm, a mobile phone ringing, or even a door slamming. You will stay in the zone and nothing will have an adverse impact on your playing.

Just notice you are ready for any eventuality and then just follow it through. Take a couple of minutes with zappers in hand to play through the remaining numbers in your set.

Denis: Yeah, I was just thinking of where there is just one bit where it's just me and drum for ages going nuts . . . and because he does so many mad rhythms, like I can't get my head around a lot of them. So, if I lose my four rhythm what will I do? Because, he won't be on the four, he will be somewhere else and no one else will know where he is . . . and then he'll come back . . . like . . . he'll always throw you off and throw you off and throw you off and you'll be like . . . where am I, where am I, where am I? And just as you think you don't know where you are, he'll just come crashing in with a four and it'll be the heaviest groove . . . because he'll build the tension like it'll stretch the time and you'll be like: Oh, what's going on, what's going on? And just as you say it, he'll be helping you to build the tension. But I was just thinking, if I manage to skip a beat on that, he'll always come back in with the . . .

Art: So, is there a word you can have with him beforehand, or a signal you can set up with him to anticipate when he is going to come in with this heaviest groove?

Denis: He is such an intuitive drummer he doesn't need any signal. I tried talking . . .

Art: . . . because I thought the minute you do that you put your hand here so what I can suggest is repeating this movement. [Movement of index finger is referred to as somatic referencing point for Denis.]

And this would get your thinking and intuition tuned in, so between the two you would be in complete harmony with the drummer.

Denis: Yeah, I'll just play . . . if he does throw you, you know that, you might be thrown, even if he throws you for four–eight bars he will always catch you back and it won't just be a little subtle "I'm back here", it'll be the base player as well and they will be on top of it.

Art: Good, good—so play it through and just notice how you want it to end. You are working up to the finale and he's just coming up to your last piece. You are going through it in your mind . . . just fast-forward to the end and notice what feelings, sensations, or thoughts come up.

Denis: Yeah, It will just be pure relief because the last two tunes are bloody tricky so it will be a matter of getting myself in the right place for that last tune or the last two tunes.

Art: So, just get yourself into the right place for those last two tunes and this is where you bring your resources to your aid, so you might think of any other good music teachers that you can imagine or that have helped you in the past. This is where you can imagine any support being there with you on the day. They don't have to be there in reality, they can be there virtually, for example, by video link. Imagine how they can help you over the hurdle of those last two tricky tunes. Notice whatever image comes up. I often get people to imagine their favourite colour of light beaming down on the parts of their body necessary to get the best out of the instrument. This is the light stream exercise and I can talk you through that later.

Denis: Probably my piano teacher or my sax teacher from back home.

Art: Right. OK. So just imagine that they are there with you. Would you like them in the audience or on stage?

Denis: Yeah, it would be nice to have them in the audience.

Art: OK. So just imagine that they are in the audience, OK? And that they are rooting for you. Remember how they nurtured your talent, brought you along and now, thanks to your talent, hard work, and determination, you are performing your jazz routine as they listen in the audience.

We are concentrating on the last two tricky tunes that will bring your set to its grand finale.

Denis: Yeah, no. The end . . . because the last tune it's all . . . it's just . . . it's really off your head . . . it's very "what's going on!" And the last bar is just four straight crotchets, it's just: baa, baa, baa, baa and that's the end. So it will be nice, because it's just me and the drummer, me and the drummer build up for ages and then a whole band will come in with the beat, doh, doh, doh, doh, doh, doh, it's like it's all polyrhythms. So it'll be nice just to get that last bar. Just have a big, simple baa daa daa daa . . . done! That will just be the finale.

Art: Just notice the relief, just get yourself relaxed and feel the nervous energy dissipate as you realise the performance is over. Do a body scan from head to toe and notice any sensations.

Denis: Just like an exhale of relief, which I can feel in my chest. [There is continued reprocessing of chest sensations with zappers.]

Art: So, what did you think of that?

Denis: Yeah, it's good! It's nice because I have visualised this all the time but I would never have gone into it in such detail. I would just be, like, I would lie in bed and I think about it, get nervous and then try to relax.

Art: So what was different about the way we simulated going through the actual performance?

Denis: You know like, you wouldn't notice, but I was singing through the tunes all in my head the whole time. But I haven't even noticed—I know, I think it's just this beep.

Art: And does the beep help focus?

Denis: Because . . . because when I had a steady beep, without even thinking of it, I'd be tapping in my head or I'll be . . .

Art: I could see you tapping out the rhythm with your right and left feet at different times.

Denis: Yeah, and I realise I can, as you're saying, how true that I was feeling as if I was visualising myself playing the solo during that whole time and playing tunes ahead of time. Yeah, that was useful! [Shy giggle.]

Art: So, do you think this could work with your other friends?

Denis: Yeah, I'd love to see it with the band. I'd like to see if you got a similar response to the whole band playing together.

Art: I'd love to try this approach with a band!

Denis: So you could see what everyone else is worried about, because everyone else is going to have different anxieties over different parts.

Art: Exactly, yeah. You could actually bring everyone's performance into harmony.

Denis: The bit I find hard someone else might find easy.

Art: You could have the band set up. My machine would be set up perfectly for the band. It's essentially plugging everyone in at the same time and then you could just let everyone do it in their head and go through it and then see what comes up for each band member.

Denis: Yeah, the thing that I would really like to find out is, could you do brain pictures?

Art: Yeah, yes.

Denis: Can you see what parts of the brain are conscious and subconscious?

Art: Yes, you can certainly see that because this is all conscious here and this entire bit is conscious, OK? [I demonstrate conscious and unconscious processing with my model of the brain.]

Denis: But, can you analyse it as it is happening?

Art: Oh, yes you can. I mean, it's hard because the scans normally have you lying down like that, but as we get better at it there will be better ways to do it and tune into the brain's reprocessing.

Denis: Because I would love to see it, because the amount you internalise during the process we have been through is dramatic.

Art: Yes, it is mostly internalised.

Denis: Because there is stuff that last year I would have really had to think about when I'm playing, whereas now I just say that was the pattern I practised for six months.

Art: But, I'm glad now that we've managed to record this because I think I'd like to get this transcribed and I think it would work fantastically well with musicians. There is so much of it that is in your head, then it gets unconsciously internalised, and then when you start to think about it, it can become blocked from the process.

Denis: Yeah, that is the thing when I was saying, like you have to read this to remind yourself to do stopping and listening. So, I am thinking: 'listen, listen, listen, listen!' Even if you forget the chord changes, you'd be better off not knowing when the chord changes and using your ear instead.

Then knowing them and only thinking about it. Like I reckon, if I just had a groove going, and you just said "jam over that groove, it's the one key you've got you can do what you want in it and, whether it's intense chord changes every two beats and you're like, aaaggrrrh, you're trying to get around them, up and in and out of them and I'm trying to get them smooth in and out and that second last tune it's literally, just chord changes every two beats [copying chord changing by clicking of fingers] that fast! I was like, deh, deh, deh, deh.

So every chord, I have to relate it to a mode. Every two beats [at] that speed I've got to think of a mode and a scale. The second one is going to be different from the first—if I hold a note from that over that one, a lot of the time it will sound horrible. But then, when you actually sit back and listen, you find all the notes that link together and you can make it sound as if it isn't just loads of unconnected notes.

Art: This language is new to me. I had no idea about music language or notation. However, you have now activated your prefrontal cortex and Broca's area in the left cerebral hemisphere. You have reflective capacity for reprocessed thoughts related to your forthcoming performance in line with BART peak performance.

Art: When you are actually doing the recital what is your happening in your mind?

Denis: Hmmm, I see the music. What I mean is, with my eyes open, like, my eyes are open but the music changes are going by my eyes. I can be looking, because I can be playing and stare in someone's eyes and it would not even register with me.

Art: Are you hearing the notes or seeing them?

Denis: Hearing them, and then visualising the musical chart. So, like, if I'm doing that tune, I'll be listening and I'll be seeing the chords go by or I'll be seeing that on a piano. Going round the changes in all their aspects.

I know that is the thing that is different about sax. On piano it's all visual. You can sing me a line and I could just play it on the piano. Whereas if you sang me a line on sax, it would take me a minute to figure it out. Because none of it is visual on the sax, it's all ears and you're like doh, dah, dah, whereas on the piano it's easy to see it.

Art: Taking it back to what we did, what do you think came out of the earlier bit that we need to reprocess? I think this would help as well by not having it interfere with your forthcoming recital.

Denis: Yes, because I have not even talked about this with myself either. [Denis had never previously processed the knife attack.]

Art: What did you learn at the start of the session?

Denis: It was interesting how it involved my throat for that memory [of the knife attack] as well as when I was imagining playing the sax.

Art: So now you can realise that that has naturally healed. [The traumatic memory of the attack by the drug addict has been dealt with.]

Denis: Yes, because if I get a lump in my throat as well I won't just not be able to talk, I won't be able to play the sax either, so I suddenly just can't afford to have this happen.

This shows that, for Denis, reprocessing his memory of the previous knife attack helped him to perfect his blowing techniques essential to get a good sound from the saxophone.

Denis: I remember when I used to play the piano, never in my life had I had sweat in between my fingers but every time before I performed, I would notice, "why am I sweating there?" It's the weirdest place to sweat, nowhere else is sweating, and I'd be here rubbing it on a napkin. Some people had bottles or buckets of ice in which they dipped their hands before they went in. Why does it happen and how does my brain know to start panicking here? You know what I mean?

Art: That is very like the meridian response we were talking about earlier. That part of your finger is probably where the meridians are. They are the ones that relate to these fingers. They are the parts that get over stimulated when you play the sax.

Denis: Because nowhere else was sweating, so you just couldn't ignore it as you may miss some notes.

Art: So how is your whole body feeling now?

Denis: I feel a little bit more relaxed now.

Art: A lot of people tell me that they feel sleepier.

Denis: I kind of want to have a rehearsal now, that's kind of what I feel like. Just want to get back and get them [the band] in a room and start. You know what I mean? Because I kind of want to put all that I have learnt during this session . . .

Art: . . . into practice.

Denis: Because I've been thinking about this so much while we are doing this; the more you think about it the more you want to play.

Art: But I think this [BART peak performance] has never been done before, so I think it will help and have a positive effect. Now that you have practised it in your head, it is as good as a performance.

Summary

This chapter has discussed the role of BART peak performance in helping clients to become expert in their chosen discipline. The key is to simulate being in the zone and can be summarised as lack of time awareness, autotelicity, the sweet spot, and automaticity. Factors relevant in developing optimal or peak performance are stressors, challenge, and meta cognition. There is a flow chart illustrating the concept of being in the zone. The role of normal and aberrant sleep architecture is explained. This can be activated via the imagery of mentally re-performing the chosen activity, for example, in sports such as golf, football, or rugby, and for those in business, on stage, or those in performing arts, where anxiety can impair performance.

Examples from the world of Champions League football are used to explain how BART peak performance could improve results. The concept of being in the zone is illustrated. I have described how BART psychotherapy is applied in achieving peak performance alongside using feedback, so that future predicted states are more accurate. The task of achieving peak performance is broken down into five parts, somewhat analogous to the five stages of BART psychotherapy. Part one focuses on achieving the transition from psychotherapy to peak performance. There is recognition of the 10,000 hours of practice it takes to become world champion in your chosen field. Part two focuses on the enjoyment needed in your chosen pursuit so that your complete absorption means losing track of time. Part three deals with the motivational aspects of peak performance, so that the chosen activity is seen as rewarding for its own sake. Part four implies that the person has reached the state of unconscious learning and is able to rely on the firing of unconscious neurons and muscle fibres. Thus, learning has progressed from cognitive to associative to, finally, automatic. The final part of BART peak performance is when the performance actually hits the chosen target and the cycle can begin again based on the next set of objectives. The problem of "yips" is discussed, with potential solutions, and the reader is encouraged to write down their own objectives. My model of using zappers is explained. The chapter concludes with a transcript of a peak performance session with a jazz saxophonist preparing for a major performance.

CHAPTER THIRTEEN

Template for comprehensive assessment of the patient or client prior to BART psychotherapy or peak performance, and use of the Hermann brain dominance instrument

Comprehensive assessment questionnaire of patient or client in preparation for BART psychotherapy and peak performance

This will take approximately two hours to complete. However, invaluable information will be collected to guide further treatment. It is adapted from the Health of the Nation Outcome Scale for Children and Adolescents designed by Professor Simon and the late Professor Richard Harrington (Gowers, Bailey-Rogers, Shore et al., 2000). I have further modified the diagnostic interview of the child. I have created the section on chronology and stresses, which was absent from the HoNOSCA. The genogram section was designed by Barry Litt and is available on www.BLitt.com. It is reprinted with permission from Barry Litt.

Client: Name ....

Address..

Post (Zip) code......................

Contact details: Tel nos. Home:................................... Mobile:............................

Work:.............................. Email:.. Age:.............

DOB:.........................

Date considered by referral co-ordinator: ....

Date allocated: ....

Care coordinator:......................

Co-therapist:...

Venue:...................................... Referred by:...................................
Name:............................... Address:...

Postcode:..........................Profession:............................... .Email:.....................................

Assessing clinician:..

Notes taken by:...

Present:... Relationship:...

PROBLEM HISTORY
(a) *List presenting complaints in child's/adolescent's own words*
In order of severity
SUDS 0 1 2 3 4 5 6 7 8 9 10
Neutral Bad Worst
Doesn't bother Bothers a bit Bothers a lot
Complete SUDS rating for each presenting complaint

(b) *History of presenting complaints (background to referral)*
Nature of symptoms, onset frequency situations (places times in which symptoms occur), severity, precipitating alleviating factor, impact on life, personal family, friends, school relationship, to current events and mental state
(c) *Parents'/guardians' view of their children/adolescent's problems and details of previous involvement with professional services*

Developmental history

1(a) *Pregnancy: planned, unplanned, feelings (physically, emotionally)*
Complications, drugs, alcohol. What were you doing during pregnancy, e.g., working? How much was baby wanted? Were you ever pregnant before? Why did you want to get pregnant at this stage of your life? When did the pregnancy seem real to you? What were your impressions about the baby during pregnancy (kicks, etc.?).

(*continued*)

What did you sense the baby might be like (gender, temperament, personality)? Reactions to and feelings about the pregnancy and the baby (same or different).

1(b) *Tell me about the labour and delivery.* How did you feel and react at the time? What was your first reaction when you saw (name of baby)? What was your reaction to having a boy/girl? How did your family react (husband, partner, siblings, others)?

1(c) *Were there any problems in the first few days after birth?* How quickly were you discharged from hospital? How did you decide to feed your baby? Why? Breast crawl reflex. This is explained by referring mothers to WHO www.breastcrawl.org. What was the experience of feeding like for you?

1(d) *What was first month at home like (feeding, sleeping, crying).* Sets emotional tone of baby's entrance into the family.

1(e) *Tell me about your baby's developmental milestones: smiling, sitting up, crawling, walking, talking.*
Motor, social, language difference: i.e., ahead or behind? What did you think of your baby's intelligence in first few years?

1(f) *Did your baby have a regular routine?* What happened if this routine was changed?

1(g) *How has...............reacted to being separated from you?* Dates and times if > 1 day in years 0–3. How did..................react? How did you feel and what did you do?

1(h) *How and when did you choose name? How well does this name fit any family naming traditions?*

2. *Does ....get upset often? How do you feel and react? What do you do?*
(a) When he/she became upset what did they do?
When sad, frightened, angry? What did you feel like doing? What did you do?

(b) Tell me when ....was physically hurt, e.g., cuts, scrape, bumps, bleeding? How did you feel? What did you do?

(c) Tell me when...................was ill, e.g., ear infection, cold/flu illnesses, etc. What was this like for you? How did you respond emotionally and behaviourally?

3(a) *Pick 5 adjectives to describe your child's personality.*
(i–v) Word .... Describe a specific incident.

4 Who does .... remind you of and in what ways? How does .... remind you of self and father? How is .... different to mother and father? What are the family characteristics on your side you see in ....'s personality? Other parent's side?

5 What is unique about .... compared to other children you know?

(continued)

6 What is hardest to handle about ....'s behaviour? Give example. How often does this happen?

7 5 words to describe your relationship with .... Describe with incident or memory.

8 What aspect of your relationship with your baby is most pleasing?

9 What would you like to change?

10 How has your relationship with .... affected their personality? Has this relationship changed over time? If so, in what ways? What is your own feeling about that change?

11 Which parent is closest to ....? How can you tell? Has it always been that way?
As .... gets older, do you expect this to change? If so, how?

12 Tell a favourite story about .... What do you like about this story?

13 Any regrets about how you have brought up ....? In hindsight, would you do anything differently?

14 Favourite age so far.

15 Most difficult time looking ahead.

16 What will .... be like as an adolescent? Why? What will be good? And what is bad about this stage of development?

17 What are your hopes and fears as .... becomes an adult?

1. *Problems with disruptive, antisocial or aggressive behaviour (conduct disorder/oppositional defiant disorder)*
Oppositional defiance, lying, stealing, running away, truancy. Oppositional to authority, fire setting, aggressive, delinquency, contact with law, tantrums.

If relevant, take forensic history and proceed to risk

Inappropriate sexualised behaviour   Assessment (e.g., sexual abuse of other children).

Include behaviour associated with any disorder, e.g., hyperkinesis, depression, drugs, alcohol, or autism. Include physical or verbal aggression (e.g., pushing, hitting, vandalism, teasing). If disruptive behaviour is due to overactivity, rate on scale 2 (below). If due to truancy, rate on scale 13. If due to self-harm, rate on scale 3. Circle the appropropriate rating scale.

0 No problems of this kind during the period noted.

1 Minor quarrelling, demanding behaviour, undue irritability, lying, stealing.

2 Mild but definite disruptive or antisocial behaviour, lesser damage to property or aggression or defiant behaviour.

(*continued*)

3 Moderately severe aggressive or antisocial behaviour such as fighting or persistently threatening, very oppositional, or more serious destruction to property, or moderate delinquent acts.

4 Disruptive in almost all activities, or at least one serious physical attack on others, or animals, or serious destruction to property.

2. *Problems with overactivity, attention, or concentration (ADHD)*

Home/school attention span distractibility. Passive, self-imposed and imposed tasks. Impulsivity, inattention. Energy anergia. Motor activity, underactivity, restless, fidgety. Coordination, e.g., feeding, dressing buttons, laces, writing.

Include overactive behaviour associated with any disorder, e.g., hyperkinetic disorder, mania, or due to drug misuse.

0 No problems of this kind during the period noted.

1 Slight overactivity or minor restlessness.

2 Mild but definite overactivity and/or attentional problems, but these can usually be controlled.

3 Moderately severe overactivity and/or attentional problems that are sometimes uncontrollable.

4 Severe overactivity.

3. *Non-accidental self-injury*

Suicidal ideation/attempts. Non-suicidal self-injury, overdose, hanging, drowning. Non-suicidal self-injury such as hitting self, self-cutting. Frequency, severity, type, meaning outcome treatment.

If scratching or picking, due to physical illness or due to SLD or physical disability, or due to drugs or alcohol misuse. Rate on scale 6.

0 No problem of this kind during the period rated.

1 Occasional thoughts about death or self-harm not leading to injury. No self-harm or suicidal thoughts.

2 Non-hazardous self-harm, such as wrist scratching, whether or not associated with suicidal thoughts.

3 Moderately severe suicidal intent (including preparatory acts, e.g., collecting tablets) or moderate non-hazardous self-harm (e.g., small overdose).

4 Serious suicidal attempt (e.g., serious overdose), or serious deliberate self-injury.

3

(*continued*)

4. *Problems with alcohol, substance/solvent misuse*

Smoking amounts, types of alcohol dependence. Physical/psychological norms. Solvent use by other members of the family. Rate aggressive/disruptive behaviour due to drugs and alcohol on scale 1.

Rate physical illness or disability due to drugs and alcohol on scale 6

0 No problems of this kind during the period rated.

1 Minor alcohol or drug use, within age norms.

2 Mildly excessive alcohol or drug use.

3 Moderately severe drug or alcohol problems significantly out of keeping with age norms.

4 Severe drug or alcohol problems leading to dependency or incapacity.

4

5. *Problems with scholastic or language skills*

Hearing, comprehension, reading, spelling, arithmetic, speech or language impairment associated with specific development disorder or hearing impairment. Social response and use of empathy, referral for speech and language therapy.
Include decreased academic performance associated with emotional or behavioural problems.

0 No problems of this kind during the period rated.
1 Minor impairment within the normal range of variation.
2 Mild but definite impairment of clinical significance.
3 Moderately severe problems, below the level expected on the basis of mental age, past performance or physical disability.
4 Severe impairment much below the level expected on the basis of mental age, past performance, or physical disability.

5

6. *Physical illness and disability problems that limit or prevent movement, impair sight or hearing, or interfere with personal functioning*

Health problems: hospitalisation, treatment, physical effects of drugs or alcohol. Fits, convulsions, meningitis. Current medication. Compliance. Side effects. Allergies to drugs, food. Physical complications of psychological disorders, e.g., loss of periods from severe weight loss. Sexual development, puberty, and menarche, include hearing or visual impairment.

Rate somatising disorders on scale 8, i.e., on-organic somatic symptoms.
Include movement disorder, medication side effects, and physical effects from drug/alcohol misuse, self-injury due to severe learning or physical disability or because of self-injury such as head banging.

(*continued*)

0 No incapacity because of physical health problem during the period rated.

1 Slight incapacity because of a health problem during the period (e.g., cold, non-serious fall, etc.).

2 Physical health problem imposes mild but definite functional restriction.

3 Moderate degree of restriction on activity due to physical health problem.

4 Complete or severe incapacity due to physical health problems.

6

7. *Problems associated with hallucination, delusions and abnormal perceptions (mental state examination)*

Delusions, primary or secondary. Derealisation, depersonalisation, dissociation.

Rate disruptive or aggressive behaviour associated with hallucinations or delusions on scale 1. Rate overactive behaviour associated with hallucinations or delusions at scale 2. Hallucinations: visual, auditory, tactile, gustatory, olfactory, bodily sensation, Hypnogogic/hypnopompic, pseudo-hallucinations/illusions. Over-valued ideas such as distorted body image. Include odd and bizarre behaviour associated with hallucinations and delusions.

0 No evidence of abnormal thoughts or perceptions during the period rated,

1 Somewhat odd or eccentric beliefs not in keeping with cultural norms.

2 Abnormal thoughts or perceptions are present (e.g., paranoid ideas, illusions, or body image disturbance) but there is little distress or manifestation in bizarre behaviour, i.e., clinically present but mild.

3 Moderate preoccupation with abnormal thoughts or perceptions or delusions, hallucinations, causing much distress and/or manifested in obviously bizarre behaviour.

4 Mental state and behaviour is seriously and adversely affected by delusions, hallucinations, or abnormal perceptions, with severe impact on child/adolescent or others.

Suspicious or paranoid thoughts, e.g., thought withdrawal, insertion, broadcasting, passivity of affects, impulse. Volition. Somatic passivity, overvalued ideas, e.g., distorted body image, obsessions, compulsions.

7

Cognition: Attention span, digit span, forwards, backwards. Draw a person, write name, days of week. Orientation: time, person, place. Concentration: memory registration, recall at 3 mins. Refer to psychological assessment if available to estimate IQ.

Insight awareness of hallucinations/delusions

Child, parent, others

(*continued*)

8. *Problems with non-organic somatic symptoms*
(Medically unexplained physical symptoms (MUPS)
Include problems with gastrointestinal symptoms, e.g., tummy ache or non-organic vomiting, diarrhoea. Cardiovascular symptoms, e.g., palpitations. Neurological symptoms, e.g., pain, dizziness, headaches. Bladder symptoms, non-organic enuresis. Bowel problems, e.g., encoporesis. Sleep problems, e.g., initial insomnia nightmares, and night terrors. Chronic fatigue syndrome/ME.

Rate movement disorders such as tics and physical illnesses that complicate MUPS on scale 6.

0 No problems of this kind during the period rated.

1 Slight problems only, such as occasional enuresis, minor sleep problems, headaches or stomach aches without organic basis.

2 Mild but definite problem with non-organic somatic symptoms.

3 Moderately severe, symptoms produce a moderate degree of restriction in some activities.

4 Very severe or symptoms persist into most activities. The child is seriously or adversely affected

8

9. *Problems with emotional and related worries*
Emotions: happy, sad, crying, irritable. Disgust, anxiety, fears, anger, phobias. Depression. Obsession ideas, rituals. and ruminations. Compulsions arising from any clinical condition, including eating disorders. Include early morning waking and diurnal mood variation. Mood scale 0–10 (highest mood). Thought content: views of self, world, future.

If aggressive, destructive, or overactive behaviours attributed to fears or phobias, rate at scale 1

Rate only the most severe clinical problem not considered previously.

Rate physical complications of psychological disorders, such as severe weight loss, at scale 6.

0 No evidence of depression, anxieties, fears or phobias during the period rated.

1 Mildly anxious, gloomy, or transient mood changes.

2 A mild but definite emotional symptom is clinically present but is not preoccupying.

3 Moderately severe emotional symptoms, which are preoccupying, intrude into some activities, and are uncontrollable, at least sometimes.

(*continued*)

4 Severe emotional symptoms, which intrude into all activities and are nearly always uncontrollable.

9

10 *Problems with peer relationships*
Friends: frequency of interaction, quality of relationships (close friends). Popularity, ignored, lonely. Assessment of empathy and ability to make friends. Boy/girlfriend. Theory of mind.

Include problems with school friends and social network, active or passive withdrawal from social relationships, over-intrusiveness, and inability to form satisfying peer relationships.

Include social rejection due to aggressive behaviour or bullying.

If peer relationship problems due to bullying or aggressive behaviour, rate on scale 1; if problems with family or siblings, rate on scale 12.

0 No significant problems during the period rated.

1 Either transient or slight problems, occasional social withdrawal.

2 Mild but definite problems in making or sustaining peer relationships. Problems causing distress due to social withdrawal, over-intrusiveness, rejection, or being bullied.

3 Moderate problems due to active or passive withdrawal from social relationships, over-intrusiveness, and/or to relationships that provide little or no comfort or support, e.g., because of being severely bullied.

4 Severe social isolation with no friends due to inability to communicate socially and/or withdrawal from social relationships.

Self-esteem (how you see yourself?)

Temperament (how others see you)
Emotional expression response to new situations and people. Adaptability affections: easy, slow to warm up, difficult.

10

Sensitivities, strengths, interests
Resilience factors

11 Chronology of stresses, traumas, and significant life events (SLEs)
Adverse life events, losses, setbacks, change—why & how? History of trauma (bereavements, abuse, witness to violence, illnesses, accidents). Timeline: from conception 0 (birth) to current age. Add in brief description of key life events.

(continued)

0 No problems during the period rated
1 Minor traumatic events (IES-R</ = 30)
2 Moderate traumatic events (30 IES-R < 45)
3 Severe traumatic events (45 </ = IES-R < 55)
4 Incapacitating complex traumatic events +/– dissociation (55 </ = IES-R < 88)
IES-R = Impact of Events Scale Revised

What is your worst memory? Is this an episodic or semantic memory? What are your 5 best memories of childhood? Are these achievements outlined here for peak performance? How did your mother react on finding out she was pregnant? Pregnancy

Trimesters Weeks of gestation

First 0 13

Second 14 27

Third 28 40

Birth details. Length of labour. Any foetal distress (Type 2 dips in foetal heart rate), APGAR score.

Type of birth: normal, water, forceps, suction.

Medical or surgical intervention (Caesarean section, neonatal intensive care unit hours to days)

Year one

0–12 months

13–23 months

Years

2 ....
3 ....
4 ....
5 ....
6 ....
7 ....
8 ....
9 ....
10 ....
11 ....
12 ....
13 ....
14 ....
15 ....
16 ....

(*continued*)

17 ....
18 ....
19 ....
20 ....
25 ....
30..
35 ....
40 ....
45 ....
50 ....
55 ....
60 ....
65 ....
70 ....
75 ....
80 ....
85 ....
90 ....
100 ....

12 *Problems with self-care and independence*

Feeding: Loss of appetite, dieting, distorted body image, fads, over-eating, weight gain/loss.

Rate the overall level of functioning, e.g., problems with basic activities of self-care, i.e., feeding, washing, dressing, toileting, and complex skills, e.g., managing money, travelling independently, shopping, etc., taking into account the norm for the child's chronological age

Include poor levels of functioning arising from lack of motivation, mood or any other disorder.

Rate lack of opportunities for exercising, intact abilities and skills, e.g., an over-restrictive family on scale 12. If due to enuresis and encoporesis, rate at scale 8

0 No problems during the period rated; good ability to function in all areas.

1 Minor problems only, e.g., untidy, disorganised.

2 Self-care adequate, but definite inability to perform one or more complex skills (see above).

3 Major problems in one or more areas of self-care (eating, washing, dressing) or inability to perform several complex skills.

4 Severe disability in all or nearly all areas of self-care and/or complex skills.

(continued)

13 *Family life and relationships/structure*

Family tree: including names, age, occupation, and health of parents, grandparents. Names, ages of siblings and other important people. Close attachments/patterns of conflict. Relationships with foster parents, social workers/teachers in residential placements. Family history: psychiatric disorder, including parental history of hyperactivity, personality problems, mental handicap, & mental illness if they affect the child. Medical condition, e.g., epilepsy, stroke, diabetes. Reported patterns of interactions with adults and sibs. Family rules, discipline, support, hostility, over-involvement, drugs, alcohol, emotional, verbal, physical, or sexual abuse, marital disharmony. Parenting care and management rules expectations, training, e.g., Webster–Stratton (developmentally appropriate, consistent, effective, flexible). Parental neglect/rejection, over-restriction. Sibling jealousy, abuse by sibling, enmeshment or over-protection. Problems associated with family bereavement, loss and subsequent family reorganisation. Accommodation history, i.e., periods away from home in the care of the local authority and/or relatives.

0 No problems during the period rated.

1 Slight or transient problems.

2 Mild but definite problem, e.g., some episodes of neglect or hostility or enmeshment or over-protection.

3 Moderate problems, e.g., neglect, abuse, hostility. Problems associated with family/carer breakdown or reorganisation.

4 Serious problems with child feeling or being victimised, abused, or seriously neglected by family.

Genogram instructions

Barry Litt, MFT (barrylittmft.com), EMDRIA approved consultant

I. Genogram history-taking questions preparation: use graph paper and begin in the upper left corner.

Questions:

1. Beginning with your mother's mother: what is/was her name? Is she deceased, what was cause of death or age? Ethnicity?

2. What was your mother's father's name? Is he deceased, what was cause of death or age? Ethnicity?

3. Were your mother's parents married to each other? Was either of them ever divorced, separated, remarried, or have children outside the marriage? If so, who, how many, etc.? Draw other partners and any offspring.

4. How many children did your mother's parents have together?

(*continued*)

5. What number was your mother in the birth order? (Draw mother's circle lower than the rank of her sibs, to distinguish her visually from the rest. List her sibs, but identify her sibs and their families (only if it seems useful at the time).

6. In your mother's lifetime, how many times has she been married? How many children did she have? (List all husbands and men with whom she became pregnant.)

7. What is/was your father's name? Note age or year and cause of death?

8. Begin father's family history as with questions above.

9. In your parents' lifetimes, were they ever divorced, separated, remarried, or have children outside the marriage? If so, who, what ages are they now?

10. How many pregnancies did your parents have with each other? Include miscarriages, stillbirths, and/or abortions. (As before, draw the client's circle or square at a lower rank than the sibs to distinguish it.)

11. Who was the first pregnancy? Present age? Are they married? How many times? Have they any children?

12. Continue with each sibling, skipping the client for now. List chronologically left to right.

13. Now begin the client's family, drawing the client on a lower rank than the sibs to distinguish him/her visibly.

14. In your lifetime, how many partners have you lived with, married, or had pregnancies with? (List these chronologically, left to right if possible.)

15. Establish custody and household membership of each child. Document marital or cohabitation partners for each child, and any offspring they may have (i.e., grandchildren).

II. Risk factors preparation: Draw a 5 × 3 grid on the paper to indicate yes or no to the following:

1. Of everybody in the family that you have named, who does or did abuse drugs and or alcohol, including prescription medication? (Indicate on genogram.)

2. Have you yourself ever had a problem with drugs and/or alcohol or medications? (If yes, then document details.)

3. Repeat questions 1 & 2 for "psychiatric illness, depression, anxiety, nervous breakdowns, 'bad nerves', or suicide attempts".

4. Repeat questions 1 & 2 for "Physical abuse, or corporal punishment neglect that would be considered excessive by today's standards".

5. Repeat questions 1 & 2 for "Sexual abuse, or inappropriate sexual behaviour, touching, or fondling".

(*continued*)

6. Repeat questions 1 & 2 for "Emotional or verbal abuse, name calling or threats".

III. Relationship assessment preparation: Use a red pen to indicate pathology, a blue or black pen to document data.

1. How would you describe your parent's marriage? (Document the quote, and then ask for elaboration)

2. What did your parents do to be helpful to one another?

3. Did your parents show affection to each other or to the kids?

4. How did your parents settle their differences? (Ascertain the tactics and defences used.)

5. Did one or the other parent seem to have more to say in decisions?

6. Did your parents have traditional gender roles?

7. Did either of your parents confide in you or one of your sibs about grievances with the other parent?

8. Did you ever feel you had to take sides with one parent over the other?

9. Which parent are you most like? With whom are/were you closer?

10. What did each parent do for you? How did they take care of you? What did they discuss, counsel, or teach you?

11. How do things go now between you and your Mum? Dad? Who initiates contact?

12. What do you do to be helpful to your Mum? Dad?

13. Is your Mum/Dad pleased with you? How do you know? What do you do to please him/her?

14. Are you able to say "no" to your parents? When have you? What does it cost you?

15. Are you worried about your Mum/Dad? If so, why? What have you done about that?

16. Who is the favourite child of each parent? Are any of the sibs "black sheep"?

17. How do you get along with your sibs now and during childhood? How were conflicts managed? What role did parents play in sib relationships?

18. What role do you play in your family?

19. What would you like to see change in your family? In your conduct with family members?

III. Relationship assessment, continued. (Relationship with children of adult clients.)

(*continued*)

20. Establish the names, genders, ages, and custody status of each child for each child in turn:

21. Was the child planned? Was this child wanted?

22. Were there any complications around the pregnancy or delivery?

23. What challenges did you face in raising this child?

24. Who contributed to raising this child?

25. What concerns do you have for this child?

27. Who is this child most like?

28. What does this child do to show care or loyalty to you? To the family?

29. Does this child know you are seeking therapeutic help? What has this child been told?

In the event of divorce or separation:

30. How does this child understand the reasons for the divorce/separation?

31. Who told the child what about this event?

32. Is this child expected to hold any secret information? If so, from whom?

33. Who was/is available to this child to help cope with the event?

34. Does this child seem to take sides? Is this child expected to take sides?

In the event of a parent's death or illness:

35. How old was this child when the parent died/became ill?

36. How does this child understand the cause/circumstances of the event?

37. Who told the child what about the event?

38. Who is emotionally available to this child about this?

39. Has the child taken part in the funeral/ill parent's care?

40. How has this affected this child?

Many of these questions may have already been answered earlier in the assessment.

13

14 *School/education*

Dates and names of nursery, primary, and secondary schools, academic progress, interaction with peers and teachers, school attendance, truancy, school report, educational psychologist, SENCo statement, strengths, weaknesses, problems, e.g., bullying, school refusal, school withdrawal or suspension. Poor school attendance rate in last two weeks. If school holiday, rate last two weeks of previous term.

0 No problems of this kind during the period rated.

1 Slight problems e.g., late for two or more lessons.

(*continued*)

2 Definite but mild problems, e.g., missed several lessons because of truancy or refusal to go to school.

3 Marked problems, absent several days during the period rated.

4 Severe problems, absent most or all days. Any school suspension, exclusion, or expulsion for any cause during the period rated.

Nursery, primary, secondary, college, university, postgraduate

14

Section B (Designed to provide guidance on prognosis)
Items 15 and 16, each with their corresponding rating scales, are concerned with problems for the child, parent, or carer relating either to lack of information or access to services. These are not direct measures of the child's health, but beneficial changes here can result in long-term benefits for the child.

15 Problems with knowledge or understanding about the nature of the child's/adolescent's difficulties (in the previous two weeks)

Include lack of useful information or understanding available to the child/adolescent, parents, or carers.

Include lack of explanation about the diagnosis, the cause of the problem, or the prognosis.

0 No problems during the period rated. Parents/carers have been adequately informed about the child's problems.

1 Slight problems only.

2 Mild but definite problem.

3 Moderately severe problems. Parents/carers have very little or incorrect knowledge about the problem which is causing difficulties, such as confusion or self-blame.

4 Very severe problem. Parents have no understanding about the nature of their child's problems.

15

16. Problems with lack of information about services or management of the child's/adolescent's difficulties

Include lack of useful information available to the child/adolescent, parents, carers, or referrers.

Include lack of information about the most appropriate way of providing services to the child, such as care arrangements, educational placements, respite care, or statementing.

(continued)

0 No problems during the period rated. The need for all necessary services has been recognised.

1 Slight problems only.

2 Mild but definite problem.

3 Moderately severe problems. Parents/carers have been given little information about appropriate services or professionals are not sure where a child should be managed.

4 Very severe problem. Parents have no information about appropriate services or professionals do not know where a child should be managed.

16

General observations of child: appearance and behaviour

Eye contact: include activity levels, restlessness, fidgety, abnormal movements, e.g., tics, rituals. Disinhibition, coordination, aocial interaction, rapport and attention.

House and neighbourhood

Type of house. Financial difficulties in family. Area, including safety amenities, crime, and drug misuse. Neighbours support.

Physical examination

Height (cm)

Weight (kg)

$$\text{BMI} = \frac{\text{weight (kg)}}{\text{Height (m)}^2}.$$

< 18.5 anorexia > 25 obese > 30 morbid obesity Normal range = 20–25

Dysmorphic features or minor physical anomalies

General examination, including: cardiovascular, respiratory, gastrointestinal, musculoskeletal, neurological, including cranial nerves, handedness, coordination, including assessment of DCD and dyspraxia.

Case formulation

Main complaint. Differential diagnosis. Predisposing, precipitating, maintaining, preventative, and resilience factors.

Consider: individual, family, social environment.

Agreement about a clear intervention goal:

What do the family want to work on? How do they want to do it? How will they know when they have reached their goal? Agree and formulate care plan.

SMARTER goals are:

Specific, Measurable, Achievable/affordable, Realistic, Time limited, Exciting, and Relevant and recorded.

(*continued*)

Decision about who is most appropriate to help
CAMHS, Adult mental health team, trauma clinic, peak performance clinic. Family to organise this themselves.

Agreement on pre-partnership goals
What can be done to change the problem before next meeting in CAMHS?

Booking into an intervention slot.

Match therapist skills to desired intervention goal for patient or client.

Further assessment required: Choice appt. ☐
Partnership appt. ☐

Referral to (tick all that apply) Partnership		*Clinician*	
ASD pathway	☐	Cognitive behaviour therapy	☐
ADHD pathway	☐	Solution-focused therapy	☐
		Family therapy	☐
Child in need, e.g.			
Child protection		Child psychotherapy	
Multi-agency conference	☐	BART psychotherapy	☐
Early intervention in psychosis	☐	Speech & language therapy	☐
Neurodevelopmental	Occupational therapy/physiotherapy		
Community paediatrics	☐	MCAST assessment	☐
		Attachment/play therapy	☐
Substance misuse service			
Motivational interview		Legal or court report	
Social Services	☐	Statement of education	☐
		Need	☐
In/outreach service	☐		
Psychiatric assessment	☐	Traumatic stress clinic	☐
Clinical psychology	☐	Eating disorders service	☐
Neuropsychology	☐	Pupil support group	☐
Watch wait & wonder	☐	Inpatient unit	☐
Self-harm group	☐		

Parent Support Group for Autism or Aspergers (ASCEND)

ICD-10 codings: ....

Axis I Clinical psychiatric syndromes.
II Specific disorders of psychological development.
III Intellectual level.
IV Medical conditions.
V Associated abnormal psychosocial situations.
VI Global assessment of psychosocial disability.

(*continued*)

At referral *at discharge, or 6 months later*

SDQ
IES-R (single traumatic event).
IES-R (average for multiple relevant traumatic experiences).
CRIES-13.
CGAS.
GAPD.

Changes in scores.

State number partnership appointments attended

After the course of intervention has been completed successfully. This section is designed to receive feedback on therapy to improve future performance:

Intervention(s) that made a difference:

(a) clinician's opinion,

(b) opinion of patient or client,

(c) opinion of carer(s).

SECTION A	*HoNOSCA (revised)*	*RATE 0– 4*	
a. *Behavioural problems* Subscale	Range of section scores	HT1	HT2
1. Disruptive, antisocial, or aggressive behaviour		☐	☐
2. Over-activity, attention, and concentration		☐	☐
3. Non-accidental self injury		☐	☐
4. Alcohol, substance or solvent misuse		☐	☐
b. *Impairment*			
5. Scholastic or language skills		☐	☐
6. Physical illness or disability problems		☐	☐
c. *Symptomatic problems*			
7. Hallucination and delusions.		☐	☐
8. Non-organic somatic symptoms.		☐	☐

(continued)

9. Emotional and related symptoms.	☐	☐
d. *Social problems*		
10. Peer relationships.	☐	☐
11. Significant life events.	☐	☐
12. Self-care and independence.	☐	☐
13. Family life and relationships.	☐	☐
14. Poor school attendance.	☐	☐
SECTION B (out of 12)		
Lack of knowledge—nature of difficulties.	☐	
Lack of information—services/management. (out of 8)	☐	☐
HT1 (HoNOSCA Time 1)	☐	
HT1 (HoNOSCA Time 2)		☐
Change in HoNOSCA scores (HT1 minus HT2		☐

Conclusion: use of the Herrmann brain dominance instrument (HBDI)

The HBDI is a system claimed to measure and describe thinking preferences in people. In his brain dominance model, Herrmann (1991) developed it as a cognitive style measurement while leading management education at General Electric's Crontonville factory. He identifies four different modes of thinking:

- A. *Analytical thinking*
  Key words: auditive, logical, factual, critical, technical, and quantitative.
  Preferred activities: collecting data, analysis, understanding how things work, judging ideas based on facts, criteria, and logical reasoning.
- B. *Sequential thinking*
  Key words: safekeeping, structured, organised, complexity or detailed, planned.
  Preferred activities: following directions, detail orientated work, step-by-step problem solving, organisation, and implementation.
- C. *Interpersonal thinking*

Key words: kinaesthetic, emotional, spiritual, sensory, feeling.
Preferred activities: listening to, and expressing, ideas, looking for personal meaning, sensory input, and group interaction.

- D. *Imaginative thinking*
  Key words: visual, holistic, intuitive, innovative, conceptual.
  Preferred activities: looking at the big picture, taking initiative, challenging assumptions, visuals, metaphoric thinking, creative problem solving, long-term thinking.

His theory was inspired by the research into left–right brain lateralisation by Roger Wolcott Sperry, Robert Ornstein, Henry Mintzberg, and Michael Gazzaniga and further developed to reflect a metaphor for how individuals think and learn. Use of that metaphor brought later criticism by brain researchers such as Terence Hines for being overly simplistic. Herrmann also coined the phrase "whole brain thinking" as a description of flexibility in using thinking styles that one may cultivate in individuals or in organisations, allowing the situational use of all four styles of thinking. Use of all four thinking styles can be encouraged using the techniques outlined in this book.

The brain is divided into four quadrants, each with their individual functionality.

A Left cerebral hemisphere.
B Left limbic hemisphere.
C Right limbic hemisphere.
D Right cerebral hemisphere

The HBDI can be completed online at www.hbdi.org. and used to find the points at which your brilliance meets what you are passionate about. These can gel to identify the unique talents that will help you to both find your element and put you in the zone. The goal, in colloquial terms, is to find both what makes you "tick" and what "floats your boat".

The theory suggests that strengthening your weaker quadrants will improve your overall creative potential.

Strategies appropriate to each quadrant of the Herrmann brain dominance instrument are outlined.

Knowledge of this can be combined with BART psychotherapy for our clients seeking to optimise their performance in school, university, work, or sport settings.

The following twelve brain functions have key associations with different Brodmann (2006) functional brain areas.

1. Visuospatial working memory involves activation of the ventrolateral frontal cortex 46 and parietal lobe 7.
2. Spatial working memory involves activation of frontal lobe 10 and posterior parietal lobe 39.
3. Focused attention engages the right prefrontal cortex 11. This occurs at the latter stages of BART psychotherapy.
4. The ability to rotate objects mentally involves the superior parietal cortex 5.
5. The brain's strategy for visuospatial working memory involves the coming together of two streams of neurological information: (a) parietal lobe (where) 5 and 7, (b) temporal lobe perception and memory for objects (what) 20, 21, and 37.
6. This is called paired associate learning, and involves linking memories such as a person's name and their telephone number. It allows the person to learn connections between related concepts.
7. Deductive reasoning involves activity in the back and outer surface of the frontal lobes and in the middle of the parietal lobe.
8. Visuospatial processing involves the parietal cortex and the higher visual areas of the occipital cortex, 17, 18, and 19.
9. Visual attention again involves activation of the visual centres at the base and back of the brain.
10. Verbal reasoning tests activate the dorsolateral frontal cortex, 46 and 47, which lie on the outer surface of the frontal lobe midway between top and bottom.
11. Verbal working memory activates the ventrolateral frontal cortex of the left hemisphere speech area.
12. Planning an activity involves the frontal lobe caudate lobe, supplementary motor area, posterior parietal lobe, and the cerebellum. All of these areas are activated at the end of BART sessions as the patient or client reviews the session and plans their next steps in either psychotherapy or peak performance.

Summary

This final chapter outlines the uses of the Hermann Brain Dominance Instrument. This is useful to combine with BART psychotherapy to monitor those quadrants that need to be targeted for improvement. The HBDI can also be used to analyse, strategise, organise, and personalise the information for each patient or client. Further resources are available at www.hbdi.org. I have included my initial comprehensive health assessment for children, adolescents, and adults, which contains the HoNOSCA-revised and a genogram section devised by Barry Litt and available from www.BLitt.com. I received permission to reprint these questions from Barry Litt.

REFERENCES

Anathaswamy, A. (2013). The knockout enigma: how your mechanical brain works. *New Scientist, 2932*: 32–35.

Assagiolis, R. (1975). *Psychosynthesis*. Winnipeg, Canada: Turnstone Press, 17.

Austin, J. H. (1999). *Zen and the Brain: Toward an Understanding of Meditation and Consciousness*. Cambridge, MA: MIT Press.

Azevedo, F. A. C., Carvalho, L. R. B., Grinberg, L. T., Farfel, J. M., Ferretti, R. E. L., Leite, R. E. P., Wilson, J. F., Lent, R. & Herculano-Houzel, S. (2009). Equal numbers of neuronal and nonneuronal cells make the human brain an isometrically scaled-up primate brain. *The Journal of Comparative Neurology, 513*: 532–541.

Bandler, R., & Grinder, J. (1975a). *The Structure of Magic Vol I: A Book about Language and Therapy*. Palo Alto, CA: Science & Behaviour Books.

Bandler, R., & Grinder, J. (1975b). *The Structure of Magic Vol II: A Book about Communication and Change*. Palo Alto, CA: Science & Behaviour Books.

Baron-Cohen, S., & Wheelwright, S. (2001). The 'Reading the Mind in the Eyes' Test Revised Version: a study with normal adults, and adults with Asperger syndrome or high-functioning autism. *Journal of Child Psychology and Psychiatry, 42*(2): 241–251.

Bauer, P. M., Hanson, J. L., Pierson, R. K., Davidson, R. J., & Pollak, S. D. (2009). Cerebellar volume and cognitive functioning in children who experienced early deprivation. *Biological Psychiatry, 66:* 1100–1106.

BBC Sport Online (2013). Rory McIlroy says management issues have been a 'distraction'. 12 November. Available at: www. bbc. co.uk/sport/0/golf/24914810 (accessed 18 March 2014).

Bernsten, D. K. B., Thomsen, Y. D., Bertelsen, M., Hoyle, R. H., & Rubin, D. C. (2012). Peace and war. Trajectories of posttraumatic stress disorder before, during and after military deployment in Afghanistan. *Psychological Science, 23*(12): 1557–1565.

Blakemore, S., & Choudhury, S. (2006). Development of the adolescent brain: implications for executive function and social cognition. *Journal of Child Psychology and Psychiatry, 47*(3): 296–312.

Blore, D. (2012). *In Search of the Antonym to Trauma.* Germany: Lambert Academic.

Briggs, D. (producer and director) (2012). *Heart v. Mind: What Makes Us Human.* First broadcast on BBC4 TV, 10 July.

Brodmann, K. (2006). *Brodmann's Localisation in the Cerebral Cortex,* L. J Garey (Trans.). New York; Springer Science and Business Media.

Buczynski, R., & Lanius, R. (2012). The neurobiology of trauma: how the brain experiences unresolved trauma: a webinar session. Available at: http://nicabm-stealthseminar.s3.amazonaws.com/Trauma2012/Lanius/NICABM-Lanius2012.pdf (accessed 4 April 2014).

Buczynski, R., & Porges, S. W. (2012). The polyvagal theory of trauma. A webinar session. Available from: www.nicabm.com (accessed 24 February 2014).

Cairns, J., Overbaugh, J., & Miller, S. (1988). The origin of mutants. *Nature, 335*: 142–145.

Calaprice, A. (2011). *The Ultimate Quotable Einstein.* Princeton, NJ: Princeton University Press.

Canli, T., Congdon, E., Constable, R. T., & Klaus, P. L. (2008). Additive effects of serotonin transporter and tryptophan hydroxylase-2 gene variation on neural correlates of affective processing. *Biological Psychology, 79*(1): 118–125.

Carey, G. W., & Perry, I. E. (2013). *God-man: The Word Made Flesh* (facsimile reprint of 1920 edition). Eastford, CT: Martino Fine Books.

Carey, S., Diamond, R., & Woods, B. (1980). Developmental course of facial recognition: a maturational component. *Developmental Psychology, 16*(4): 257–269.

Carlyle, T. (1922). *Death of Goethe.* Love is ever the beginning of knowledge, as fire is of light. Quote cited in Hoyt, J. K, & Roberts, K. L. (1922). *Hoyt's New Cyclopedia of Practical Quotations. New* York: Funk & Wagnall's.

Cavdar, S., Onat, F., Aker. R., Şehirli, U., Şan, T., & Yananli, H. R. (2001). The afferent connections of the posterior hypothalamic nucleus in the rat using horseradish peroxide. *Journal of Anatomy, 198*(4): 463–472.

Cechetto, D., & Saper, C. (1987). Role of the cerebral cortex in autonomic function. In: A. Loewy & K. Spyer (Eds.), *Central Regulation of Autonomic Function* (pp. 208–223). Oxford: Oxford University Press.

Cherkassky, V. (2007). Functional and anatomical cortical under connectivity in autism: evidence from an fMRI study of an executive function task and corpus callosum morphometry. *Cerebral Cortex, 17*(4): 951–961.

Cherry, N. (2002). Schumann resonances, a plausible biophysical mechanism for the human health effects of solar/geomagnetic activity. *Natural Hazards, 26*(3): 279–331.

Childre, D., & Rozman, D. (2002). *Overcoming Emotional Chaos: Eliminate Anxiety, Lift Depression and Create Security in Your Life*. San Diego, CA: Jodere Group.

Colvin, G., (2008). *Talent is Overrated: What Really Separates World-Class Performers from Everybody Else*. London: Nicholas Brealey Publishing.

Conservative Party (2010). *Invitation to Join the Government of Britain: The Conservative Manifesto 2010*. London: Conservative Campaign Headquarters.

Cox, B. (2013). *Wonders of Life*. London: HarperCollins.

Cryan, J., & Dinan, T. (2012a). Mind-altering microorganisms: the impact of the gut micro biota on brain and behaviour. *Nature Reviews Neuroscience, 13*: 701–712.

Cryan, J., & Dinan, T. (2012b). An evaluation of neuropsychological performance in irritable bowel syndrome (IBS): relationship between altered visuo-spatial memory function, salivary cortisol levels and tryptophan metabolism along the kynurenine pathway. *Neurogastroenterology & Motility, 24, Special Issue:* Abstracts of the Joint International Neurogastroenterology and Motility Meeting, 6–8 September 2012, Bologna, Italy: 175.

Csikszentmihalyi, M. (1990). *The Psychology of Optimal Experience*. London: HarperCollins.

Dalai Lama (2012). *His Holiness the Dalai Lama UK visit*. [Teachings by his holiness the Dalai Lama; pamphlet issued on the occasion of the Dalai Lama's talk at the Manchester Arena, UK, 18 June 2012.

Damasio, A. R. (1996). Somatic motor hypothesis and the possible functions of the prefrontal cortex. *Philosophical Transactions of the Royal Society B, Biological Sciences, 351*: 1413–1420.

Damasio, A. R. (2006). *Descartes' Error: Emotion, Reason and the Human Brain*. London: Vintage.

Damasio, A. R. (2010). *Self Comes to Mind: Constructing the Conscious Brain.* London: William Heinemann.

Darwin, C. (1872). *The Expression of the Emotions in Man and Animals.* London: John Murray.

Davidson, R. (2004). Well-being and affective style: neural substrates and biobehavioural correlates. *Philosophical Transactions of the Royal Society of London B: Biological Sciences, 359*: 1395–1411.

De Bellis, M. D., Baum, A. S., Birmaher, B., Keshavan, M. S., Eccard, C. H., Boring, A. M., Jenkins, F. J., & Ryan, N. D. (1999). Developmental traumatology: Part I biological stress systems. *Biological Psychiatry, 45*(10): 1259–1270.

Donne, J. (1987). *Devotions upon Emergent Occasions,* A. Raspa (Ed. and commentary). New York: Oxford University Press.

Ekman, P. (2003). *Unmasking the Face: a Guide to Recognizing Emotions from Facial Expressions.* Los Altos, CA: Malor Books.

Ellis, J., Brandimonte, M., Einstein, G. O., & McDaniel, M. (Eds.) (1996). *Prospective Memory: Theory and Applications.* Mahwah, NJ: Lawrence Erlbaum Associates.

Ericsson, K. A., & Lehmann, A. (1996). Expert and exceptional performance: evidence on maximal adaptations on task constraints. *Annual Review of Psychology, 47*: 273–305.

Ericsson, K. A., Krampe, R. T., & Tesch-Römer, C. (1993). The role of deliberate practice in the acquisition of expert performance. *Psychological Review, 100*(3): 363–406.

Fifield, D. (2013). Chelsea back in old routine thanks to Ramires double at Steau Bucharest. Available at www.theguardian.com/football/2013/oct/01/steaua-bucharest-chelsea-champions-league (accessed 13 April 2014).

Filler, A. (2007). A historical hypothesis of the first recorded neurosurgical operation: Isis, Osiris, Thoth, and the origin of the djed cross. *Neurosurgical Focus, 23*(1): *1–6.*

Flavell, J. (1979). Metacognition and cognitive monitoring: a new area of cognitive–developmental inquiry. *American Psychologist, 34*(10): 906–911.

Fletcher, D., & Sarker, M. (2012). A grounded theory of psychological resilience in Olympic champions. *Psychology of Sport and Exercise, 13*: 669–678.

Fox, N. (1991). If it's not left, it's right: electroencephalograph asymmetry and the development of emotion. *American Psychologist, 46*(8): 863–872.

Freud, S. (1900a). *The Interpretation of Dreams. S.E., 4–5.* London: Hogarth.

Freud, S. (1905d). *Three Essays on the Theory of Sexuality. S.E., 7*: 125–145. London: Hogarth.

Gardner, H. (1993). *Frames of Mind: The Theory of Multiple Intelligences* (10th anniversary edn). New York: Basic Books.

Garfinkel, S. N., & Critchley, H. D. (2013). Interoception, emotion and brain: new insights link internal physiology to social behaviour. Commentary on: Anterior insular cortex mediates bodily sensibility and social anxiety. *Social Cognitive and Affective Neuroscience, 8*(3): 231–234.

Garfinkel, S. N., Barrett, A., Minati, I., Dolan, R. J., Seth, A., & Critchley, H. (2013). What the heart forgets: cardiac timing influences memory for words and is modulated by metacognition and interoceptive sensitivity. *Psychophysiology, 50*(6): 505–512.

Ghosh, P. (2014). Earliest footprints outside Africa discovered in Norfolk. BBC News Online, 7 February. Available at: www.bbc.co.uk/news/science-environment-26025763 (accessed 7 April 2014).

Gilbert, P., & Choden, K. (2013). *Mindful Compassion. Using the Power of Mindfulness and Compassion to Transform our Lives.* London: Constable & Robinson.

Gladwell, M. (2008). *Outliers. The Story of Success.* New York: Little, Brown.

Gogtay, N., Giedd, J. N., Lusk, L., Hayashi, K. Greenstein, D., Vaituzis, A. C., Nugent, T. F. (III), Herman, D. H., Clasen, L. S., Toga, A. W., Rapoport, J. L., & Thompson, P. M. (2004). Dynamic mapping of human cortical development during childhood through early adulthood. *PNAS, 101*(21): 8174–8179.

Gowers, S., Bailey-Rogers, S. J., Shore A., & Levine, W. (2000). The health of the nation outcome scales for child and adolescent mental health (HoNOSCA). *Child Psychology & Psychiatry Review, 5*(2): 50–56.

Hanson, J. L., Suh, J. W., Nacewicz, B. M., Sutterer, M. J., Cayo, A. A., Stodola, D. E., Burghy, C. A., Wang, H., Avants, B. B., Yushkevich, P. A., Essex, M. J., Pollak, S. D., & Davidson, R. J. (2012). Robust automated amygdala segementation via multi-atlas diffeomorphic registration. *Frontiers in Neuroscience, 6*(166).

Hebb, D. (1949). *The Organization of Behaviour.* New York: Wiley & Sons.

Hering, H. (1910). A functional test of heart vagi in man. *Menschen München Medizinische Wochenschrift, 57*: 1931–1933.

Herrmann, N. (1991). The creative brain. *Journal of Creative Behaviour, 25*(4): 275–295.

Hess, W. (1949). Nobel Prize acceptance speech: for medicine/physiology. (Online.) Available at: http://www.nobelprize.org/nobel_prizes/medicine/laureates/1949/press.html (accessed 18 March 2014).

Hogenboom, M. (2013). Blow to multiple human species idea. BBC News Online, 17 October. Available at: www.bbc.co.uk/news/science-environment-24564375 (accessed 7 April 2014).

Jung, C. G. (1964). Civilization in transition, *C.W., 10*. London: Routledge.

Keats, J. (1817). Letter to Benjamin Bailey, 22 November 1817. In: R. Gittings (Ed.), *Letters of John Keats*. Oxford: Oxford University Press, 1970.

Kennedy, P., Clarke, G., O'Neill, A., Groeger, J., Quigley, E., Shanahan, F., Schachter, S., & Singer, J. (1962). Cognitive, social, and physiological determinants of emotional state. *Psychological Review, 69*: 379–399.

Kennedy, P., Clarke, G., Quigley, E. M., Groeger, J. A., Dinan, T. G., & Cryan, J. F. (2012). Gut memories. Towards a cognitive neurobiology of irritable bowel syndrome. *Neuroscience and Biobehavioral Reviews, 36*: 310–340.

Keyes, K. (1984). *The Hundredth Monkey*. Camarillo, CA: DeVorss.

Kinsbourne, M. (1988). Hemisphere interactions in depression. In: M. Kinsbourne (Ed.), *Hemisphere Function in Depression* (pp. 133–162). Washington, DC: American Psychiatric Association.

Koestler, A. (1964). *The Act of Creation*. London: Hutchinson.

Langley, J. (1921). *The Autonomic Nervous System. Part 1*. Cambridge: W. Heffer.

Laub, B., & Shapiro, E., (2008). Early EMDR intervention (EEI); a summary, a theoretical model and the recent traumatic episode protocol (RTEP). *Journal of EMDR Research and Practice* 2(2): 79–96.

Leadbetter, C. (2013). *The Chakras, A Monograph*. Wheaton, IL: Quest Books.

Leonard, P. (producer and director) (2010). *What Happened Before the Big Bang? Horizon*: BBC2, first broadcast on 11 October 2010.

Lerner, E. L. (1991). *The Big Bang Never Happened*. New York: Vintage Books.

Lipton, B. H. (2001). Nature, nurture and human development. *Journal of Prenatal and Perinatal Psychology and Health, 16*(2): 167–180.

Lipton, B. H. (2011). *The Biology of Belief: Unleashing the Power of Consciousness, Matter and Miracles*. London: Hay House.

Lipton, B. H. (2013a). *The Honeymoon Effect. The Science of Creating Heaven on Earth*. London: Hay House.

Lipton, B. H. (2013b). YouTube clip: Bruce Lipton: Full conference/ Genes don't control your reality! Your perception controls genes. Accessed January 2014.

Lipton, B. H., & Bhaerman, S. (2011). *Spontaneous Evolution: Our Positive Future (and a Way to Get There from Here)*. London: Hay House.

Littleton, K., & Mercer, N. (2013). *Interthinking: Putting Talk to Work*. Abingdon: Routledge.

Lordkipanidze, D., Ponce de León, M. S., Margvelashvili, A., Rak, Y., Rightmire, G. P., Vekua, A., & Zollikofer, C. P. E. (2013). A complete skull from Dmanisi, Georgia and the evolutionary biology of early *Homo*. *Science*, *342*: 326–331.

Lovett, J. (1999). *Small Wonders: Healing Childhood Trauma with EMDR*. New York: Free Press.

Luthar, S. S., Cicchetti, D., & Becker, B. (2000). The construct of resilience: a critical evaluation and guidelines for future work, *Child Development*, *71*(3): 543–562.

Malone, D. (2012). Documentary film. *Horizon. Heart vs Mind: What Makes Us Human*? BBC Four, 6 July.

Mantyh, F. (1982). Forebrain projections to the periaqueductal grey in the monkey, with observations in the cat and rat. *Journal of Comparative Neurology*, *206*(2): 146–158.

Maslow, A. (1943). A theory of human motivation. *Psychological Review*, *50*(4): 370–396.

McCraty, R., Atkinson, M., & Tomasino, D. (2001). *Science of the Heart. Exploring the Role of the Heart in Human Performance*. Boulder Creek, CA: Heartmath Research Center.

McGilchrist, I. (2009). *The Master and His Emissary: The Divided Brain and the Making of the Western World*. New Haven, CT: Yale University Press.

McGilchrist, I. (2010). The divided brain and the making of the western world. Available at: www.thersa.org_data/assets/pdf_file/0006/1533615/RSA-Lecture-Iain-McGilchrist-transcript.pdf (accessed 18 March 2014).

McGivern, R., Andersen, J., Byrd, D., Mutter, K. L., & Reilly, J. (2002). Cognitive efficiency on a match to sample task decreases at the onset of puberty in children. *Brain and Cognition*, *50*(1): 73–89.

Meer, F. (1990). *Higher Than Hope: the Authorized Biography of Nelson Mandela*. London: Hamish Hamilton.

Mercer, N., & Littleton, K. (2007). *Dialogue and the Development of Children's Thinking: A Sociocultural Approach*. London: Routledge.

Molden, D., & Hutchinson, P. (2007). *Brilliant NLP: What the Most Successful People Know, Do and Say*. Harlow: Pearson Education.

Muir, E., Lojkasek, M., & Cohen, N. (1999). *Watch, Wait and Wonder: A Manual Describing a Dyadic Infant-led Approach to Problems in Infancy and Early Childhood*. Toronto: Hincks-Dellcrest Institute.

National Health Service North West (2011). *Improving Outcomes and Ensuring Quality: Guide for Commissioners and Providers of Pernatal and Infant Mental Health Services*. NHS North West.

Nelson, E. E., Leibenluft, E., McClure, E. B., & Pine, D. S. (2005). The social re-orientation of adolescence: a neuroscience perspective on the process and its relation to psychopathology. *Psychological Medicine, 35*(2): 163–174.

Newton, I. (1675). Letter to Robert Hooke, 5 February 1675. The Newton project. *From Memoirs of the Life, Writings and Discoveries of Sir Isaac Newton* (1), Edinburgh 1855. Letter written Cambridge, 5 February 1675. [Online.] Available at: www. newtonproject. sussex. ac. uk/ view/texts/normalized/OTHE00101 (accessed 24 February 2014).

New Zealand Folksong (2011). Ka Mate. Available at: http://folksong. org.nz/ka_mate/1chant.html (accessed 4 April 2014).

Noesselt, T., Driver J, Heinze, H. J. & Dolan, R. (2005). Asymmetrical activation in the human brain during processing of fearful faces. *Current Biology, 15*(5): 424–429.

Nosarti, C., Reichenberg, A, Murray, R. M., Cnattingius S., Lambe, M. P., Yin, L., & MacCabe, J. (2012). Preterm birth and psychiatric disorders in young adult life. *Archives of General Psychiatry, 69*: 610–617.

Ogden, P., Pain, C., & Minton, K. (2006). *Trauma and the Body: A Sensorimotor Approach to Psychotherapy*: New York: W. W. Norton.

Ohno, S. (1972). So much junk DNA in our genome. *Brookhaven Symposia on Biology, 2*: 366–370.

O'Malley, A. G. (2011). Workshop on The Art of Bart. *Proceedings of the Annual Conference of the International Society for the Study of Trauma and Dissociation*. Montreal.

Oppenheim, D., & Goldsmith, D. F. (Eds.) (2007). *Attachment Theory in Clinical Work with Children: Bridging the Gap between Research and Practice*. New York: Guilford Press.

Panksepp, J. (1988). *Affective Neuroscience: The Foundations of Human and Animal Emotions*. New York: Oxford University Press.

Panksepp, J., & Bernatsky, G. (2002). Emotional sounds and the brain: the neuro-affective foundations of musical appreciation. *Behavioural Processes, 60*: 33–155.

Parnell, L. (2013). *Attachment Focused EMDR. Healing Relational Trauma*. New York: W. W. Norton.

Pascal, B. (1958). *Pascal's Pensées*. New York: E. P. Dutton.

Peters, S. (2012). *The Chimp Paradox. The Mind Management Programme for Confidence, Success and Happiness*. London: Vermilion.

Pollak, S. (2012). Lecture presented at University of Manchester, Department of Speech and Language Therapy. Developmental Neuroscience seminar series, November.

Porges, S. W. (1995). Orienting in a defensive world: mammalian modifications of our evolutionary heritage. A polyvagal theory. *Psychophysiology, 32*: 301–318.

Porges, S. W. (2001). The polyvagal theory: phylogenetic substrates of a social nervous system. *International Journal of Psychophysiology, 42*: 123–146.

Porges, S. W. (2006). Social engagement and attachment: a phylogenetic perspective. *Annals of the New York Academy of Sciences 1008 [Roots of Mental Illness in Children]*: 31–47.

Porges, S. W. (2009). The polyvagal theory: new insights into adaptive reactions of the autonomic nervous system. *Cleveland Clinic Journal of Medicine, 76*(suppl. 2): S86–S90.

Porges, S. W., & Doussard-Roosevelt, J. (1999). Sleep state and vagal regulation of heart period patterns in the human newborn: an extension of the polyvagal theory. *Psychophysiology, 36*(1): 14–21.

Poynder, M. (1992). *Pi in the Sky: A Revelation of the Ancient Wisdom Tradition*. London: Rider.

Pujol, J., Vendrell, P., Junqué, C., Martí-Vilalta, J. L., & Capdevila, A. (1993). When does human brain development end? Evidence of corpus callosum growth up to adulthood. *Annals of Neurology, 34*(1): 71–75.

Raichle, M. E., & Snyder, A. Z. (2007). A default mode of brain function: a brief history of an evolving idea. *Neuroimage, 37*: 1083–1090.

Rizzolatti, G., Forgassi, L., & Gallese, V. (2001). Neurophysiological mechanisms underlying the understanding and imitation of action. *Nature Reviews*: *Neuroscience, 50*: 661–670.

Roberts, R. M. (1989). *Serendipity: Accidental Discoveries in Science*. New York: Wiley.

Robinson, K. (2009). *The Element. How Finding Your Passion Changes Everything*. London: Penguin.

Rossi, E. L. (2004). The genomic science foundation of body psychotherapy. *USA Body Psychotherapy Journal*, 3(2): 30–49.

Rusbridger, A. (2014). Interview with Professor Ray Dolan (online). Available at: http://alanrusbridger. com/playitagain/interviews/ interview-professor-ray-dolan-frs (accessed 18 March 2014).

Russell, B. (1945). *A History of Western Philosophy*. New York: Simon and Schuster.

Sayed, M. (2011). *Bounce. The Myth of Talent and the Power of Practice*. London: HarperCollins.

Schutter, D. J., & van Honk, J. (2006). An electrophysiological link between the cerebellum, cognition and emotion: frontal theta EEG activity to single-pulse cerebellar TMS. *Neuroimage, 33*(4): 1227–1231.

Schwaller de Lubicz, R. A. (1949). *The Temple in Man*. Rochester, VT: Inner Traditions, Bear.

Searl, J. (1990). Review. *The Mystery of Consciousness*. New York: New York Review of Books.

Seung, S. (2012). *Connectome: How the Brain's Wiring Makes Us Who We Are*. London: Penguin.

Shakespeare, W. (1979). *Macbeth*, K. Muir (Ed.). London: Methuen, 1979.

Shankoff, J. P., & Phillips, D. A. (Eds.) (2000). *From Neurons to Neighborhoods: The Science of Early Childhood Development*. Washington, DC: National Academies Press.

Shapiro, F. (2001). *Eye Movement Desensitization and Reprocessing (EMDR): Basic Principles, Protocols, and Procedures* (2nd edn). New York: Guilford Press.

Sheldrake, R. (1988). Extended mind, power and prayer. Morphic resonance and the collective unconscious—Part III. *Psychological Perspectives, 19*(1): 64–78.

Sherrington, C. (1906). *The Integrative Action of the Nervous System*. New Haven, CT: Yale University Press.

Simon-Thomas, E. R., Role, K. O., & Knight, R. T. (2005). Behavioural and electrophysiological evidence of a right hemisphere bias for the influence of negative emotion on higher cognition. *Journal of Cognitive Neuroscience, 17*(3): 518–529.

Sitchin, Z. (1976). *The 12th Planet*. New York: Stein and Day.

Stickgold, R. (2002). EMDR: a putative neurobiological mechanism of action. *Journal of Clinical Psychology, 58*(1): 61–75.

Stringer, C. (2012). *The Origin of Our Species*: London: Allen Lane.

Toga, A., & Thompson, P. (2003). Mapping brain asymmetry. *Nature Reviews Neuroscience, 4*: 37–48.

Tsuchiya, N., & Adolphs, R. (2007). Emotion and consciousness. *Trends in Cognitive Sciences, 11*(4): 158–167.

Verhoeven, J., Revesz, D., Epel, E. S., Lin, J., Wolkowitz, O. M., & Penninx, B. W. (2013). Major depressive disorder and accelerated cellular aging: results from a large psychiatric cohort study. *Molecular Psychiatry, 19*: 895–901.

Villa, P. M., Hämäläinen, E., Maki, A., Räikkönen, K., Pessonen, A.-K., Taipale, P., Kajantie, E., & Laivuori, H. (2013). Vasoactive agents for the prediction of early- and late-onset preeclampsia in a high risk cohort. *BMC Pregnancy and Childbirth, 13*: 110.

Wan, Y., Qu, K., Zhang, Q. C., Flynn, R. A., Manor, O., Ouyang, Z., Zhang, J., Spitale, R. C., Snyder, M. P., Sega, E., & Chang, H. Y. (2014).

Landscape and variation of RNA secondary structure across the human transcriptome. *Nature, 505*: 706–709.

Waters, O. (2013). Doing by not doing. *Spiritual Dynamics Newsletter* [online]. Available at: www.spiritualdynamics.net/articles/author/owen/ (accessed 18 March 2014).

Williams, P. L., Bannister, L. H., Berry, M. M., Collins, P., Dussek, J. E., Dyson, M., & Ferguson, M. W. J. (Eds.) (1995). *Gray's Anatomy: The Anatomical Basis of Medicine and Surgery*. London: Churchill Livingstone.

Wimmer, H., & Perner, J. (1983). Beliefs about beliefs: representation and constraining function of wrong beliefs in young children's understanding of deception. *Cognition, 13*: 103–128.

Wittgenstein, L. (1967). *Philosophical Investigations*, G. E. M. Anscome (Trans.). Oxford: Wiley-Blackwell.

Wundt, W. (1902). *Principles of Physiological Psychology. Morphological Development of the Central Organs*, E. B. Titchener (Trans.). New York: Macmillan.

Wulf, G., McConnell, N., Gärtner, M., & Schwarz, A. (2002). Enhancing the learning of sport skills through external-focus feedback. *Journal of Motor Behavior, 34*(2): 171–182.

Zecevic, N., & Rakic, P. (2001). Development of layer I neurons in the primate cerebral cortex. *The Journal of Neuroscience, 21*(15): 5607–5619.

INDEX

abuse, xvi, xix, 10, 81, 97, 99–101, 103, 105, 113, 126, 253, 256
child, 81
drug, 257
emotional, 258
physical, 257
sexual, 11, 248, 256–257
sibling, 256
verbal, 258
Adolphs, R., 70
affect(ive), 43, 131, 157, 204, 215, 251
awareness, 130
discharge, 195
distress, 127
disturbance, 170
dysregulated, 39, 42, 150, 157, 167, 204
emotional communication, 128
experience, 3, 130
expression of, 104, 221
intense, 157
negative, 12, 92, 195
neuroscience, xiii, xvi, xix, 67, 208
positive, 12, 62, 92
primacy of, 134
regulation, 104, 126, 130, 186, 201
reprocessing, xix, 3, 20, 141, 186, 193
state, 186
stimuli, 13, 152
tolerance, 101, 104, 106, 149, 169, 186, 193, 229, 235
aggression, 98, 104, 192, 200–201, 248, 252
behaviour(al), 230, 248, 250–251, 253, 263
manner, 97
response, 196
severe, 249
state, 36
verbal, 248
Aker, R., 154
alcoholic(s), 246, 248, 250, 256–257
dependence, 250
misuse, 110, 249–250, 263

Andersen, J., 109
anger, 34–36, 60–61, 106, 109, 122, 125, 192, 221, 223, 230, 247, 252
anxiety, 7, 9, 41, 71, 106, 148, 213, 222, 231, 240, 243, 252, 257 *see also*: regulation
  mild, 252
  performance, 213
  resolution, 6
Assagiolis, R., 26, 30
Atkinson, M., 14
attachment, 19, 61, 65, 86, 94, 206, 262
  close, 256
  disorder, 103, 151
  disorganised, 80
  insecure, 34
  interview, 161
  patterns, 92, 103
  relationship, 58, 151
Austin, J. H., xviii, 185, 189
autism, xvi, 74, 77, 97–99, 101, 103–105, 117, 122–123, 141–142, 248, 262 *see also*: disorder
Avants, B. B., 105
Azevedo, F. A. C., 135

Bailey-Rogers, S. J., 161, 245
Bandler, R., 163
Bannister, L. H., 167
Baron-Cohen, S., 123
Barrett, A., 66
Bauer, P. M., 79
Baum, A. S., 81
BBC
  News, 50
  Sport Online, 229
Becker, B., 214
behaviour(al), xviii, 67, 78, 87, 105, 108, 110, 120, 170, 188, 192, 201, 203, 247–248, 251, 261 *see also*: aggression
  adaptive, 94, 222
  anti-nociceptive, 154
  antisocial, 111, 248, 249
  autistic, 99
  automatic, 68
  bad, 29
  bizarre, 251
  calming, 82
  conscious(ness), 91
  deceptive, 248
  defensive, 103
  demanding, 248
  destructive, 24
  discerning, 36
  disruptive, 248, 250
  escape, 90
  feigning death, 84
  fight or flight, 85
  functions, 85
  good, 29
  oppositional, 94
  organisation, 28
  overactive, 249, 251–252
  patterns, 203
  playful, 97
  problems, 250, 263
  programmed, 68, 177
  reciprocity, 97–98
  risk-taking, 110
  self-soothing, 125
  sexual, 120, 248, 257
  social, 81, 120, 122
  spontaneous, 104
  stereotypical, 104
  unhelpful, 68
Bernatsky, G., 128
Bernsten, D. K. B., 187
Berry, M. M., 167
Bertelsen, M., 187
Bhaerman, S., 175
Birmaher, B., 81
Blakemore, S., 123
Blore, D., 16
Boring, A. M., 81
brain (*passim*)
  adolescent, 110, 113
  developing, xvi, 10

divided, 119
emotional, 120
foetal, 59, 73, 120
fore, 44, 89, 120, 133, 154
function, xx, 22, 80, 127, 135, 266
gut, 4–7, 11, 13–15, 19, 29, 36–37, 49, 59, 62, 66, 75, 83, 92, 101, 112–113, 136, 150, 176
head, xv, xx, 3–6, 9–15, 19, 27, 29, 36–37, 49, 62, 65–66, 75, 83, 92, 112–113, 119, 136, 150, 165, 176–177, 195, 208, 225
heart, 4–6, 11, 13, 15, 17, 19, 27, 29, 37, 49, 59, 75, 83, 101, 112–113, 136, 150, 176
hind, 120
-mediated disorder, 59
mid, xvii, 20, 44, 89, 120, 134, 146, 154, 197
physical, 4
processing, xvii
pubertal, 110
-stem, xvi–xix, 6, 8, 19, 21, 37, 44–45, 47, 50, 53, 56, 62, 67, 78–78, 83–87, 89, 94–95, 101–103, 106, 115, 119, 121, 150–151, 154, 162–163, 172, 194, 197–199, 203–204, 207–208
whole-, 192, 265
Brandimonte, M., 108
Briggs, D., 63
Brodmann, K., 266
brain areas, xx, 135
Buczynski, R., xix, 95
Buddhism, 24–25, 54, 66
Burghy, C. A., 105
Byrd, D., 109

Cairns, J., 183
Calaprice, A., 118, 201
Canli, T., 92
Capdevila, A., 107
Carey, G. W., 20
Carey, S., 109
Carlyle, T., 66
Carvalho, L. R. B., 135
case examples
Example 1, 44
Example 2, 49–50
Example 3, 155, 157
Example 4, 165–166
Example 5, 166
Example 6, 200–201
Cavdar, S., 154
Cayo, A. A., 105
Cechetto, D., 154
cerebellum, xvi, 5, 19–23, 29, 44, 47, 53, 63, 67, 74, 79, 87, 89, 95, 105–106, 113, 119, 152, 154, 197, 199, 203, 223, 266
chakras, xv, 24, 27, 31, 33–34, 36–37, 48–49, 53–56, 68, 71, 152, 155, 158, 195, 204, 206–207, 209, 213, 219
body, 31, 152, 155–156
brow, 23, 46–48
central, 64
crown, 31–32, 46–50, 54, 94, 155, 158, 168, 198
earth star, 31–32, 48, 55, 169
energy, 153, 183
fields, 151
points, xiii, xv, 11, 18, 49, 55, 149, 206
systems, 152, 169, 207–208
forehead, 5, 54, 121, 153
heart, 8, 31–32, 37–40, 53, 149, 197, 206
higher, 17, 27, 39, 44, 150, 152
lower, 44
Muladhara, 34
root, 31–32, 34, 55, 150, 168, 198
sacral, 8, 17, 31–32, 35, 54–55, 69, 168, 198
sixth, 23
solar, 31–32, 35–36, 168, 197
soul star, 31, 50
spinal chord, 55

splenic, 54
stellar gateway, 31–32, 51, 53, 168
subpersonal, 31
third eye, 23, 31–32, 44, 46, 49, 54, 152, 153, 164, 168–169, 181, 198, 207
throat, 23, 31–32, 39–41, 55, 94, 149, 152, 168, 197, 204
universal gateway, 31–32, 51
Chang, H. Y., 182
Cherkassky, V., 75
Cherry, N., 16
Childre, D., 14
Choden, 25
Choudhury, S., 123
Cicchetti, D., 214
Clarke, G., 12–13
Clasen, L. S., 53
Cnattingius S., 161–162
Cohen, N., 126
Collins, P., 167
Colvin, G., 224
complex, 26
bidirectional vagal, 199
cognitive processes, 105
dorsal motor, 92
dorsal vagal (DVC), 84–85, 87–88, 92, 102–103
K-, 216
polyvagal, 96
trauma, xvii, 67, 254
traumatic stress, 172
ventral vagal, 85, 92, 102–103
Congdon, E., 92
conscious(ness), 14, 20, 24, 26–27, 37, 41, 44, 48, 54, 56, 94, 112, 115–116, 134, 142, 149, 155, 175, 193, 240 *see also*: behaviour, unconscious(ness)
awakening of, 36
awareness, 1, 19, 24–25, 38, 48, 54, 69–70, 142, 149, 161, 192, 195, 203
centre of, 68
concepts of, 25, 30
content of, 62
continuity of, 49
control, xvii, 203
cosmic, 48
planes of, 155
creativity, 35
experience, 13, 62
individual, 143
learning, 223, 234
level of, 62, 90, 200–201, 204
mind, 115, 135
origin of, xvii, 134, 145
self-, 27, 109
shift in, 17
state, 78
sub-, 234–235, 240
thought, xvii, 141, 145, 213–214
time, 212
unity of, 200–201
will, 129–130
Conservative Party, 192
Constable, R. T., 92
cortex, 13, 20–21, 30, 43, 74, 77, 86–87, 105, 115, 119, 134, 204
adrenal, 207
allo-, 119
archi-, 119
association, 115
auditory, 164–165
central nervous system, 49
cerebral, 62, 65–66, 78–79, 82, 84–85, 108, 113, 120, 135, 162, 197
cingulate, 67, 73, 75, 129, 223
anterior, 59, 73, 184, 199
middle, 73
posterior, 62, 73, 184–185
frontal, xvi, 12, 39, 73, 95, 104, 108, 119–120, 123, 203
dorsolateral, 266
orbito-, 62, 69, 110, 152, 229

pre-, xvii, 12, 14, 19, 23, 37, 45, 53, 60, 62, 67–68, 79, 90, 100, 105–108, 110, 119, 126, 131, 152, 163, 170–172, 184–185, 196, 202, 213, 223, 226–227, 241, 266
pubertal, 109
ventrolateral, 266
frontotemporal, 122
gustatory, 12
insular, 8, 11–13, 62, 93, 101, 106, 112, 154
anterior, 12, 107
posterior, 12
neo-, 105, 119–120
occipital, 163, 185, 266
outer, 119
paloe-, 119
parietal, 164, 266
superior, 266
posterior, 119
retrosplenial, 73
temporal, 84
Cox, B., 44, 183
Critchley, H. D., 66, 75
Cryan, J. F., 7, 12, 59
Csikszentmihalyi, M., 218

Dalai Lama, 24–25, 30
Damasio, A. R., 110, 115–116, 130, 199
Darwin, C., 53, 81, 177, 189
Davidson, R. J., 12, 79, 105
De Bellis, M. D., 81
depression, 23, 40, 49, 60, 64, 126, 248, 252, 257
postnatal, 125–126
severe, 155, 157, 167
development(al), xx, 16, 49, 71, 81, 91–92, 103, 107–111, 113, 123, 128, 131, 142, 155, 185, 187, 196, 256
age, 197
brain, 92, 105, 113, 161, 196
cerebellar, 105, 113
childhood, 60
delay, 125
disorder, 92, 103–104, 250
dynamic, 184
embryonic, 83, 120, 130
emotional, 106–107, 111
evolutionary, 108
foetal, 58
healthy, 125
history, 172, 246
hormonal, 60
infant, xvi, 59, 103
intellectual, 105
language, 98, 105, 107, 128, 131
milestones, 247
moral, 125
muscle, 225
neuro, 75, 77, 103, 106, 262
anatomical, xix
-logical, 150, 211
normal, 59, 81
of memory, 138
of resilience, 28
personal, 214
process, 74
psychological, 112, 262
sensory, 59
sexual, 250
social cognition, 109
somato-motor, 104
stage, xix, 130, 200, 248
steps, xvii
synaptic, 109, 128
trauma, xvii
Diamond, R., 109
Dinan, T. G., 7, 12, 59
disorder, 59, 127, 248–250, 255, 262
see also: attachment, development(al), trauma(tic)
attention deficit hyperactivity (ADHD), 60
autism spectrum, 97, 99, 113, 141
brain-mediated, 59

conduct, 248
dissociative identity, xvii, 195
eating, 252, 262
gastrointestinal tract, 8
gut, 12
hyperkinetic, 249
mood, 134
movement, 250, 252
neurodevelopment, 77
oppositional defiant, 248
personality, 103
multiple, 141
psychiatric, 105, 161–162, 256
psychological, 250, 252
Dolan, R. J., 66, 92
Donne, J., 135
Doussard-Roosevelt, J., 82
Driver, J., 92
Dussek, J. E., 167
Dyson, M., 167

Eccard, C. H., 81
ego, xx, 26–27 *see also*: therapy
-centric, 185–186
personal, 48
state, 100, 195
Einstein, G. O., 108
Ekman, P., 109
Ellis, J., 108
Epel, E. S., 167
Ericsson, K. A., 211, 223
Essex, M. J., 105

Farfel, J. M., 135
Ferguson, M. W. J., 167
Ferretti, R. E. L., 135
Fifield, D., 221
Filler, A., 67
Flavell, J., 214
Fletcher, D., 214
Flynn, R. A., 182
Forgassi, L., 109
Fox, N., 92
Freud, S., 25, 173

Gallese, V., 109
Gardner, H., 62
Garfinkel, S. N., 66, 75
Gärtner, M., 214
Ghosh, P., 52
Giedd, J. N., 53
Gilbert, P., 25
Gladwell, M., 224
glands
adrenal, 11, 69, 154–155
endocrine, 20, 34–36, 38, 40, 47, 49, 152, 155, 158, 207
hypothalamic, 5
lacrimal, 165
mammary, 93
Gogtay, N., 53
Goldsmith, D. F., 161
Gowers, S., 161, 245
Greenstein, D., 53

grief, 8, 37, 198
delayed, 5
traumatic, 10, 149–150, 152, 186, 198
unresolved, 204
Grinberg, L. T., 135
Grinder, J., 163
Groeger, J. A., 12–13

Hämäläinen, E., 59
Hanson, J. L., 79, 105
Hayashi, K., 53
Hebb, D., 135, 137, 196
Heinze, H. J., 92
Herculano-Houzel, S., 135
Hering, H., 102
Herman, D. H., 53
Herrmann, N., xx, 264–265
Hess, W., xvi, 81, 95
Hoyle, R. H., 187
Hutchinson, P., 163

instinct(ive), 67, 71, 134, 148, 157, 204, 229
drives, 134

experience, 13
gut, 5, 7–8, 11, 13, 36, 68, 112, 152, 182, 215
movement, 157
reactions, 37, 71–72, 95, 148, 199
reflexes, 79, 121
response, xvii, 2, 19, 90, 106, 172, 178, 193, 204
survival, 34, 89, 121
intervention, 91, 162, 263
early, 79, 262
goal, 261–262
slot, 262
surgical, 254
therapeutic, 96

Jenkins, F. J., 81
Jung, C. G., 25–26, 30, 46, 127, 143
Junqué, C., 107

Kajantie, E., 59
Keats, J., 66
Kennedy, P., 12–13
Keshavan, M. S., 81
Keyes, K., 17
Kinsbourne, M., 119
Klaus, P. L., 92
Knight, R. T., 92
Koestler, A., 143
Krampe, R. T., 223

Laivuori, H., 59
Lambe, M. P., 161–162
Langley, J., xvi, 81, 95
Lanius, R., xix
Laub, B., 167
Leadbetter, C., 53–56
Lehmann, A., 211
Leibenluft, E., 64, 110
Leite, R. E. P., 135
Lent, R., 135
Leonard, P., 25, 142
Lerner, E. L., 142
Levine, W., 161, 245
Lin, J., 167
Lipton, B. H., xviii, 80, 175–177, 183, 188
Littleton, K., xvi, 112
Lojkasek, M., 126
Lordkipanidze, D., 51
Lovett, J., 2
Lusk, L., 53
Luthar, S. S., 214

MacCabe, J., 161–162
Maki, A., 59
Malone, D., 66
Manor, O., 182
Mantyh, F., 154
Margvelashvili, A., 51
Martí-Vilalta, J. L., 107
Maslow, A., 48, 71, 158, 206
McClure, E. B., 64, 110
McConnell, N., 214
McCraty, R., 14
McDaniel, M., 108
McGilchrist, I., 75, 116, 118, 127–129, 134, 138–139, 192, 205
McGivern, R., 109
Meer, F., 64
Mercer, N., xvi, 111–112
Miller, S., 183
Minati, I., 66
Minton, K., 2, 151
Molden, D., 163
Muir, E., 126
Murray, R. M., 161–162
Mutter, K. L., 109

Nacewicz, B. M., 105
National Health Service North West, 80
Nelson, E. E., 64, 110
New Zealand Folksong, 218
Newton, I., 136
Noesselt, T., 92
Nosarti, C., 161–162
Nugent, T. F. (III), 53

object, 26, 116, 134, 185, 266
objective/objectivity, xx, 4–5, 134, 230, 244
  strategic, 179–180
  thought, 5
Ogden, P., 2, 151
Ohno, S., 182
O'Malley, A. G., 37, 41
O'Malley, S., 148, 171, 178
Onat, F., 154
O'Neill, A., 13
Oppenheim, D., 161
Ouyang, Z., 182
Overbaugh, J., 183

Pain, C., 2, 151
Panksepp, J., 128, 130, 134
Parnell, L., 169
Pascal, B., 65–66
Penninx, B. W., 167
Perner, J., 122
Perry, I. E., 20
Pessonen, A.-K., 59
Peters, S., xvi, 67, 223
Phillips, D. A., 125
Pierson, R. K., 79
Pine, D. S., 64, 110
Pollak, S. D., 79, 105–106
Ponce de León, M. S., 51
Porges, S. W., xvi, 61, 82–86, 95, 98–99, 101, 113
Poynder, M., 181
Pujol, J., 107

Qu, K., 182
Quigley, E. M., 12–13

Raichle, M. E., xviii, xix, 184, 189
Räikkönen, K., 59
Rak, Y., 51
Rakic, P., 107
Rapoport, J. L., 53
regulation, 20, 43, 82–84, 87–88, 92, 94, 97, 99, 102–103, 122, 125, 153–154, 182, 222 *see also*: affect(ive)
  auto, 125
  biological, 119, 130
  cooperative, 125
  down-, 155
  dys-, 8, 12, 39, 125, 157, 167, 204, 232
  emotional, xv, 101, 104, 106, 127, 149, 169, 186, 229, 235
  interactive, 125
  neurological, 83, 104, 151
  of anxiety, 7
  of regulation, 7
  thermo-, 153
  viscera-motor, 104
Reichenberg, A., 161–162
Reilly, J., 109
Revesz, D., 167
Rightmire, G. P., 51
Rizzolatti, G., 109
Roberts, R. M., 143
Robinson, K., 215, 223
Role, K. O., 92
Rossi, E. L., 171–172
Rozman, D., 14
Rubin, D. C., 187
Rusbridger, A., 13
Russell, B., xvii, 138
Ryan, N. D., 81

Şan, T., 154
Saper, C., 154
Sarker, M., 214
Sayed, M., 223
Schachter, S., 13
Schumann resonances, 16–18, 29, 197
Schutter, D. J., 105
Schwaller de Lubicz, R. A., 20
Schwarz, A., 214
Searl, J., 116
Sega, E., 182
Şehirli, U., 154

self, 13, 36, 49, 73, 103, 115–116, 141, 185–186, 247, 252 *see also*: behaviour(al), conscious(ness)
-actualisation, 48, 71
autobiographical, 116, 130, 199
-awareness, 46
-belief, 220
-blame, 260
-care, 255, 264
-centred, 24
-control, 36
core, 116, 130, 199
-cutting, 249
-destruction, 182
dislike, 58
-esteem, 34, 38, 71, 253
-expression, 206
genetic, 193
grounding of, 115
-harm, 92, 110, 141, 248–249, 262
higher, 38, 49
-identity, 186
image of, 26, 151
-imposed, 249
-injury, xvii, 249–250, 263
-interest, 24
-loathing, 185
-motivated, xx
-perception, 142
proto-, 116, 130
-realisation, 46
-referential, 185
-reflection, 101, 106, 111, 186
-reinforcing, 18
-related, 186
representation of, 151
sense of, 13, 185–186
-soothing, 82, 85, 102, 125
-stages, 130
symbol of, 26
-tapping, 170
-worth, 186
Seth, A., 66
Seung, S., xvii, 134–138
sexual, 195 *see also*: abuse, behaviour(al), development(al)
assailant, 162
assault, 150
sexuality, 35, 154
innate, 168
Shakespeare, W., 67
Shanahan, F., 13
Shankoff, J. P., 125
Shapiro, E., xviii, 167
Sheldrake, R., 16, 81
Sherrington, C., 119
Shore A., 161, 245
Simon-Thomas, E. R., 92
Singer, J., 13
Sitchin, Z., 51
Snyder, A. Z., xviii, xix, 184, 189
Snyder, M. P., 182
Spitale, R. C., 182
Stickgold, R., 150
Stodola, D. E., 105
Stringer, C., 22, 52
subject(ive), 23, 61, 73, 115, 147, 173, 222
inter-, 124
Suh, J. W., 105
Sutterer, M. J., 105
symbol(-ism), xvi, 34–36, 38–39, 43–44, 46, 64, 67–68, 72, 139, 183, 207
bindi, 56
caduceus, 54, 181, 206, 209
mystical, 139
ouroboros, xx, 198–199, 208
spiral, xix, 181
Tau, 34
synapses, 7, 43, 107–109, 135–136, 196–197, 203, 216
excitatory, 137
neural, 43, 45
olfactory nerve, 162
raphe nucleus, 154
system
antagonism, 81

auditory, 98
belief, 177
biological, 17
brain, 195
cardiovascular, 154
chakra energy, 152, 169, 195, 207–208
circulatory, 72
cognitive appraisal, 110
endocrine, xv, 9–11, 14, 91, 103, 204, 207–208
neuro-, 207
gastrointestinal, 8
hierarchical, 192
human body, 14, 99
immune, 7, 12, 14, 99, 104, 177, 207, 208
limbic, 53, 73, 112, 119–120, 203
motor, 81
nervous, 6, 15, 81, 84, 90–91, 94–95, 97–99, 150, 152, 176, 206, 208
autonomic, xvi, 12–15, 75, 81, 85, 91, 95, 102, 154, 194, 195, 228
cardiac, 5, 11, 29, 112
central, 5, 7–8, 12, 14–15, 29, 36, 49, 53, 59, 62–63, 110, 119, 155, 197, 208
enteric, 7, 8, 12, 15, 29, 195
gut, 112
human, x, 5
integrated, 81
intrinsic, 10, 66
parasympathetic, 5–6, 90, 127
peripheral, xv, 5, 27, 54, 83, 119, 141, 157, 197, 216
sympathetic, 36, 82, 84–85, 89, 103, 127, 196
neuromuscular, 170
perceptual, 99
phylogenetic, 84
physiological, 225
reticular acting, 87, 89
sensorimotor, 119
social engagement (SES), 82, 84–86, 93, 98, 101, 113
somato-motor, 104
sympathetic–adrenal, 102

Taipale, P., 59
Tesch-Römer, C., 223
thalamus, 12, 19–21, 39, 43, 67, 77, 84, 120, 204
epi-, 120
hypo-, 40, 62, 85, 120, 153–154, 207–208
intralaminar, 62
sensory, 20, 112, 197
sub-, 120
theory, xvii, 25, 82, 134, 143, 191, 214, 265
Darwinian, 53
lineage, 52
of cerebellar processing, 112
of mind, 109, 121–123, 130, 142, 184, 253
of morphogenetic fields, 16
of natural selection, 177, 189
of vibratory intelligence, xvi
polyvagal, xvi, 82, 85–86, 95, 101–102, 113
quantum, 25
string, 51
super-, 143
vagal paradox, 83
therapy (*passim*) *see also*: trauma(tic)
cognitive behavioural (CBT), 2, 24, 53, 131, 262
couple, xx
effectiveness of, 172
ego state, xx, 195
end of, 206
eye movement desensitisation and reprocessing (EMDR), xiii, xviii, xx, 2, 78, 89, 127, 151, 165, 172, 256
family, 262
lack of progress in, 212

occupational, 262
onset of, 71
parent–infant dyadic, 126
play, 262
process of, 151
psycho-, xv, xviii, 2–3, 18, 133, 141, 143, 158, 166, 172, 244, 266
child, 262
sensorimotor, xiii, 2, 78, 150–151, 164
readiness for, 61
sessions, 23, 212
solution-focused, 262
speech and language, 250
successful, 172
"watch, wait and wonder", 126
Thompson, P. M., 53, 121
Thomsen, Y. D., 187
Toga, A. W., 53, 121
Tomasino, D., 14
trauma(tic) (*passim*) *see also*: development(al)
blocks, 197
childhood, 99, 103
circumstances, 58
complex, 67
emotions, 100
episode, xviii, 162
event, 39, 59, 100–101, 104, 110, 147, 169, 185, 193–194, 199, 202–203, 254, 263
experiences, 28, 72, 87, 92, 106, 123, 148, 152, 158, 165, 167, 171–172, 194, 197, 199, 263
life, 43, 152
feeling, 149
-focused
cognitive behaviour, 2, 78, 172, 194
therapy, xv, xix, 2, 53, 78, 126, 131, 173
grief, 10, 149–150, 152, 186, 198
history, 147, 162, 165, 172, 231
images, 157
intensity, 152
issues, 126
memories, xviii, 2, 23, 41, 137, 143, 148–150, 152, 194, 200, 242
post, xv, 16
preverbal, 161
psychotherapy, xviii
reprocessing, 78, 164–165, 168, 171, 197
resolution, 2, 13, 25, 86, 158, 194
sensation, xviii
sensori-motor, 2
sensory information, 87
significant, 161
stress, 4, 16, 37, 53, 100, 120, 126, 158, 162, 172, 187, 198, 217, 228
clinic, 172, 262
disorder, xvi, xviii, 99, 113
symptoms, 201
therapy, 4, 43
unresolved, 126, 162
Tsuchiya, N., 70

unconscious(ness), 14, 22, 69, 94, 98, 203, 240–241 *see also*: conscious(ness)
activity, 145
attention, 139
awareness, 141
biological, 26
regulation, 119
collective, 25–26, 41, 46, 48, 143
control, 164
cultural, 26
fear, 58
learning, 217, 223, 227–229, 234, 244
memory, 149, 212
mind, 46
movements, 165, 169
neuroception, 103
neurons, 244
personal, 26
process, 84, 91, 227, 234, 240

Vaituzis, A. C., 53
van Honk, J., 105
Vekua, A., 51
Vendrell, P., 107
Verhoeven, J., 167
Villa, P. M., 59

Wan, Y., 182
Wang, H., 105
Waters, O., 217
Wheelwright, S., 123

Williams, P. L., 167
Wilson, J. F., 135
Wimmer, H., 122
Wittgenstein, L., 129
Wolkowitz, O. M., 167
Woods, B., 109
Wulf, G., 214
Wundt, W., 102

Yananli, H. R., 154
Yin, L., 161–162
Yushkevich, P. A., 105

Zecevic, N., 107
Zhang, J., 182
Zhang, Q. C., 182
Zollikofer, C. P. E., 51